Towards More Sustainable Investment Frameworks

EVALUATING THE FEASIBILITY OF SUSTAINABLE INVESTMENT FACILITATION AGREEMENTS WITH SOUTHERN NEIGHBOURHOOD COUNTRIES

OECD
BETTER POLICIES FOR BETTER LIVES

This document, as well as any data and map included herein, are without prejudice to the status of or sovereignty over any territory, to the delimitation of international frontiers and boundaries and to the name of any territory, city or area.

The statistical data for Israel are supplied by and under the responsibility of the relevant Israeli authorities. The use of such data by the OECD is without prejudice to the status of the Golan Heights, East Jerusalem and Israeli settlements in the West Bank under the terms of international law.

Note by the Republic of Türkiye
The information in this document with reference to "Cyprus" relates to the southern part of the Island. There is no single authority representing both Turkish and Greek Cypriot people on the Island. Türkiye recognises the Turkish Republic of Northern Cyprus (TRNC). Until a lasting and equitable solution is found within the context of the United Nations, Türkiye shall preserve its position concerning the "Cyprus issue".

Note by all the European Union Member States of the OECD and the European Union
The Republic of Cyprus is recognised by all members of the United Nations with the exception of Türkiye. The information in this document relates to the area under the effective control of the Government of the Republic of Cyprus.

Please cite this publication as:
OECD (2024), *Towards More Sustainable Investment Frameworks: Evaluating the Feasibility of Sustainable Investment Facilitation Agreements with Southern Neighbourhood Countries*, OECD Publishing, Paris, https://doi.org/10.1787/411468b9-en.

ISBN 978-92-64-94216-5 (print)
ISBN 978-92-64-98951-1 (PDF)
ISBN 978-92-64-42994-9 (HTML)
ISBN 978-92-64-64113-6 (epub)

Photo credits: cover © AlxeyPnferov / Getty Images

Corrigenda to OECD publications may be found at: https://www.oecd.org/en/publications/support/corrigenda.html.

Foreword

The present Report provides a stocktaking of the current investment climates of five selected Southern Neighbourhood countries (Algeria, Egypt, Jordan, Morocco and Tunisia), benchmarked against key investment facilitation standards enshrined in the Sustainable Investment Facilitation Agreement (SIFA) signed between the European Union (EU) and Angola in late-2023. The Report aims at informing the EU and interested partners of the region on the potential of future SIFA negotiations for the improvement of local business climates, to promote mutually beneficial investments.

This Report was prepared by the OECD Secretariat (Directorate for Financial and Enterprise Affairs, Investment Division) with financial assistance from the European Commission. It was drafted by Rima Bugaighis and Faraz Moosa under the general guidance of Ana Novik (Head of the OECD Investment Division) and Hélène François (Investment Division). It also benefited from input by Martin Wermelinger, Fernando Mistura and Fares Al Hussami (Investment Division). Annex B of the Report was prepared by Petra Kelly (Directorate for Science, Technology and Innovation, Science and Technology Policy Division), with significant input and guidance by Deger Saygin (Environment Directorate, Finance, Investment and Global Relations Division) and was reviewed by Alec Fiorini (OECD Secretariat, Directorate of Global Relations, Middle East & Africa Division). The Report also benefited from valuable research contributions by Theresa Dammann, Hesham Omar and Kimberley Sesen.

Information for this Report was collected from publicly accessible government sources, in particular legislation, parliamentary documentation, and public reports, as well as OECD work in the MENA region and other publicly available information by International Organisations. Translations of legislation and similar material are provided for convenience and have no legal value. They are based on unofficial translations made available by governments or other authoritative sources or occasionally machine translation tools.

Countries whose rules and practices are described throughout the Report and in the Annexes, as well as the European Commission, have had an opportunity to comment on their respective draft sections. The material and feedback received under these processes, for which the OECD is grateful, has been incorporated in this Report, which otherwise continues to reflect the situation as of September 2023. The findings of the Report were also presented at the meeting of 15 May 2024 of the Union for the Mediterranean (UfM) Regional Platform on Trade and Investment. The Report was finally circulated to the OECD Investment Committee delegates on 30 May 2024.

Table of contents

FIGURES

TABLES

BOXES

Abbreviations and acronyms

AAPI	Algerian Investment Promotion Agency
ANDI	Algerian National Investment Development Agency
APII	Agency for the Promotion of Innovation and Industry
APSI	Algerian Agency of Promotion, Support and Follow-up of Investment
BIT	Bilateral Investment Treaty
CRI	Regional Centre for Investment
CRUI	Regional Unified Investment Commissions
EPA	Economic Partnership Agreement
EU	European Union
FDI	Foreign direct investment
FET	Fair and Equitable Treatment
FIPA	Tunisian Foreign Investment Promotion Agency
GAFI	General Authority for Investment and Free Zones
GATT	General Agreement on Tariffs and Trade
IEC	Incentives and Exemptions Committee
IFD	Investment Facilitation for Development Agreement
IIA	International Investment Agreement
ILO	International Labour Organization
IMF	International Monetary Fund
IPA	Investment Promotion Agency
ISC	Egypt Investor Service Centre
JIC	Jordan Investment Commission
MENA	Middle East and North Africa
MNE	Multinational enterprise
MoI	Ministry of Investment
OECD	Organisation for Economic Co-operation and Development
OSS	One-stop-shop

PFI	Policy Framework for Investment
PNI	Projects of national interest
PPP	Public-Private Partnership
RBC	Responsible Business Conduct
SDG	Sustainable Development Goal
SIFA	Sustainable Investment Facilitation Agreement
SME	Small and Medium-sized Enterprise
TIA	Tunisian Investment Agency
TPR	Trade Policy Review
USAID	United States Agency for International Development
USD	United States Dollar
WJP	World Justice Project
WTO	World Trade Organization

Executive summary

Foreign direct investment (FDI) can be an important contributor to enhance economic growth and innovation, create quality jobs and develop human capital, including for women, and raise living standards and environmental sustainability in host economies. Recent geopolitical and economic tensions combined with the economic drawbacks caused by the COVID-19 pandemic – which themselves follow a longer period of stagnant or even declining global FDI flows which began with the Global Financial Crisis of 2008/2009 – have nevertheless significantly disrupted global trade and investment flows.

To harness investment for inclusive and sustainable economic growth and allow a resilient post-crisis recovery, a comprehensive investment facilitation framework is necessary to guide government action and improve local investment climates to create favourable conditions for FDI to contribute positively to host economies. In this context, negotiations between the EU and Angola for a new Sustainable Investment Facilitation Agreement (**SIFA**), concluded in November 2023. This template SIFA (**the EU-Angola SIFA**) aims to create such favourable conditions to attract more and better investments and promote mutually beneficial investments.

Southern Neighbourhood countries could constitute strategic partners for SIFA negotiations, in light of the European Union's (**EU**) priorities to deepen its cooperation with its regional partners. The EU's new *Agenda for the Mediterranean* of 2021 called for the strengthening of the Union's ties with its southern neighbours as being a strategic imperative, especially in areas of investment facilitation and sustainable development, such priorities having not been sufficiently addressed in their trade and investment agreements concluded in the 1990s and the 2000s. As such SIFAs with the Southern Neighbourhood countries – namely, Algeria, Egypt, Jordan, Morocco and Tunisia – considered in the context of this Report – could help create favourable conditions to attract more and better investments.

Over the last years, all five selected Southern Neighbourhood countries have directed important resources towards enhancing their legal and regulatory frameworks for investment, including by introducing reforms designed to bring about further transparency and predictability in their respective frameworks, and to further streamline investment-related authorisation processes with a view to ease administrative procedures and reduce discretionary application of rules. Despite these recent improvements, investment conditions in the five selected Southern Neighbourhood countries in some respects remain somewhat challenging. For one, the outsized role of privileged firms – such as some state-owned enterprises or politically-connected private-sector firms – benefitting from special regulatory treatment and selective enforcement of rules has often been pointed out as a key challenge hampering competitive markets in many Southern Neighbourhood countries. Along with other cross-cutting factors, such practices have limited the potential for higher levels of growth and investment, and more inclusive development in the region. Continued policymaking aimed at improving the overall transparency and predictability of investment-related rules and procedures in the selected Southern Neighbourhood countries would allow them to bolster the development of their private sectors and create favourable conditions for investment to contribute to more inclusive and sustainable development.

The present Report provides a stocktaking of the current investment climates of the five selected Southern Neighbourhood countries, benchmarked against investment facilitation standards reflected in the EU-

Angola SIFA, with a view to ultimately inform the EU and those countries of the potential capacity for future negotiations. To achieve this, the Report reviews the state of readiness of each of the selected Southern Neighbourhood countries in light of the SIFA's key facilitation standards, based on a – principally desk-based – assessment of their respective domestic legal and regulatory frameworks and institutional arrangements for investment. More specifically, the report outlines and describes the key facilitation standards enshrined in the EU-Angola SIFA, relating specifically to the transparency and predictability of domestic regulatory frameworks and the streamlining of investment authorisation procedures, and how these standards are reflected in each of the selected countries, by way of legal, regulatory and institutional channels.

The approach adopted is transversal and thematic: it provides a functional description of how transparency, predictability and streamlining-related standards and provisions are incorporated and operationalised across the selected countries' domestic frameworks for investment. This includes but is not limited to how each of the countries' adopt and deploy the legal and regulatory measures and institutional arrangements that seek to enhance the transparency and predictability of the domestic framework for investment, by what means the domestic frameworks intend to promote the transparency of relevant investment incentives, and the architecture of administrative and authorisation procedures processes. Finally, the report also provides an overview of the EU-Angola SIFA's approach to investment and sustainable development, as reflected in its Chapter 5, against the key policy orientations of the OECD FDI Qualities Policy Toolkit. In a self-standing Annex B, the Report specifically addresses the framework conditions for investment in renewable energy and green hydrogen in the selected Southern Neighbourhood countries.

The OECD Secretariat has reached out to competent authorities and other relevant stakeholders in the selected Southern Neighbourhood countries. Input has been received from a number of these countries (Egypt, Morocco) and private sectors stakeholders in other countries (Algeria). Comparative business surveys have also been relied on – and cited – to shed light on practical considerations linked to facilitation standards considered in this Report. While an opportunity to review Annex A's country sections and comment on these has been provided to competent authorities and stakeholders in the five selected Southern Neighbourhood countries, the Report is however principally desk-based and as such outlines investment facilitation measures and initiatives in place rather than hose these have been effectively implemented, or shortcomings in their effective implementation.

An ongoing parallel project is being carried out by the OECD in collaboration the EU Commission's DG TRADE, which intends to specifically map out comprehensively the EU-Angola SIFA's Chapter 5 provisions to support the incorporation of a wider spectrum and more ambitious sustainability considerations into future SIFA iterations as well as to offer guidance to governments for the implementation of domestic reforms and measures to maximise the impact of such treaty provisions on the quality of FDI.

1 Context, structure and key findings

A comprehensive investment facilitation framework is necessary to create favourable conditions for FDI to benefit host economies and societies. Sustainable Investment Facilitation Agreements (SIFA), such as the one concluded by the EU with Angola in late 2023, could be useful tools to promote facilitation practices and mutually beneficial investments between parties. This Report aims at informing the EU and interested countries of the Southern Neighbourhood region (Algeria, Egypt, Jordan, Morocco and Tunisia) on the potential and opportunity of future SIFA negotiations. This introductory chapter sets the context, structure and key findings of the Report on investment facilitation practices in the Southern Neighbourhood countries and their alignment with key provisions of the EU-Angola SIFA.

Context

Foreign direct investment (FDI) can be an important contributor to enhance economic growth and innovation, create quality jobs and develop human capital, including for women, and raise living standards and environmental sustainability in host economies (OECD, 2022[1]). By linking domestic firms – especially small and medium-sized enterprises (SMEs) – to multinational enterprises (MNEs), it can also encourage technology spillovers and be a conduit for domestic firms to access international markets and integrate global value chains (OECD, 2023[2]).[1] The OECD FDI Qualities Policy Toolkit provides policy guidance to governments to leverage the catalytic role of FDI in financing Sustainable Development Goals (SDGs), fulfil their commitments made under the Paris Agreement, and optimise the strength and quality of post-crisis recovery.

However, recent geopolitical and geoeconomic tensions that follow a longer period of stagnant or even declining global FDI flows which began with the Global Financial Crisis of 2008/2009 have significantly disrupted global trade and investment flows. Several events with global implications have contributed to such disruptions: the COVID-19 pandemic, which exacerbated the vulnerabilities of global supply chains to external shocks (OECD, 2021[3]), Russia's war of aggression against Ukraine, which impacted energy and food security and the clean energy transition, and the conflict in the Middle East, whose long-term implications are yet to be assessed (OECD, 2022[4]). In this context, enterprises are re-evaluating the implications of their supply chains, and some seek to re-shore or near-shore the sources of their inputs. These factors had and continue to have implications for FDI.

The overall economic environment remains challenging, and increased concerns about the sustainability and resilience of supply chains continue shaping investment policymaking around the world, including that of the EU. Such concerns are reflected in the EU's Trade Policy Review prepared by the European Commission in 2021, which called for a new trade strategy for the Union based on a more *"open, sustainable and assertive trade policy"* (European Commission, 2021[5]). In this context, the EU's new Global Gateway strategy aims at creating opportunities for smart investments by the EU Member States' private sectors in sustainable and quality infrastructure in partner countries, whilst ensuring their positive contribution to local communities and the enforcement of high environmental and labour standards. The strategy is underpinned by several core principles, including the need to foster 'equal partnerships' through projects driven by local needs and opportunities as well as the EU's own strategic interests in five key sectors, which include digitalisation, health, climate and energy, transport, as well as in education and research (European Commission, 2021[6]).

To harness investment for inclusive and sustainable economic growth, a comprehensive investment facilitation framework is necessary to guide government actions and align more closely investment policy with sustainability objectives. Host economies may also miss out on the positive benefits of FDI to advance their SDGs if investors regularly face hurdles and practical impediments in establishing, operating or expanding their projects in a country. Specifically tailored policies aimed at improving local investment climates are thus required to create favourable conditions for FDI to contribute positively to host economies.

Investment facilitation – understood broadly as a "combination of tools, policies and processes that foster a transparent, predictable and efficient regulatory and administrative framework for investment that maximises the benefits to the host economy" (Novik and de Crombrugghe, 2018[7])[2] – allows host economies to cut down investors' transaction costs, reduce complex administrative burdens, and increase legal predictability and certainty for investors which could drive further investment opportunities (OECD, 2015[8]). Facilitation policies can also promote investments by smaller firms which generally enjoy fewer resources than larger MNEs to establish and operate in foreign markets. The OECD's work on investment facilitation and the OECD Council Recommendation on FDI Qualities for Sustainable Development adopted at Ministerial level in June 2022 calls for Adherents to take steps to ensure that their domestic policy, legal, and regulatory frameworks support positive impacts of investment on sustainable development, and to facilitate and promote investment for sustainable development opportunities by addressing information failures and administrative barriers.[3]

Investment Facilitation Agreements, such as those negotiated by the EU, could be a useful tool to harness the positive effects of FDI and promote mutually beneficial investments. Investment facilitation has historically received significantly less policy consideration in comparison to other domains of investment policy, such as investment *protection* or, to a lesser extent, investment *liberalisation*. International Investment Agreements (IIAs) – especially early generation IIAs – have primarily focused on investment protection, although they may have included standard language on the facilitation of investments, especially within their preambles.[4] At the same time, investor protection standards are not entirely disconnected or impermeable to investment facilitation objectives.[5] Some investment protection standards typically included in IIAs, such as the obligation to accord 'fair' and 'equitable' treatment (FET) to qualifying investments, may be supported or strengthened by facilitation efforts.[6] Inversely, an absence or lack of measures seeking to facilitate investment may – in some cases and depending on the specific design and scope of a given IIA's standard of treatment – entail a state's liability under its international commitments.[7] Extensive interpretative practices by arbitral tribunals may further increase the probability of such a scenario, especially in cases where protection standards are vaguely worded in the stock of earlier generation investment treaties currently into force.[8]

Investment facilitation has only recently emerged as a policy priority in global investment governance, especially since 2017 with discussions over a plurilateral "*Investment Facilitation for Development (*IFD*) Agreement*" being hosted by the World Trade Organization (WTO).[9] The launch of discussions over a plurilateral WTO IFD Agreement follows a perceptible shift in global investment governance priorities, as more recent IIAs – whether investment chapters of FTAs or bilateral/regional investment agreements –[10] have increasingly included a wider range of investment facilitation provisions,[11] especially relating to the transparency of domestic investment frameworks, and to a lesser extent, the streamlining of administrative processes;[12] and regional initiatives had led to the adoption of framework agreements recommending good practices to facilitate investment.[13] The maturation of the EU's investment policy also led to the incorporation of investment facilitation as a policy priority within future Economic Partnership Agreements (EPAs) with the EU's economic partners of the African, Caribbean and Pacific regions. The EPAs' negotiating directives now refer to the need to establish a framework with relevant partners based on principles of non-discrimination, openness, transparency and stability to *"facilitate, enhance and stimulate mutually beneficial sustainable investment between them"*.[14] In November 2023, the EU and Angola concluded a Sustainable Investment Facilitation Agreement (SIFA), which represents the first bilateral agreement of its kind negotiated by the Union that reflects such priorities.

The EU-Angola SIFA shows an ambitious approach to investment facilitation and sustainable development, similar to that observed in more recent investment facilitation agreements. The Agreement's overarching objectives state, similar to other investment facilitation agreements, that it aims at "facilitating the attraction, expansion and retention of FDI between the Parties *for the purposes of economic diversification and sustainable development*". However, its real innovation resides not only in developing more detailed provisions on key investment facilitation principles, but also in its Chapter 5 which exemplifies the Agreement's approach to investment and sustainable development. The Agreement goes beyond just formulating recommendations to create favourable conditions for FDI to contribute to SDGs, which would be the result of 'broad' investment facilitation efforts. It also encourages Parties to align their domestic legal frameworks with international labour and environmental standards as well as responsible business conduct principles (RBC) to maximise the benefits of FDI; and calls for Parties to use FDI itself as a lever to advance their SDGs by promoting and facilitating investment projects with sustainable outcomes.

Southern Neighbourhood countries could be strategic partners for SIFA negotiations, in light of the EU's priorities to deepen its cooperation with its regional partners and promote and encourage mutually beneficial investments. The EU's new *Agenda for the Mediterranean* calls for the strengthening of the

Union's ties with its southern neighbours as being a strategic imperative, especially in areas of investment facilitation and sustainable development (European Commission, 2021[9]).

The EU has maintained strong economic ties with its Southern Neighbours: it is the first origin of inward FDI in Southern Mediterranean countries, holding in average a third of their respective inward FDI stocks in 2021, followed by countries of the MENA region Figure 1.1, Panel A). EU member states are often within the top five jurisdictions of origin of inward FDI stock in Southern Mediterranean countries, among which France, Italy and Spain (Figure 1.1, Panel B).

Figure 1.1. Inward FDI stock in the selected Southern Neighbourhood countries

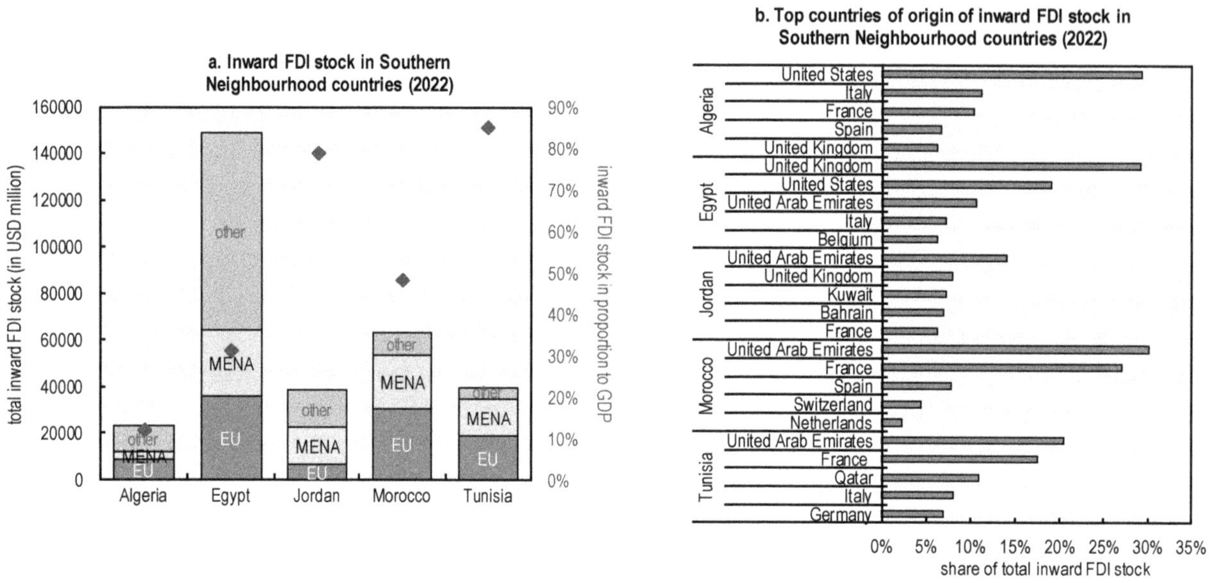

Note: Year of latest available data for individual countries. FDI stock data for Tunisia excludes the energy sector.
Source: OECD elaboration from IMF (Coordinated Direct Investment Survey and International Investment Positions), World Bank (World Development Indicators) and data reported by national authorities.

At the same time, SIFAs with the selected Southern Neighbourhood countries could help create favourable conditions to attract more and better investments as their overall FDI performance has been stagnating since the turn of the 2010 decade in light of the global financial crisis of 2008/2009 and the political and social instability resulting from the Arab Spring movements of 2010-2011. Whilst all of the selected Southern Neighbourhood countries had showed promising signs of post-crisis recovery from the twin shocks of 2008 and 2011, FDI flows in the region do not appear to have regained their pre-crisis levels, as the Covid-19 pandemic further strained such recovery efforts (Figure 1.2, Panel A).

In this context, the efforts to attract *more* and *better* FDI are important. Political shocks of the last decade have skewed the sectoral composition of FDI in the Southern Neighbourhood towards their extractive industries which have shown to be relatively impervious to political instability (OECD, 2021[10]; Burger, Ianchovichina and Rijkers, 2013[11]). However, there has been a positive shift in the region the last years towards sectors and activities that are more aligned with the achievement of SDGs, with renewable energy projects significantly outweighing fossil fuels in the share of announced greenfield FDI in the MENA region from 2019 onwards (OECD, 2023[12]) (Figure 1.2, Panel B).

Figure 1.2. Recent FDI inflows trends in Southern Neighbourhood countries

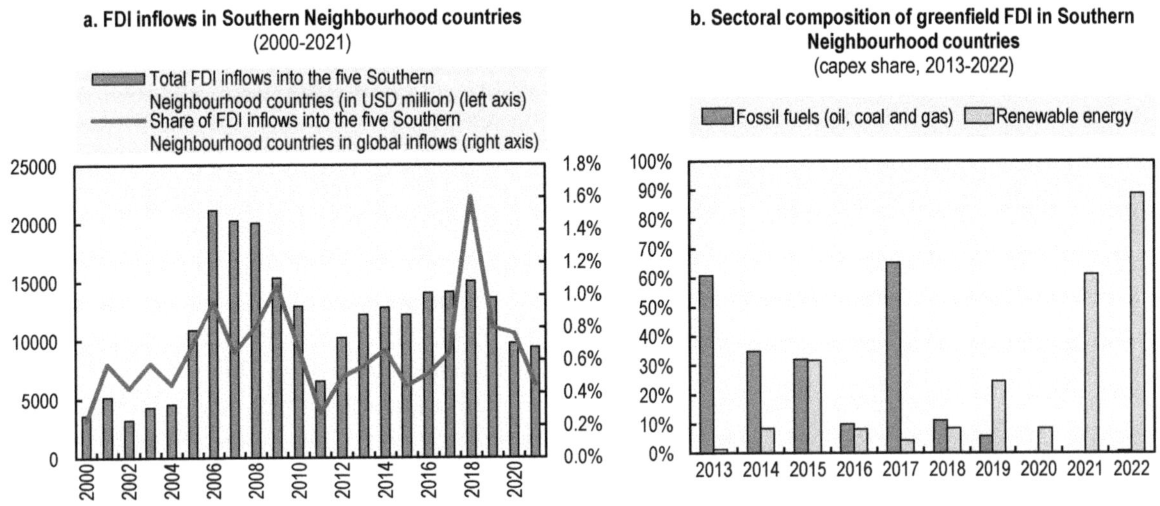

Note: The important increase in 2018 of the share of FDI inflows into the five Southern Neighbourhood countries in proportion to global FDI inflows (Panel A) appears to have been driven by a sharp decrease in global FDI inflows in that year due to large repatriations of earnings by US parent companies in response to tax reforms in the United States (see OECD, *FDI in Figures – October 2018*). Percentages in Panel B represent shares of capital expenditure (capex) of announced greenfield FDI projects.
Source: OECD elaboration from IMF BOP/IIP statistics, World Bank (Panel A) and the FT's fDi Markets database (Panel B).

Over the last years, all of the selected five Southern Neighbourhood countries have directed important resources to enhance their legal and regulatory frameworks for investment and made notable improvements to streamline regulations for investors or ease administrative procedures to reduce discretionary application of rules. Despite recent improvements, investment conditions in the five selected Southern Neighbourhood countries remain challenging in some respects. The outsized role of privileged firms – such as some state-owned enterprises or politically-connected private-sector firms – benefitting from special regulatory treatment and selective enforcement of rules has often been pointed out as a key challenge hampering competitive markets in many Southern Neighbourhood countries (OECD, 2021[10]). Along with other cross-cutting factors, such practices have limited the potential for higher levels of growth and investment, and more inclusive development in the region. Further policies aimed at improving the overall transparency and predictability of investment-related rules and procedures in the focus countries would allow Southern Neighbourhood countries to bolster the development of their private sectors and create favourable conditions for investment to contribute to more inclusive and sustainable development. Other organisations, such as the International Monetary Fund (IMF), have also called for the need to implement structural reforms in Middle East and North Africa (MENA) countries – such as those aimed at making their private sectors more 'investment-friendly' and lifting bureaucratic red tape – to raise their potential for growth in the context of tight monetary and fiscal policies that were recently put in place (IMF, 2023[13]).

The European Commission has called upon the OECD to assess the extent to which the legal, regulatory and institutional frameworks for investment in selected Southern Neighbourhood countries,[15] are aligned with the objectives, requirements and key investment facilitation standards enshrined in the EU-Angola SIFA. By providing a gap analysis of investment facilitation shortcomings in the selected Southern Neighbourhood, this aims at guiding the European Commission and the Southern Neighbourhood partners on potential future SIFA negotiations.

Structure

The present report is organised in two main sections:

- **Section 2** provides a stocktaking of investment facilitation practices within the selected Southern Neighbourhood countries benchmarked against the standards laid out in the EU-Angola SIFA, especially relating to regulatory transparency and predictability (Chapter 2 of the Agreement), the streamlining of investment authorisation procedures (Chapter 3) and their frameworks aimed at promoting and encouraging investments with sustainable outcomes (Chapter 5).[16]
- **Section 3** outlines a country-by-country assessment of each of the selected Southern Neighbourhood countries' domestic frameworks and their current level of alignment with the above-cited standards and requirements, with a view to guide the EU Commission on future key partners for SIFA negotiations. The assessment considers in which instances the existing domestic frameworks of the selected countries go further than how these standards are articulated in the EU-Angola SIFA, and in which instances these standards appear too distant from the existing domestic frameworks of the selected countries.

It is complemented by two Annexes:

- **Annex A** sets out the domestic legal frameworks for investment of each of the selected Southern Neighbourhood countries, which outline the findings of extensive desk-based research and analysis into their legal, regulatory and institutional investment frameworks. The Report's benchmarking, gap analysis rely on the findings outlined in this Annex.
- **Annex B** informs the potential for future SIFA negotiations with the five selected Southern Neighbourhood countries, specifically with respect to investment into renewable energy and green hydrogen sectors.

Key findings

The Report's key summary findings include the following:

- From an **institutional perspective**, approaches as to how facilitation standards and mechanisms have been incorporated into domestic investment frameworks vary significantly. Some countries have adopted a decentralised, region-based approach to investment facilitation, whereas others feature centralised, nation-wide investment promotion agencies (**IPA** or **IPAs**) and/or one-stop shops (**OSS**). Further, while some countries feature a single IPA, others operate several IPAs with either sector-specific jurisdictions or investor-specific mandates; the same observation goes for OSS. The institutional foundations of IPAs themselves vary from framework to framework: some countries operate IPAs that are independent administrative agencies, while others have entrusted IPA-related mandates and functions to government ministries.
- The selected Southern Neighbourhood countries' respective **OSS act as focal points**, providing information and assistance to investors on establishment and operation procedures and administrative authorisations. Their mandates are primarily defined by reference to their membership, i.e., competent authority representatives either entrusted with processing and issuing authorisations that fall within their jurisdiction *or* acting as points of contact between investors and their respective authorities. Enhanced transparency on OSS membership would clarify their effective mandates and enhance the predictability of domestic investment frameworks.
- The EU-Angola SIFA features a number of standards geared towards enhancing the **transparency** and **predictability** of domestic investment frameworks. These are reflected into the domestic frameworks of each of the selected Southern Neighbourhood countries in different manners:

- All five selected Southern Neighbourhood countries have to varying degrees formalised arrangements for the **publication of investment-related measures legislation**, or effectively do so in practice without specific reference to any institutional or legislative requirement. The availability of regulatory material (including specifically investment-related material) remains uneven across the countries, as access to investor-relevant regulatory material is at times hampered in practice (e.g., website user-friendliness and/or paywall considerations; issues in accessing consolidated and up-to-date regulatory material). Measures and arrangements seeking to ensure easy and free access to relevant and up-to-date investment-related laws and regulations would further enhance the transparency and predictability of domestic investment frameworks.
- **Participative policymaking arrangements** (advance publication of investment-related legislation, opportunity to comment to investors and stakeholders) are formalised by way of legislation or carried out on an *ad hoc*, informal basis, or in some instances inexistent. Some practical considerations hinder access to draft legislation (e.g., websites for online publication are not regularly updated and/or comprehensive). Formalised participative policymaking arrangements would further enhance the transparency and predictability of domestic investment frameworks.
- The **overall transparency of each of the five countries' domestic investment frameworks** is positive and encouraging but uneven across the selected Southern Neighbourhood Countries. All five countries operate single portals: these generally provide sufficient information relating to investment laws and regulations and relevant contact information, but the availability of comprehensive and easily accessible information on FDI restrictions and practical information on business operation is uneven. Arrangements to enhance the **transparency of investment incentives** is similarly inconsistent. Most but not all the selected countries provide a general overview of the different incentives offered to investors, either through their IPAs' websites or their OSS, but the granularity of this information (e.g., with respect to application procedures and requirements, institutional arrangements and relevant contact information) varies. Similarly, information on domestic suppliers with a view to establish **host economy linkages** is available in varying degrees of transparency and depth. Further efforts to ensure easy access to core information on the countries' investment frameworks would improve their transparency and predictability.

- The EU-Angola SIFA also features a number of standards geared towards **streamlining authorisation procedures** relevant to domestic investment frameworks. These are reflected into the domestic frameworks of each of the selected Southern Neighbourhood countries in different manners:
  - Two **complementary approaches to streamlining** are observed in practice: an underlying – and encouraged – "whole-of-government" approach to achieve overall administrative efficiency, and a complementary approach to facilitate specific investment-related procedures. Investment-specific streamlining solutions across selected Southern Neighbourhood countries include a variety of measures, e.g.: establishment of dedicated OSS to guide and assist investors in respect of investment-related authorisations; bestowing OSS the powers to directly process some or all administrative investment-related authorisation requests or facilitate their obtention; and clarifying authorisation application processes and eligibility criteria.
  - While most domestic frameworks feature arrangements that **centralise single-authorisations applications**, this is not carried out in a uniform manner across selected Southern Neighbourhood countries. OSS either act as focal points, pointing investors towards competent authorities, or are themselves mandated to directly grant or facilitate the obtention of investment-related authorisations. Depending on the frameworks, multiple processes of applications may be required for single authorisations and/or authorisation applications may or

may not be submitted electronically, for example. This may bring about burdensome authorisation procedures. The adoption of complementary measures to ensure that applications across sectors and types of projects are centralised, either via an OSS or other government agency, with a view to connect investors to competent authorities via a single portal, would further strengthen streamlining mechanisms.

   - Most selected Southern Neighbourhood countries feature **standardised measures for the processing of investment authorisation applications**, e.g., capped timeframes for the processing of authorisation applications, tacit approval mechanisms, measures to swiftly address incomplete investor applications, including recourse mechanisms. Formalised and harmonised requirements – whether whole-of-government or investment-specific – could further enhance the streamlining of authorisation applications. Further, enhanced transparency on such requirements and authorisation processes and related fees (e.g., via a comprehensive negative list enshrined by way of regulation or sector-specific licensing guides) would help further streamline investment frameworks.

- While FDI has had generally **positive spillovers in the four SDG areas** considered by the OECD *FDI Qualities Indicators*, the five countries of the Southern Neighbourhood are harnessing these benefits unevenly and at different paces, whether it be in terms of productivity and innovation, creating quality jobs, advancing gender equality principles or advancing decarbonisation goals.

Strengthening Southern Neighbourhood's investment facilitation frameworks could help countries not only attract more FDI, but also harness its potential positive benefits. The Report hence identifies potential room for improvement in the five selected Southern Neighbourhood countries and underlines the extent to which each of their domestic frameworks align with the EU-Angola SIFA's key facilitation standards, with a view to guide the EU Commission and interested partners in the region on potential future SIFA negotiations.

References

Burger, M., E. Ianchovichina and B. Rijkers (2013), *Risky Business: Political Instability and Greenfield Foreign Direct Investment in the Arab World*, Policy Research Working Paper, http://documents.worldbank.org/curated/en/450971468110956873/Risky-business-political-instability-and-greenfield-foreign-direct-investment-in-the-Arab-world. [11]

European Commission (2021), *Communication From the Commission to the European Parliament, the Council, the European Economic and Social Committee and the Committee of the Regions: Trade Policy Review - An Open, Sustainable and Assertive Trade Policy*, COM(2021) 66 final, https://eur-lex.europa.eu/resource.html?uri=cellar:5bf4e9d0-71d2-11eb-9ac9-01aa75ed71a1.0001.02/DOC_1&format=PDF. [5]

European Commission (2021), *Joint Communication to the European Parliament, the Council, the European Economic and Social Committee and the Committee of the Regions on a Renewed partnership with the Southern Neighbourhood*, https://www.eeas.europa.eu/sites/default/files/joint_communication_renewed_partnership_southern_neighbourhood.pdf. [9]

European Commission (2021), *Joint Communication to the European Parliament, the Council, the European Economic and Social Committee, the Committee of the Regions and the European Investment Bank*, JOIN/2021/30 final, https://eur-lex.europa.eu/legal-content/EN/TXT/?uri=CELEX%3A52021JC0030&qid=1653525883495. [6]

European Commission (2021), *Joint Communication to the European Parliament, the Council, the European Economic and Social Committee, the Committee of the Regions and the European Investment Bank: The Global Gateway*, https://eur-lex.europa.eu/legal-content/EN/TXT/?uri=CELEX%3A52021JC0030&qid=1653525883495. [14]

IMF (2023), *Safeguarding Macroeconomic Stability amid Continued Uncertainty: Regional Economic Outlook of the Middle East and Central Asia*, https://www.imf.org/en/Publications/REO/MECA/Issues/2023/04/13/regional-economic-outlook-mcd-april-2023. [13]

Novik, A. and A. de Crombrugghe (2018), *Towards an international framework for investment facilitation*, OECD Investment Insights, https://www.oecd.org/investment/Towards-an-international-framework-for-investment-facilitation.pdf. [7]

OECD (2023), *FDI Qualities in the Middle East and North Africa: A mapping of policies and institutions that can strengthen sustainable investment*, Background document for the regional seminar on sustainable investment in the MENA region, 19 and 20 June 2023, OECD Istanbul Centre, Türkiye, https://www.oecd.org/mena/eu-oecd-mediterranean-investment/FDI-Qualities-MENA.pdf. [12]

OECD (2023), *Policy Toolkit for Strengthening FDI and SME Linkages*, OECD Publishing, Paris, https://doi.org/10.1787/688bde9a-en. [2]

OECD (2022), *FDI Qualities Indicators 2022*, OECD Publishing, Paris, https://www.oecd.org/en/topics/investment.html. [1]

OECD (2022), *International investment implications of Russia's war against Ukraine*, OECD Publishing, Paris, https://doi.org/10.1787/a24af3d7-en. [4]

OECD (2021), *Fostering economic resilience in a world of open and integrated markets: Risks, vulnerabilities and areas for policy action*, https://www.oecd.org/newsroom/OECD-G7-Report-Fostering-Economic-Resilience-in-a-World-of-Open-and-Integrated-Markets.pdf. [3]

OECD (2021), *Middle East and North Africa Investment Policy Perspectives*, OECD Publishing, Paris, https://doi.org/10.1787/6d84ee94-en. [10]

OECD (2015), *Policy Framework for Investment, 2015 Edition*, OECD Publishing, Paris, https://doi.org/10.1787/9789264208667-en. [8]

Notes

[1] OECD, in collaboration with the European Commission (Directorate General for Regional and Urban Policy – DG REGIO), is currently conducting a multi-year project to offer tailored policy advice to countries and regions on how to develop linkages between FDI and local SMEs how to strengthen FDI-SME ecosystems to create more opportunities for productivity and innovation spillovers. On the OECD's work in this policy area, see: https://www.oecd.org/industry/smes/fdi-sme.htm.

[2]. Investment facilitation should thus be distinguished from investment *liberalisation* which refers to the process by which restrictions imposed to foreign investors – such as foreign equity caps, screening or licensing requirements, minimum capital requirements or limitations to the appointment of key foreign personnel – are phased out or partially alleviated in a given country. Investment facilitation provisions do not usually encompass disciplines on market access for foreign investors. Similarly, while investment *facilitation* and investment *promotion* are often used interchangeably, these two terms cover nevertheless two distinct investment policy areas. Investment *promotion* is principally concerned with generating investments by promoting a country or its regions as investment destinations ('image building'), while investment *facilitation* focuses on policies to foster an enabling investment climate and ease the establishment, operation and expansion of investment projects. Investment *promotion* and investment *facilitation* are also temporally distinct: while promotion is rather about attracting potential investors that have not yet selected an investment destination, investment facilitation starts at the pre-establishment phase, when an investor has already shown interest in a location or a country.

[3] For more information on the OECD's work in this policy area, see, https://www.oecd.org/investment/sustainable-investment/.

[4] On such standard language, see e.g., the Egypt-Germany BIT (2005): "*intending to create favourable conditions for investments by investors of either State in the territory of the other State*"; or more recently, the Japan-Jordan BIT (2018): "*intending to further create stable, equitable, favourable and transparent conditions for greater investment by investors of a Contracting Party in the Area of the other Contracting Party*".

[5] Investment facilitation agreements have tended to explicitly limit such interactions. For instance, the EU-Angola SIFA states on its scope that it "*does not create or modify commitments related to the liberalisation of investments, nor does it create or modify rules on the protection of established investors in the territory of Parties, or of their investments, or on investor-state dispute settlement*" (Article 2(3)). Such matters were also explicitly excluded early on from the scope of discussions on the Investment Facilitation for Development Agreement in the context of the WTO.

[6] For instance, the Comprehensive Economic and Trade Agreement (CETA) between Canada, of the one part, and the EU and its Member States, of the other part, includes "fundamental breach of due process, including a fundamental breach of transparency in judicial and administrative proceedings" or even "manifest arbitrariness" within its FET clause (Article 8.10) which could be theoretically avoided by the rationalisation of administrative decisions.

[7] See e.g., *CMS Gas Transmission Company v. The Argentine Republic*, ICSID Case No. ARB/01/8, Award, 12 May 2005, in which the Tribunal held that "*a stable legal and business environment is an essential element of fair and equitable treatment*" (para. 274). In *Metaclad Corporation v. The United Mexican States* (ICSID Case No. ARB(AF)/97/1, Award, 30 August 2000), the Tribunal found that the administration of measures in the case was in breach of NAFTA's transparency requirements which subsequently amounted to a breach of the Agreement's FET clause. The scope of the NAFTA FET clause was further clarified following the *Metaclad* award by the NAFTA Free Trade Commission in 2001 which stated that FET does not require treatment "*in addition to or beyond that which is required by the customary international law minimum standard of treatment of aliens*" and that the determination of a breach of another NAFTA provision or of a separate international agreement does not establish a breach of NAFTA's FET clause. While the note did not explicitly state that the FET standard in NAFTA excludes regulatory transparency requirements, it inherently limited the possibility of importing foreign legal provisions – such as the Agreement's transparency provisions – within the customary international law minimum standard

treatment of aliens. Such specifications were subsequently reflected in recent investment treaty designs, including in the USMCA (Investment Chapter, Article 14.6) which replaced NAFTA.

[8] On specifications of FET provisions in recent investment treaty language, see OECD (2023), "*'Fair' and 'equitable' treatment provisions in investment treaties: a large-sample survey of treaty provisions*" (forthcoming), to be published on https://oe.cd/foit.

[9] See, Joint Ministerial Statement on Investment Facilitation for Development, 13 December 2017. Negotiations on the text of this agreement, which formally started in 2020, have only very recently (July 2023) concluded with an agreement reached on the final text of an IFD Agreement (see, WTO Structured Discussions on Investment Facilitation for Development – Statement by the Co-ordinators, 6 July 2023). The final text of the WTO IFD Agreement has not yet been made public at the time of publication in November 2023 but the OECD Secretariat has been able to consult it.

[10] Regional agreements with investment facilitation provisions include the EU-Kazakhstan EPCA (2015); the EU-Armenia CEPA (2017); the Investment Chapter of the PACER Plus (2017) ; the Hong Kong (China)-ASEAN Agreement on Investment (2018) ; the USMCA (2020); and the Regional Comprehensive Economic Partnership (2020) (RCEP). These follow earlier initiatives to include investment facilitation provisions in regional IIAs, e.g., the Framework Agreement on the ASEAN Investment Area (1998) and its subsequent replacement, the ASEAN Comprehensive Investment Agreement (2009), and the subsequent series of ASEAN Agreements concluded with partners (e.g., the ASEAN-China Investment Agreement (2009);

[11] This shift in global investment treaty making priorities is especially reflected by some countries' model investment agreements. Brazil appears to have pioneered such approach; its IIAs were indeed the first set of treaties that directly incorporated key facilitation provisions in parallel to investor protection standards, including regulatory transparency requirements and the establishment of national focal points to support investors. Additional countries have started incorporating key facilitation provisions within their model agreements: see the India Model BIT (2015), and more recently, the Canada Model FIPA (2021).

[12] The regulatory transparency-related provisions in recent IIAs have essentially focused on basic publication requirements for relevant laws and regulations. Only a few IIAs concluded in the past ten years have featured facilitation provisions specifically relating to providing stakeholders with an opportunity to comment on relevant investment laws and regulations, on arranging for reasonable time periods between the publication of a law and its application, and requirements to explain the rationale of an investment-related law or regulation. Similarly, IIAs that address administrative streamlining are relatively rare (see e.g., the Investment Agreement of the China-Hong Kong (China) CEPA (2017)).

[13] See e.g., the Intra-MERCOSUR Investment Facilitation Protocol (2017) and the ASEAN Investment Facilitation Framework (2021). The Investment Protocol to the African Continental FTA (AfCFTA) was adopted in February 2023 but its final text is not yet available. The latest publicly available drafts of the text shed lights on the text's ambitions, namely with respect to investment facilitation (e.g., the publication of relevant laws and regulations, entry and sojourn requirements, general requirement to streamline administrative procedures, the institution of national focal points), investment promotion (e.g., incentives for sustainable investments), and investment protection (e.g., national treatment, most-favoured nation treatment, administrative and judicial treatment, physical protection and security). The last draft also features a chapter dedicated to sustainable development-related issues.

[14] Council Decision (EU) 2020/13 of 19 December 2019, OJ L 6, 10.1.2020, p. 101-111. The EU's Global Gateway strategy also refers to the need to improve local investment climates to improve conditions for attracting quality investments in partner countries (European Commission, 2021[14]).

[15] Lebanon has not been included in the scope of this Report, in the light of the important economic and legislative reforms, and improvements to its transparency mechanisms, which are expected to benefit from the financial support of the International Monetary Fund (IMF), and which have not to date been implemented, but which could entail comprehensive reforms and considerable adjustments to Lebanon's domestic legal framework for investment. A stocktaking of Lebanon's current investment-related laws and regulations would thereby soon become obsolete. In that regard, Lebanon's investment legal framework does not appear to have witnessed any significant changes since the Investment Law No. 360 was issued in 2001.

[16] The present Report's consideration of Chapter 5 of the EU-Angola SIFA (Investment and Sustainable Development) primarily focuses on providing a broad assessment of FDI trends and policies in the selected Southern Neighbourhood countries' to boost the positive benefits of FDI to their sustainable development, but it does not include a benchmarking assessment of the provisions specifically set out in Chapter 5. Further work is currently being conducted by the OECD in the context of a separate project to comprehensively identify avenues of improvement of the model agreement's approach to investment and sustainable development specifically (forthcoming).

2 The incorporation of key investment facilitation standards in Southern Neighbourhood countries

Investment facilitation is key to creating favourable conditions for mutually beneficial investments. While the EU's Southern Neighbourhood countries have shown significant strides in recent years to improve their overall investment climates, their respective approaches to investment facilitation have varied significantly and yielded uneven results. This Chapter provides an overview of these approaches, benchmarked against the standards enshrined in the EU-Angola SIFA, specifically with regards to the transparency and predictability of investment frameworks, the streamlining of authorisation procedures, and principles to encourage and promote mutually beneficial sustainable investments.

Transparency and predictability

A fair, transparent, clear and predictable regulatory framework for investment is a critical determinant of investment decisions and a cornerstone to a stable investment climate. Principles of transparency and predictability are central to effective regulation, to enhancing investor confidence in a country's legal and regulatory environment by allowing for informed decision-making at investor level, and to ensure regulatory compliance. Evidence suggests that investors are more likely to invest in a country which provides a stable regulatory environment (World Bank Group, 2017[1]),[1] i.e., where investment-related laws and regulations are readily available through public online sources, and where investment policies are developed in a participatory manner, including based on stakeholder comments and consultations. A predictable and transparent legal framework is critical to enable smooth business operations and is thus as important at the post-investment operational phase as at the pre-investment establishment phase.

Transparency and predictability of legal frameworks for investment may be achieved or enhanced through several ways (OECD, 2015[2]), e.g.:

- Making investment-related laws and regulations clear and readily available and accessible, and arranging for advance publication of draft texts prior to their adoption.
- Developing registers of existing and proposed regulations; expanding the use of electronic dissemination of regulatory material; publishing and reviewing administrative decisions.
- Simplifying and streamlining legislation and drafting in plain language; translating these into English and other languages relevant to investors.
- Developing and maintaining a proactive investment policymaking strategy and making publicly available expected regulatory changes and their underpinning rationales.
- Consulting systematically with interested stakeholders, for instance through institutionalised consultation mechanisms that enable investors and other stakeholders to participate in the design and monitoring of business-related laws and regulations (OECD, 2021[3]).
- Assessing and communicating the potential impact – environmental, social and economic – of new regulations before their adoption; periodically reviewing regulations to assess their effectiveness in facilitating investment.

The focus of the EU-Angola SIFA's Chapter 2 relates to regulatory transparency and predictability. The Agreement founds transparency and predictability requirements on three core pillars or principles which govern the administration of investment-related measures: *reasonableness*, *objectivity,* and *impartiality*.[2] These are also enshrined in the Article VI:1 WTO General Agreement on Trade in Services, which appears to have inspired the wording of the EU-Angola SIFA's Article 6:

EU-Angola SIFA, Article 6:

Each Party shall ensure that all measures of general application falling within the scope of this Agreement are administered in a reasonable, objective and impartial manner.

The scope of these three core principles, as reflected in Article 6 of the EU-Angola SIFA, is rather broad and can be understood as applying to all phases of the investment policy life cycle, starting with its strategic elaboration, to its drafting, adoption, implementation, application, maintenance, and even its phasing-out.[3] The Agreement does not define what these principles encompass specifically in terms of procedural or substantive requirements, which leaves ample room for interpretation. As such, all three core principles may be understood as addressing distinct aspects of regulatory transparency and predictability – albeit with potential overlaps:

- ***Reasonableness*** can relate to both procedural and substantive requirements of regulatory transparency and predictability. Administering investment-related measures *with reason* can entail, for instance, outlining the rationale underpinning existing business-related measures or proposed regulatory changes and publishing sufficient information on the investment framework to avoid informal or excessively discretionary processes that could lead to arbitrary or discriminatory outcomes.[4] Reasonableness can also entail more practical aspects of policymaking, e.g., publishing proposed regulatory changes in advance to provide stakeholders with an opportunity to comment to ensure that they are not disproportionately affected by the proposed measures and ensure overall regulatory stability.
- ***Objectivity*** requirements may overlap in part with a number of substantive aspects of the reasonableness principle, as well as the procedural contours of the principle of impartiality, outlined below. Objectivity could for example entail developing clear policy *objectives* to existing or proposed investment-related measures. An objective administration of investment-related measures implies that Parties review their existing investment frameworks to ensure that measures adequately serve their intended purpose, and to align those that do not with their policy priorities and strategies.
- ***Impartiality*** requires *inter alia* that investment-related measures are not developed or applied in a way that would unfairly favour or restrict an investor or a category of investors. It entails that measures should be administered in such a manner that benefits all investors in like circumstances indiscriminately.[5] An objective administration of investment-related measures would ensure that this administration is aligned not on discretionary factors or considerations, but rather, on clear, reasonable and objective criteria, and thus administered *impartially*, e.g., with respect to investors' access to investment incentives.

The unspecified nature of these principles together with their broad scope of application to all phases of the investment policy life cycle translates into a wide range of possible implementing solutions. While some of these practical solutions may be specifically tailored to achieve particular principles, others may serve several of these core principles synchronously. Regulatory transparency and predictability of investment policy can also be the result of a broader effort to improve a country's regulatory governance in the context of a "whole-of-government" approach. As such, overarching shortcomings relating to transparency and predictability of a regulatory framework would shed some light onto the transparency and predictability of investment-related regulations specifically. Separately, disparities in practical solutions to enhance regulatory transparency and predictability may be observed between countries, but also sometimes at the sub-national level itself, given the variety of approaches to governance and local idiosyncrasies. Despite these variations, international good practices have emerged to effectively foster transparency and predictability in policymaking and policy administration.

Chapter 2 of the EU-Angola SIFA outlines a list of practical measures or solutions which Parties should implement to achieve and enhance regulatory predictability and transparency of investment-related measures of general application. These practical applications of the principles of reasonableness, objectivity, and impartiality concern specifically the publication of investment-related measures of general application (Article 7), the advance publication of draft laws and regulations and the provision of a reasonable opportunity to comment on such drafts (Article 8), enhancing access to information on the investment framework (Article 9), as well as the incentives regime (Article 10). The Agreement also encourages parties to provide information on domestic suppliers to encourage linkages with the host economy (Article 11).

Such practical solutions to enhance regulatory transparency and predictability are at the time of writing in September 2023 implemented through various measures, and to varying degrees, throughout the five selected countries of the Southern Neighbourhood. Comparative surveys highlight significant differences in the perceptions of regulatory transparency and predictability in all five countries of the EU's Southern Neighbourhood. Figure 2.1 features their scores in the World Justice Project (**WJP**)

Rule of Law Index (2022), specifically in respect of factors relating to regulatory governance that are closely related to matters addressed in Chapter 2 of the EU-Angola SIFA.[6] These concern *inter alia* undue influence over government officials in the executive and legislative branches and in the application of government regulations, publication of laws and government data, right to information, civic participation in the law making processes.

Figure 2.1 Selected Southern Neighbourhood countries' scores in the WJP Rule of Law Index (2022): regulatory governance

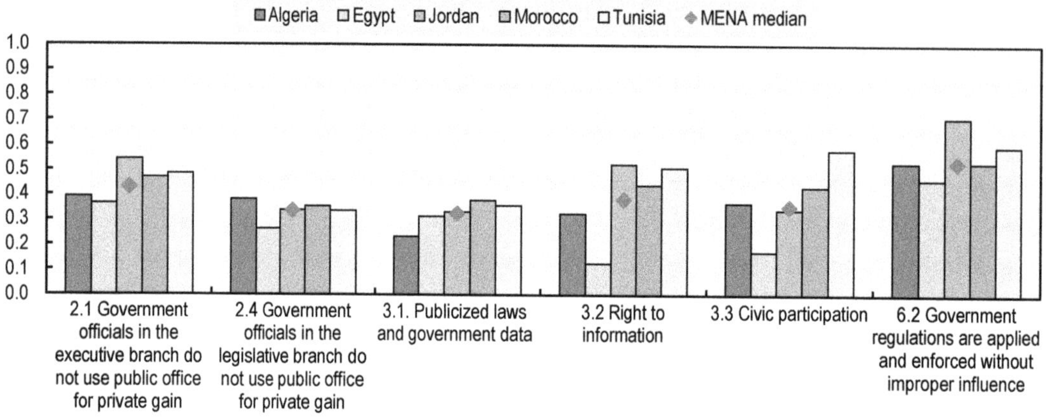

Note: Scores range from 0 (worst) to 1 (best). The WJP Rule of Law Index measures rule of law adherence across 140 jurisdictions worldwide. The country scores and rankings are built from more than 500 variables drawn from the assessments of more than 150 000 households and 3 600 legal experts. They capture the experiences and perceptions of ordinary citizens and in-country professionals concerning the performance of the state and its agents and the actual operation of the legal framework in their country. Given the broad scope of 'regulatory governance', only indicators that were closely linked to topics covered by the EU-Angola SIFA Chapter 2 were included in the graph. The MENA median was calculated using the scores of MENA countries covered by the Index, namely Algeria, Egypt, Iran, Jordan, Lebanon, Morocco, Tunisia and the United Arab Emirates.
Source: OECD elaboration based on the WJP Rule of Law Index (2022).

Although the WJP Rule of Law Index as well as other comparative surveys cover broad governance issues, they may nevertheless give a strong indication as to the state of regulatory governance of business and investment-related measures in the countries. As such, the assessment of the Tunisian and Jordanian regulatory environments highlight the significant strides taken by the two countries in addressing undue influence over law-making processes and the enforcement of regulations, as well as over access to information. Overall, while sensible differences may be observed in the selected Southern Neighbourhood countries' scores on the different factors, important shortcomings appear to affect all their domestic regulatory environments.

The following sections provide an overview of the practical solutions recommended by the EU-Angola SIFA Chapter 2 with regards to regulatory predictability and transparency of investment-related measures, and to what extent such solutions have been implemented in practice in the selected Southern Neighbourhood countries.

Publication requirements

Official publication of laws and regulations is the first basic – albeit critical – element of a transparent and predictable legal framework. Publication of investment-related measures of general application creates predictability for investors as it is a precondition of regulatory compliance: through published regulatory material, investors understand what regulations apply to them and what requirements they must comply with to establish or operate in the country. The opacity of domestic regulatory environments could also disproportionately affect smaller firms – which are less likely to enjoy the resources necessary to afford services to help them navigate the frameworks of foreign markets, including in respect of access conditions and requirements – who in turn are likely to bear the costs of poor regulatory governance (OECD, 2021[4]). The publication of regulatory material also holds the potential of limiting regulatory agencies' discretion in applying such measures, thus fostering administrative accountability.

Publication requirements of measures of general application are a quasi-universal feature of agreements with investment and/or trade facilitation provisions,[7] including some early-generation investment treaties.[8] They have become increasingly common in recent investment treaty designs.[9] Such transparency requirements also featured in the General Agreement on Tariffs and Trade (**GATT**) (1947), Article X, which provides that trade-related measures *"shall be published promptly in such a manner as to enable governments and traders to become acquainted with them"*. Transparency requirements in the GATT extended beyond domestic regulatory material, to include the publication of international agreements affecting the contracting parties' international trade policy.

EU-Angola SIFA, Article 7:

Each Party shall publish promptly or otherwise make publicly available in writing and, except in emergency situations, at the latest by the time of their entry into force, all relevant measures of general application falling within the scope of this Agreement in such a manner as to enable investors to be informed of them.

Publication of investment-related measures is the first practical solution addressed by Chapter 2 of the EU-Angola SIFA to achieve regulatory transparency, and ultimately, regulatory predictability. Article 7 rests on two alternative solutions to ensure that publication requirements are met by parties: they *"shall publish promptly or otherwise make publicly available in writing"* (emphasis added) all investment-related measures of general application falling within the scope of the Agreement. Although the Agreement does not specify the medium for publication requirements (in an Official Journal, online, on through a single portal), such publication shall aim at "*enabl[ing] investors to be informed of*" the investment-related measures. Publication of measures in a medium with restricted access would thus not appear to meet the standard laid out under Article 7 of the EU-Angola SIFA – the purpose of such publication being to enhance access to regulatory information by all investors and relevant stakeholders.[10]

Article 7 of the EU-Angola SIFA does not fall short of including recently implemented regulations within its requirements, in addition to setting a framework for the publication in advance of draft laws and regulations. The Agreement time-bars the publication requirements of recent regulatory changes, at the latest, by the time of their entry into force, except in emergency situations. Such requirements are further supported by the recommended provision of a latency period between the publication of a measure and its entry into force to enhance predictability and allow investors to comply with recently implemented regulations (EU-Angola SIFA, Article 8(6)).

The availability of published regulatory material via official channels – including investment-related regulatory material – is uneven across the five countries of the selected Southern Neighbourhood. While all five countries appear to require their authorities to publish regulatory material in the national official journals, access to these publications can be hampered in practice, including in respect of availability of translations of original Arabic-language legislation. More particularly, while **Algeria**, **Morocco** and **Tunisia** publish, via official channels, French translations of their laws, regulations, decrees and other instruments, **Egypt** does not appear to do so. Selected **Jordanian** laws and regulations are available through ministry websites rather than via a centralised platform (e.g., official journal) and often provides English translations of main instruments. Further, official journals are readily available online and free-of-charge in the five countries of the Southern Neighbourhood, except in **Egypt** where access to the Official Journal is hindered by paywalls. The user-friendliness of websites publishing material from official journals can also vary from one country to another, potentially hindering access to regulatory information. Some countries have resorted to publication of investment-specific measures through their national IPAs' websites, when available. While this approach is more targeted towards investment-related measures and can be more cost-efficient than the implementation and maintenance of a centralised legal repository, measures published by IPAs can often be outdated and may not have sufficient coverage due to the variety of laws and regulations having potential bearing on investments. This is explored further in the context of this section's assessment of Article 9 of the EU-Angola SIFA.

Publication in advance and opportunity to comment

Building on the practical solutions enshrined in the previous Article 7, Article 8 of the EU-Angola SIFA outlines the requirement for the advance publication of proposed regulatory measures, *"whether in the form of a law, regulation, rule, procedure, decision, administrative action or other"*. The rationale of the provision lays in enhancing the predictability of a country's investment framework, and ensuring that proposed changes serve the public interest, do not disproportionately affect some stakeholders, and are informed by their legitimate needs (OECD, 2012[5]).

The design and scope of Article 8 is similar to provisions featured in recent trade agreements.[11] The scope and ambition of such provisions vary when featured in IIAs. Reference is often made to publication in advance and opportunity to comment requirements, but less so to requirements pertaining to providing explanations as to the purpose and rationale of a proposed measure, or affording reasonable time between the publication of a measure and its application and entry into force.[12]

The practical solutions provided by Article 8 are limited to what Parties may *"to the extent practicable"* achieve in a manner that is *"consistent with [their] legal system"*. They pertain to the advance publication of proposed measures (i.e., that they be made publicly available in advance of their adoption); that stakeholders be provided with a reasonable opportunity to comment on such measures before their adoption, and their comments be considered; that the rationale and purposes of these measures be explained; and that investors be provided with a reasonable time between the publication and entry into force of such measures. While some of the countries' selected framework do feature formal requirements aligned with those of Article 8, these are not systematically implemented in practice.

Advance publication of proposed measures

EU-Angola SIFA, Articles 8(1) and (2):

1. To the extent practicable and in a manner consistent with its legal system for adopting measures, each Party shall publish in advance:

(a) the proposals for laws and regulations of general application to be adopted in relation to matters falling within the scope of this Agreement; or

(b) documents that provide sufficient details about the proposals referred to in point (a) to allow investors and other interested persons to assess whether and how their interests might be significantly affected.

2. To the extent practicable and in a manner consistent with its legal system for adopting measures, each Party is encouraged to apply paragraph 1 to procedures and administrative rulings of general application it proposes to adopt in relation to matters falling within the scope of this Agreement."

Article 8(1) and (2) require that proposed measures or alternatively, documents "that provide sufficient details about the proposals referred to [in the above sub-paragraph (a)] to allow investors and other interested persons to assess whether and how their interests might be significantly affected", be published prior to their adoption and entry into force. A footnote to the provision notes that Parties may have different systems in place to consult on certain regulatory and other measures before they are adopted, and the two alternative requirements are designed to accommodate this diversity.

Advance publication of drafts or proposals – or documents that provide sufficient details on – measures is principally carried out by the selected Southern Neighbourhood countries via the websites of the countries' regulatory authorities: **Jordan, Morocco** and **Tunisia**'s frameworks feature arrangements – both formal and informal – for the advance publication of proposed measures via government and/or legislative websites. These websites are however not always regularly updated and/or comprehensive: in effect, while drafts of the Jordanian Investment Environment Law were published prior to its adoption, this is not entirely clear in respect of drafts of the Moroccan and Tunisian investment laws.[13] It thus remains unclear as to whether and when drafts have been made available prior to their adoption, and indeed whether these arrangements are given effect in practice. Tunisian local press has recently reported that a new investment law is currently under elaboration (African Manager, 2023[6]). This had not at the time of writing in September 2023 been reported via official government channels, nor had any drafts of measures have been shared with the public.

Such formal arrangement is not a feature of the **Algerian** framework; however, in practice, the websites of the Algerian People's National Assembly and Council of the Nation both have dedicated web pages where draft legal texts prior to their adoption are published. Draft(s) of Algeria's 2022 Investment Law and implementing decrees could however not at the time of writing in September 2023 be located thereon. Similarly, no formal requirement exists under the **Egyptian** framework, and drafts of its 2017 Investment Law could not be located on any official government portal.

Finally, and except in the case of Jordan, no documents that outline either the rationale and/or sufficient detail about the drafts of measures to be adopted could be located.

Reasonable opportunity to comment

EU-Angola SIFA, Articles 8(3) and (4):

3. To the extent practicable and in a manner consistent with its legal system for adopting measures, each Party shall provide investors and other interested persons, on a non-discriminatory basis, a reasonable opportunity to comment on proposed measures or documents published under paragraph 1 or 2.

4. To the extent practicable and in a manner consistent with its legal system for adopting measures, each Party shall consider comments received pursuant to paragraph 3.

Article 8 of the EU-Angola SIFA also requires that Parties provide relevant stakeholders – *"investors and other interested persons"* – with a *"reasonable opportunity to comment"* on proposed measures and/or documents as defined in Article 8, and that Parties consider such comments.[14] The provision does not outline any practical ways by which such opportunities are to be provided or how a *"reasonable"* opportunity to comment is to be ensured, i.e., if comments are to be actively encouraged or promoted by the parties, if consultations are to be carried out within a brief timeframe prior to the adoption of measures so as to allow parties to consider the comments received, or if consultations are to extend over a sufficiently long period of time to allow for extensive consultations with relevant stakeholders. While flexibility in SIFA language is pivotal for Parties to implement this practical solution in a variety of ways and in accordance with their domestic frameworks, Article 8 could lay out nonprescriptive examples of how a reasonable opportunity to comment may be afforded to investors and other stakeholders, e.g., government-led consultations via public websites or platforms (such as government websites, newspapers, official gazettes), government-led consultations via public meetings, and/or targeted outreach to select stakeholders.

Some of the selected Southern Neighbourhood countries have put in place a variety of different arrangements to afford the public and relevant stakeholders a reasonable opportunity to comment on draft bills before their adoption. The frameworks of **Algeria** and **Egypt** do not feature any formal requirement to provide a reasonable opportunity to comment and/or conduct consultations during the elaboration of a measure and prior to its adoption. Publicly available information confirms however that some limited consultations may have been carried out with respect of each of the countries' investment laws although detailed information on these is not readily available.

In contrast, the frameworks of **Jordan**, **Morocco** and **Tunisia** do feature these requirements – these are either institutional (in the case of Jordan) or formalised into the regulations of the legislative body (in the case of Morocco and Tunisia). It is unclear however how this opportunity was provided, and how these consultations were carried out. In that regard, all three countries are currently engaged in programs that seek to develop public participation and engagement in the regulatory and legislative fields.[15]

Except in the case of Jordan, where the consultative processes which led to the adoption of its 2022 Investment Law were considered by some stakeholders to have been particularly rich, it is unclear on the face of publicly available information how extensive and/or inclusive these processes were in other Southern Neighbourhood countries, including whether an opportunity to comment was equally provided to all relevant stakeholders and interested persons, whether this opportunity was deemed *"reasonable"*, and whether comments received were effectively reflected into the elaboration process of these laws.

Explaining the purpose and rationale of proposed measures

EU-Angola SIFA, Article 8(5):

5. In publishing a law or regulation of general application referred to in paragraph 1, or in advance of such publication, to the extent practicable and in a manner consistent with its legal system for adopting measures, each Party shall endeavour to explain the purposes and rationale of that law or regulation.

Under Article 8(5) of the Agreement, Parties shall also *"endeavour"* to explain the purpose and rationale of laws and/or regulations of general application adopted in relation to matters falling within the scope of the SIFA, either at the time of their publication or in advance of that time. The wording of the provision again provides flexibility to the Parties as to arrangements framing this requirement, and does not set out a minimum of information required to be shared with the public.

No overarching legal requirement to explain the purpose or rationale of a proposed measures, prior to or at the time of its adoption, appears to exist in the legal frameworks of any of the selected Southern Neighbourhood countries. Nevertheless, **Algeria**, **Jordan** and **Morocco** have through various channels and within different timeframes – either before or after the adoption of their investment laws – sought to provide background and explanations regarding the purpose and rationale of laws and regulations making up their respective investment frameworks, e.g., by way of Cabinet communiqué in Algeria, accompanying explanatory notes in Jordan, and a full-fledged report and explanatory statement in Morocco.

Reasonable time between the publication of a text and the date of its application to investors

EU-Angola SIFA, Article 8(6):

6. Each Party, to the extent practicable, shall endeavour to allow a reasonable time between the publication of a law or regulation referred to in paragraph 1 and the date of its application to investors.

The text of Article 8 also provides that Parties shall *"endeavour"* to allow for a *"reasonable time"* between the publication of proposed measures, and the date upon which investors are to comply with them.[16] While the provision seeks to enhance regulatory predictability by ensuring that investors are sufficiently familiarised with obligations and requirements applicable to them before these become effective, it does not define the limits of such a *"reasonable"* period of time, and instead leaves its assessment to the Parties' discretion – e.g., a *"reasonable"* period of time could correspond to the combined timeframes between the advance publication of a draft measure, stakeholder consultations and the adoption and subsequent entry into force of a measure; alternatively, it could also correspond to a defined transitional period following the entry into force of a measure to allow time for investors to acquaint themselves with new requirements and obligations thereunder prior to compliance requirements.

Across the selected Southern Neighbourhood countries, the timeframe between publication of investment-related measures and their entry into force varied significantly.

Further, **Algeria**'s, **Egypt**'s and **Jordan**'s current investment frameworks provide that investments made under the previous legislation continue doing so for their entire lifecycle. While such mechanisms seek to address predictability objectives, such *"stabilisation"* clauses are not necessarily required if extensive arrangements are maintained by countries to enhance regulatory predictability, including those recommended under Article 8 of the EU-Angola SIFA. Such clauses could fragment the legal landscape, where investments in the countries would fall under different legal frameworks and be subject to potentially contradicting requirements, and also carry the potential of impeding the implementation of meaningful regulatory changes, especially where regulatory changes aim at strengthening labour or environmental standards and responsible business conduct principles. As such, reforms seeking to permeate law-making practices with enhanced transparency – in line with the requirements set out in Article 8 of the EU-Angola SIFA – may be more appropriate in tackling concerns of regulatory unpredictability.

In contrast, the **Moroccan**, **Tunisian** and **Jordan** investment frameworks in theory repeal and replace most if not all of the provisions of the previous investment instruments, while some feature a transitional period to investment benefiting from incentives under the previous regime – see e.g., Tunisia.

Transparency of the investment framework

Beyond general requirements pertaining to the publication of both investment-specific laws and general measures of relevance – as well as the requirement to publish proposed bills in advance, together with the provision of a reasonable opportunity to comment while developing such instruments – the investment framework itself must be readily accessible to investors and other relevant stakeholders. While publication requirements generally relate to the publication via official government gazettes – such as Official Journals or Official Bulletins – of public and legal instruments (including laws, regulations, decrees, rules and other instruments that may carry either direct or general relevance to investors, among others), the transparency of the investment framework specifically concerns making available to investors *information* directly relevant to them and their investment projects, thereby further enhancing an investment framework's transparency. Indeed, the overall transparency of an investment framework also hinges on the availability such specific information relevant to investors interested in establishing and/or operating into a country. The availability of such information further enhances predictability for investors who seek to understand which regulations, restrictions and conditions are relevant to establishing their investment, and which authorisations they would require to operate in a given jurisdiction.

IIAs featuring facilitation – and more specifically, transparency – chapters or provisions have often included general transparency requirements. In most instances, these have generally specifically called for the publication of laws and regulations. IIAs geared towards investment facilitation specifically have introduced investment framework transparency requirements also in the context of "single digital platform" provisions, for example.[17]

EU-Angola SIFA, Article 9:

1. Each Party shall make available via electronic means such as a website and, where practicable, accessible through a single portal, and update to the extent possible and as appropriate, the following:

   a) laws and regulations specifically concerning investment
   b) restrictions and conditions applying to investment
   c) contact information of relevant competent authorities for the authorisation of investment.

2. Each Party shall make available, where practicable via electronic means such as a website and accessible through the single portal referred to in paragraph 1, and update to the extent possible and as appropriate, a description that informs investors and other interested persons of the practical steps needed to invest in its territory including the requirements and procedures related to:

   a) company establishment and business registration
   b) connecting to essential infrastructure such as electricity and water supply
   c) the acquisition and registering of property such as land ownership rights
   d) construction permits
   e) resolving insolvency
   f) capital transfers and payments
   g) convertibility of currency
   h) the payment of taxes
   i) access to finance, especially for MSMEs.

3. No fee shall be imposed on any investor in a Party's territory for access to the information provided under this Article or under Article 7.

In that regard, Article 9 of the EU-Angola SIFA requires that Parties make available – via electronic means, and *"where practicable"* through a single portal – up-to-date information concerning the laws and regulations specifically concerning investment, the restrictions and conditions applying to investment, and the contact information of relevant competent authorities responsible for authorising investments. It also prescribes that Parties make available – *"where practicable"*, electronically and via a single portal – information relevant to the practical steps required to invest in a jurisdictions, including requirements and procedures relevant to company establishment, connecting to essential infrastructure, the acquisition and registration of property rights, construction permits, resolving resolution, capital transfers and payments, currency convertibility, tax payments, and access to finance (including for MSMEs). In that regard, the provision could also consider requiring that Parties also provide information relating to the temporary entry and sojourn requirements for investors and key personnel.

While Article 9 addresses practical considerations that seek to achieve transparency objectives, it does not consider matters that relate to *substantive* policy coherence which Parties could also consider when developing their respective legal and regulatory investment frameworks. Further, the matters covered by Article 20 of the EU-Angola SIFA could also have been considered in the scope of this Article 9, as indeed ensuring that information necessary for investors among others in the context of application procedures – such as licensing and qualification requirements and procedures, authorisation fees, contact information of the relevant competent authorities, and information on appeal procedures, among others – *also* enhances the transparency and predictability of the investment framework.

All five selected Southern Neighbourhood countries operate single portals which meet to varying degrees the requirements set out in Article 9. **Algeria** publishes only its new Law on Investment (2022) via its IPA's website (AAPI) in English, French and Arabic; the government's Secretariat General's website however outlines legislation alongside all of its relevant implementing and other instruments, in a comprehensive and easy-to-access manner. **Jordan**'s Ministry of Investment (**MoI**) publishes the Investment Environment Law (2022) and the Public-Private Partnership Law (2020) along with their relevant implementing decrees, in Arabic and in English.[18] **Tunisia**'s Investment Agency (**TIA**) also publishes selected instruments through its website and its OSS portal, in both French and Arabic; these include the 2016 Investment Law and its Public-Private Partnership (**PPP**) Law, accompanied by some, but not all relevant regulations. **Egypt**'s GAFI publishes the most regulatory material among its regional peers, including investment, trade and customs, financial services, companies, environmental, fiscal, labour, finance, and protection of intellectual property rights instruments; these are generally available both in Arabic and in English. However, the investment legislation which it makes available does not reflect all its latest regulatory amendments. Finally, and due to the country's decentralised approach to investment facilitation, the dissemination of investment-related regulatory material in **Morocco** is not centralised through a unique website. Rather, its regional CRIs disseminate regulatory material on their websites although with little consistency between CRIs operating in the country. These websites also feature contact information either directly relevant to the competent authorities for the authorisation of investment (**Morocco**, **Tunisia**), or the contact details of their IPA's OSS that plays a role in facilitating authorisation procedures (**Algeria**, **Egypt**, **Jordan**).

With respect to restrictions, **Algeria** provides information on applying to foreign investors specifically in commercial activities via the website of its Ministry of Commerce. Information on restrictions applying in non-commercial activities, however, does not seem to be readily available on Algerian official websites. In **Jordan**, legislation enacted pursuant to the country's new Investment Law in 2022 sets out two negative lists of restricted sectors – a list of activities in which foreign investments are prohibited; and a list of activities in which a foreign ownership cap of 50% applies; while these are not available electronically and/or through a single portal, the lists significantly enhance transparency and predictability in respect of restrictions and conditions applying to foreign investment. **Egypt, Morocco** and **Tunisia** on the other hand do not make available – via electronic means, a single portal or otherwise, including in a negative list – any consolidated information on the restrictions and conditions applying to foreign investment.

Finally, and with respect to information relevant to practical steps needed to invest in a given territory, the online portals of the IPAs and/or OSS of each of the five countries provide information as well as facilitation and support services relating to company incorporation and business registration. Information on other practical steps crucial to the investor experience – e.g., connection to essential infrastructure, acquisition and registration of property, construction permits, among others – is difficult to identify and access, and so investors must consider each of these with the relevant competent authorities directly instead. In that regard, **Tunisia** is currently working towards developing a range of online administrative services at sectoral level, including services specifically intended for investors; these would include among others the filing and processing of administrative permits, social security affiliation, customs, and tax formalities.[19]

Transparency of investment incentives

Building upon transparency requirements for parties' investment framework, Article 10 of the EU-Angola SIFA relates to the transparency of the investment promotion framework, specifically of incentives available to investors. The benefits of transparency are recognised among tax and investment policy communities (IMF-OECD-UN-World Bank, 2015[7]). The OECD Declaration on International Investment and Multinational Enterprises adopted in 1976 had at the time stressed the need to strengthen international cooperation in this policy area and thereby encouraged adhering governments to make information on incentives as transparent as possible.[20] The OECD's Task Force on Tax and Development has also identified the need for a more effective global transparency framework for tax incentives for investment (OECD, 2013[8]).

While investment incentives – e.g., favourable tax treatment, grants and/or other benefits – are widely relied on by economies to attract private investment and direct it into certain sectors, activities and locations, these should be carefully designed and administered so as to avoid their costs outweighing their benefits. Tax incentives can potentially create redundancies by subsidising firms that would have invested without favourable treatment, and can as such constitute a significant cost for governments in terms of revenue forgone. Carefully designed and targeted incentives may help correct market failures and advance certain development goals, such as supporting renewable energy or skills and technology upgrades, enhancing the positive impact of investment (OECD, 2022[9]).

Despite their widespread use, there is often a lack of public information on the provision, administration, and governance of investment incentives. Many governments do not make readily available, or regularly update, lists of all available incentives and practical information for investors. Transparency of incentives allows governments to promote such good practices for the administration of their incentives by ensuring coordination across agencies to avoid potential overlaps or inefficiencies, and reducing implementing authorities' discretion in awarding incentives and opportunities for rent-seeking and corruption. Transparency of incentives can also allow for a better assessment of their effectiveness, to ensure that they adequately serve their intended policy purposes (OECD, 2023[10]).

EU-Angola SIFA, Article 10:

1. Each Party shall make available via electronic means such as a website and, where practicable, accessible through a single portal, and update to the extent possible and as appropriate, information on investment incentives.

2. The information referred to in paragraph 1 shall cover all the incentives available to investors, including financial incentives, fiscal incentives as well as in-kind transfers, including non-financial incentives.

3. The information referred to in paragraph 1 shall include the following elements:

a) The legal basis of the incentive
b) The form of the incentive
c) The eligibility requirements of the incentive
d) The application process for the incentive, including the required forms and documents
e) Contact information of the competent authority.

The scope of the EU-Angola SIFA Article 10 is relatively broad, as it covers all types of incentives available to investors, including financial, fiscal as well as *"non-financial"* incentives. The scope of information on incentives which Parties are required to make available is clearly set out. Such information should include the legal basis of incentives – i.e., the regulatory measures in which they are outlined should also be published or made available per the publication requirements of Article 7 – the form of the incentives, eligibility requirements, application process with forms and documents, and contact information of competent authorities. [21] The Article also sets a requirement to render information accessible through electronic means, and, if practicable, through a "single portal", such as on a national IPA's website or an investor platform.

All but one of the five selected Southern Neighbourhood offer financial support for investment costs in activities related to sustainable development, environmental protection or renewable energy (**Algeria**, **Egypt**, **Morocco**, **Tunisia**), as well as other incentives based on a variety of eligibility criteria (Ampntel Chafiz, 2023[11]). However, approaches to enhancing the transparency of incentives is not consistent throughout the countries. Most selected Southern Neighbourhood countries provide a general overview of the different financial and fiscal incentives offered to investors, either through their IPAs' websites (**Algeria**, **Egypt**), or on their nation-wide investor platforms (**Algeria**, **Morocco**, **Tunisia**). Nevertheless, the granularity of information featured on these portals varies significantly, especially when benchmarked against Article 10 of the EU-Angola SIFA. **Tunisia** and **Morocco** appear to provide the most comprehensive information on incentives out of the five countries, including a contact information of a competent agent for **Tunisia**. In contrast, information on application procedures, documents, and institutional settings for incentives are not provided by **Algeria** and **Egypt**.

At the time of writing in September 2023, **Jordan** was the only country that did not maintain such a portal, even though its previous IPA had successfully implemented an 'incentives inventory' with the support of the World Bank in 2016.[22] The country's current priorities include addressing such shortcomings through a dedicated online investor portal, as reflected by the MoI's Investment Promotion Strategy (2023-2026) published in June 2023.[23]

Linkages with the host economy

Anchoring investors through deep linkages with the local economy, especially with domestic MSMEs and suppliers, can be an effective investment retention strategy. It can also strengthen a country's investment ecosystem: linkages allow for technology transfers, knowledge and managerial and technical skills, which in turn boosts the local private sector. Business surveys have in that regard highlighted the value which investors have found in the existing capacity and skills of local suppliers, as well as government support in that area, e.g., availability of information on relevant local suppliers (World Bank Group, 2017[1]). By way of context, **Morocco and Egypt** for example source more than 60% of their inputs domestically, whereas **Jordan**'s **and Tunisia**'s rates hover significantly lower, at around 30-40% (OECD, 2023[12]).

Public policies seeking to enhance spillovers run across a range of policy areas, including investment promotion and facilitation. In that regard, the OECD (2023) Policy Toolkit for Strengthening FDI and SME Linkages was developed to provide policy advice to governments as to how to increase knowledge and technology benefits from FDI on domestic small-and-medium enterprises and their local economy more generally. This facilitation requirement has been featured in a number of multilateral investment agreements; in some instances, such a requirement has been introduced in a *development goals* and *sustainability* context. [24]

EU-Angola SIFA, Article 11:

Each Party is encouraged to make available to investors and persons seeking to invest information on domestic suppliers with a view to strengthening linkages with the local economy, increasing the competitiveness of domestic suppliers and enhancing the contribution of investment to sustainable development.

Article 11 of the EU-Angola SIFA *"encourages"* Parties to make available to investors information on domestic suppliers, thereby enhancing transparency for information relevant to investors. The stated objective of the provision is to strengthen local economy linkages, increase the competitiveness of domestic suppliers and further, enhance the contribution of investment to sustainable development. Nevertheless, Article 11 falls short of outlining or providing specific examples of the means by which such *"information"* should be made available, or further define specifically what *"information"* is envisaged under the provision – e.g., matchmaking services, platforms and events, local supplier databases, among others.

Egypt's investment law does not explicitly address this particular policy area, and on the face of publicly available information, neither its IPA nor its OSS make available to potential or existing investors any information on domestic suppliers with a view to strengthening local economy linkages. **Jordan**'s investment law does, but in passing only. However, the Jordan Enterprise Development Corporation (JEDCO), in collaboration with local chambers of commerce and business associations, implements the National Linkages Programme, which connects large manufacturers with local SME suppliers, facilitates their interaction and provides technical and financial support to ensure that locally sourced inputs meet the needs of MNEs operating in Jordan (OECD, 2023[12]). Based on its mandate, **Algeria**'s IPA must make available to investors information relevant to the realisation of their investment projects, including databases on domestic business opportunities and resources, as well as setting up a business matchmaking service and promote business and partnership opportunities. These services were however at the time of writing in September 2023 not yet available through the AAPI website. **Morocco**'s regions have undertaken regional efforts to provide information on domestic suppliers relevant to investors.[25] These efforts are aligned with the mandate country's regional CRIs, which are missioned among others with making available data and information on regional investment and cooperation opportunities. **Tunisia** has also undertaken similar – but centralised – efforts, namely via two of its IPAs, the TIA and the APII. Further, Tunisia's 2016 Law re-organising the country's Ministry of Development, Investment and International Cooperation established a general investment framework committee (*comité d'encadrement général de l'investissement*) that is among others responsible for developing investment promotion policies and partnerships with domestic and foreign investment promotion actors and entities. How this objective has been implemented in practice is not clear on the face of publicly available information.

Streamlining of investment authorisation procedures

Effective regulation does not necessarily entail less regulation but rather, the streamlining of administrative processes with a view to simplify and improve the efficiency of procedures that may be required throughout an investment project's life cycle (OECD, 2015[2]). Heavy administrative and bureaucratic procedures may render business establishment and operation cumbersome for investors and could even represent practical impediments that ultimately deter investors from pursuing their projects. As such, the streamlining of administrative applications and procedures is another cornerstone of investment facilitation, as it guarantees the efficiency and predictability of a country's legal and regulatory framework by reducing bureaucratic "*red tape*", and enhances investors' confidence by requiring that authorisation procedures are administered objectively, impartially and with independence by the host state's administrative authorities.

Given the sheer variety of administrative procedures that apply to all steps of an investment life cycle, and which can sensibly differ from one investment to another depending on the economic sector, activity, or location of a project, the streamlining of administrative processes is critical to both business establishment (i.e., admission requirements and formalities, company establishment, etc.) as well as business operation or expansion (e.g., licencing requirements, the granting of permits and other authorisations), and would thus require a "whole-of-government" approach.

Streamlining is a common feature of trade and investment facilitation, and both policy areas are complementary to the extent that businesses wishing to carry out exporting activities could also face significant obstacles in obtaining trade licenses. But where streamlining efforts in the context of trade facilitation focus primarily on export or import licenses and customs procedures, investment facilitation efforts are broader by nature, and relate to the general administrative efficiency of a country, starting from the establishment and company incorporation phase, all the way to the obtaining a wide range of general and investment-specific licences, permits and other authorisations. Investment facilitation provisions featured in IIAs concluded in recent years have generally related specifically to transparency and publication requirements. In more recent years however, a number of IIAs have also featured general calls for efforts to streamline applications and authorisations procedures;[26] some have also outlined more technical requirements that seek to achieve the objective of streamlining, comparable to the EU-Angola SIFA's Chapter 3.[27]

Two complementary types of practical solutions for streamlining administrative authorisations are observed in practice: an underlying – and necessary – "whole-of-government" approach to administrative streamlining that seeks to achieve overall administrative efficiency; and a complementary investment-specific approach which seeks to facilitate specific investment-related procedures. Investment-specific streamlining solutions can for example include:

- The establishment of a dedicated agency developed to guide and provide aftercare services to investors, e.g., via a unified IPA with an OSS for investors, via which information on required establishment and operation authorisations can be identified.
- Bestowing IPAs and OSS with the mandate to directly process – some or all – administrative authorisation requests and grant such authorisations (e.g., the OSS is either provided with the mandate to issue such authorisations directly, or alternatively, hosts administrations' and public authorities' representatives that carry such mandate); or alternatively, facilitate the obtention of authorisations (i.e., liaising on behalf of investors with relevant competent authorities, assisting investors in meeting requirements for the granting of necessary authorisations, etc.).
- Clarifying eligibility criteria underlying authorisation applications with a view to enhance legal, regulatory, and administrative predictability and reduce administrative agencies' discretion in the granting of authorisations. This can be achieved, e.g., by clearly defining and making publicly available eligibility conditions, timeframes and fees relevant to authorisation applications, as well as the authorities competent to process such applications; by providing clarity throughout application processes and allowing applicants to complete their applications further to initial submission, if and when relevant; by clearly outlining appeal and/or resubmission mechanisms where applications are rejected; and by institutionalising 'tacit approval' principle (if and when relevant) whereby authorisations for complete applications are deemed granted beyond a specific timeframe, with a view to lighten the administrative burden.
- Clarifying authorisation application processes for investors with a view to enhancing the efficiency of application processes. This can be done through a variety of means, e.g., via the creation of an online, unified investor platform allowing for online applications and their follow-up; enhanced communication between authorities and investors; and enhanced communication and coordination between competent authorities when authorisations fall within several authorities' jurisdictions.
- Ensuring that officials responsible for applying regulations and processing applications have the adequate credentials, are well-trained, shielded from undue influence of interested groups,

provided with fair salaries, and have sufficient resources for carrying out their tasks (OECD, 2015[2]).

Chapter 3 of the EU-Angola SIFA (Articles 13 to 21) outlines a number of measures and recommendations for Parties to streamline "investment authorisation" procedures. Authorisations are defined under the Agreement as the *"permission[s] to pursue any economic activity related to an investment, resulting from a procedure an investor must adhere to in order to demonstrate compliance with the necessary requirements"*. The scope Chapter 3 would thus pertain to authorisation procedures at the establishment and operation phases of investments.[28]

Authorisation procedures could arguably fall within the scope of Article 6 of the EU-Angola SIFA, which calls for a *reasonable, objective and impartial* administration of investment-related measures of general application. Chapter 3 of the Agreement however provides for separate – but not unrelated – principles that govern the adoption, maintenance and application of authorisation-related measures. Article 19 of the EU-Angola calls for *objective*, *impartial* and *independent* decision-making processes on investment authorisation applications by administrative authorities; and Article 21 provides for some disciplines on the *design* as well as the *administration* of authorisation processes to ensure good practice by relevant authorities.[29]

EU-Angola SIFA, Article 19:

If a Party adopts or maintains a measure relating to authorisation, it shall ensure that the competent authority concerned processes an application, reaches and administers its decisions objectively, impartially and in a manner independent from the undue influence of any person carrying out the economic activity for which authorisation is required.

EU-Angola SIFA, Article 21:

If a Party adopts or maintains measures relating to authorisations, it shall ensure that:

a) those measures are based on clear, objective and transparent criteria, which may include the competence and ability to carry out the economic activity, including in compliance with a Party's regulatory requirements such as health and environmental requirements, it being understood that competent authorities may assess the weight to be given to each criterion;
b) the procedures are impartial, easily accessible to all applicants, and adequate to allow applicants to demonstrate whether they meet the requirements; and
c) the procedures do not in themselves unjustifiably prevent fulfilment of the requirements.

Further streamlining of investment authorisation processes is directly relevant to Southern Neighbourhood countries. The outsized role of privileged firms – e.g., state-owned enterprises or politically-connected private-sector firms benefitting from special regulatory treatment and selective enforcement of rules – has often been pointed out as a key challenge hampering competitive markets in these countries (OECD, 2021[13]). In parallel, business operators have reported facing important challenges in obtaining investment-related authorisations, whether it be for operating licences, trade licences or construction permits; although perceptions of the effects of these administrative inefficiencies over day-to-day operations vary significantly across the selected countries. The respective shares of **Moroccan** and **Tunisian** firms surveyed by the World Bank in 2019 and 2020 that identified business licensing and permits as a "major" constraint are among the highest of the MENA region. By contrast, almost no foreign-invested enterprises in **Jordan**, and only a few in **Egypt**, had identified it as a major constraint hampering their operations (Figure 2.2).

Figure 2.2. Percent of firms identifying business licensing and permits as a major constraint in the selected Southern Neighbourhood countries (by firm type)

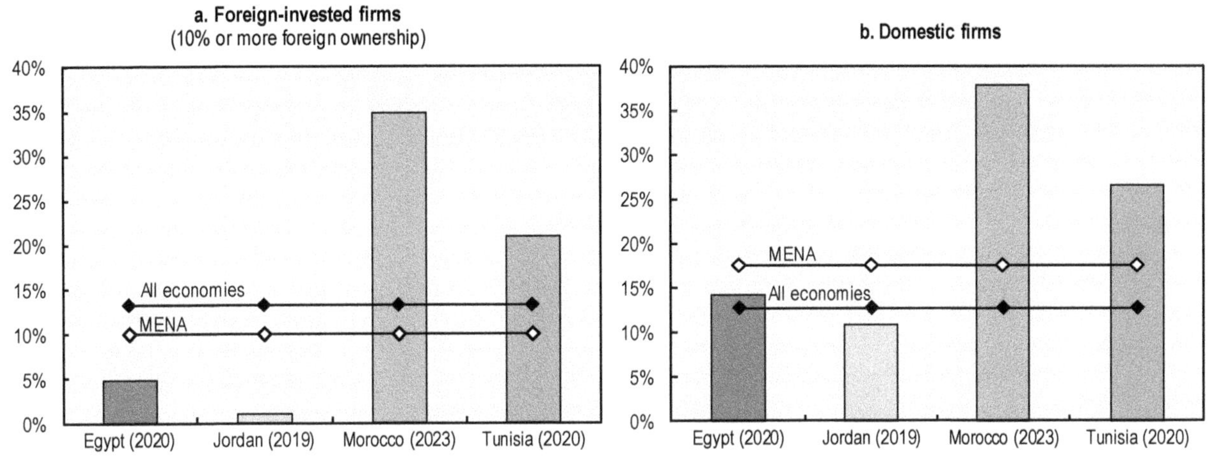

Note: The Enterprise Surveys collect a wide array of qualitative and quantitative information through face-to-face interviews conducted by the World Bank and its partners with firm managers and owners regarding the business environment in their countries and the productivity of their firms. The surveys are administered to a sample of firms (small, medium and large) in selected regions within a country that represent the largest centres of production and business enterprise. Surveyed firms operate in the entire manufacturing sector, the services sector, and the transportation and construction sectors. They exclude enterprises in public utilities, government services, health care, and financial services. Surveys conducted after 2006 have followed a uniform Global methodology. Enterprise Surveys in the MENA region are jointly funded with the European Bank for Reconstruction and Development (EBRD) and the European Investment Bank (EIB). Regional averages are computed using the latest available year of survey data for surveys posted between 2010-2017 and following the global methodology. Years in parentheses indicate latest available data for individual countries. Country-level data unavailable for Algeria.
Source: OECD elaboration from World Bank Enterprise Surveys.

Survey responses also show a notable contrast between the perceptions of domestic firms and foreign-invested ones conducting business in the countries. A higher proportion of domestic firms surveyed compared to foreign-invested ones identify business licensing and permits as a major constraint in the selected countries. While such difference is insignificant on a global scale, such trend can be observed across the MENA region, where some contrasts appear striking, e.g., in **Egypt** and **Jordan** (Figure 2.2). Similarly, differences in perceptions may be observed following the location of investors, potentially signalling uneven facilitation efforts across the territories. The issue is most notable in **Morocco** where practically no firms operating in the regions of Marrakech-Safi, Rabat-Salé-Kénitra or Tanger-Tétouan-Al Hoceïma reported having issues with business licensing, whereas nearly half of firms surveyed in the regions of Fès-Meknès, Souss-Massa or in the Oriental identified it as a major constraint.

Overall, delays in obtaining investment-related authorisations in Southern Neighbourhood countries are generally shorter than those observed on average in the MENA region, especially for operating licences and construction permits. They are the highest in **Egypt** among all the countries covered by this Report, and across all types of authorisations; followed by **Tunisia**. Authorisation procedures in **Morocco**, and in **Jordan** especially, appear to be swift in contrast (Figure 2.3).

Figure 2.3. Days to obtain authorisations in the selected Southern Neighbourhood countries: (by authorisation type)

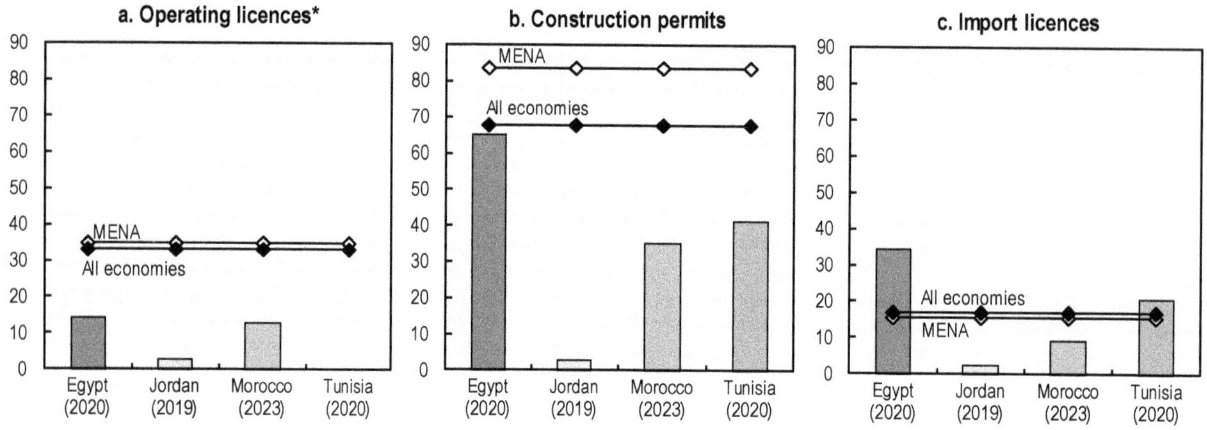

Note: See note under Figure 2.2. *Incomplete data for operating licences in Tunisia.
Source: OECD elaboration from World Bank Enterprise Surveys.

With the exception of **Jordan**, where it appears to be rare, investors have occasionally reported facing some corruption in carrying out their authorisation procedures in the Southern Neighbourhood countries. In recent years, procedures relating for construction permits appear to be the most affected, for which a significantly higher proportion of surveyed firms – domestic and foreign – reported being expected to give gifts to obtain them compared to the average proportion in the region (Figure 2.4).

Figure 2.4. Percent of firms expected to give gifts to obtain authorisations in the selected Southern Neighbourhood countries (by authorisation type)

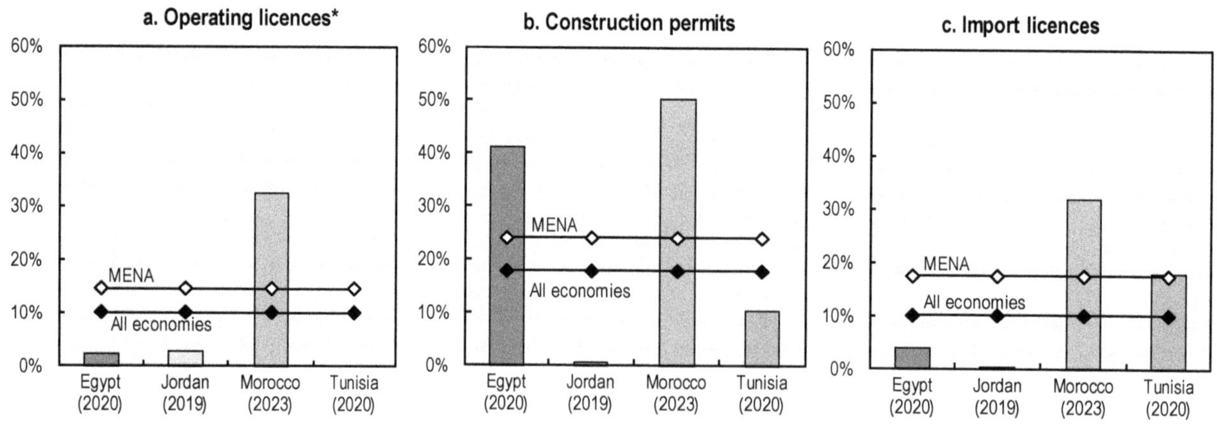

Note: See note under Figure 2.2. *Incomplete data for operating licences in Tunisia.
Source: OECD elaboration from World Bank Enterprise Surveys.

The practical solutions provided under Chapter 3 and which seek to streamline authorisation procedures concern modalities pertaining to the submission of applications (Article 14), including the possibility for electronic applications (Article 16), application timeframes (Article 15), and authorisation fees (Article 18). It also outlines the specific arrangements to be considered and implemented in the context of the processing of applications, including indicative timeframes, updates on applications and available arrangements in the case of incomplete applications, among others (Article 17). Such practical solutions to streamline authorisation procedures are implemented to varying degrees throughout the five selected countries of the Southern Neighbourhood. The following sections provide an overview of these practical solutions.

Submission of applications, timeframes, electronic applications and acceptance of copies

The principles embodied in Articles 14 to 16 of the EU-Angola SIFA establish a general structure for the authorisation of investments and upon which procedures for such authorisations rest. These overarching principles seek to promote predictability and efficiency, by avoiding duplicate and/or overlapping applications for single authorisations, by providing certainty to investors as to the timeframes of their applications, and by allowing investors to use their resources more efficiently by allowing for electronic authorisation applications. Indeed, in addition to being transparent and predictable, practical solutions centred around streamlining seek to simplify and render efficient these procedures and requirements, for both investors and competent authorities.[30] As noted above, to date, only a few IIA have set out specific streamlining requirements analogous to Articles 14-16 of the EU-Angola SIFA which address technical requirements of how authorisation applications should be processed.[31]

The handling of multiple applications for single authorisations, the timeframes envisaged for applications, and the acceptance of electronic applications and copies, are the first three practical solutions addressed by Chapter 3 of the Agreement to achieve the objective of streamlining authorisation procedures. These practical solutions are intentionally broad by nature, allowing for flexibility as to how Parties should consider implementing them; indeed, the language of these provisions encourages Parties to implement such practical solutions with a view to enhancing the streamlining of their respective authorisation procedures, *"to the extent practicable"* or *"to the extent possible*". The former would seem to afford a broader degree of discretion to Parties in implementing a given practical measure, i.e., by taking into account considerations that go beyond *feasibility* and that could also factor in practical considerations including technical, institutional and human resources related considerations.

EU-Angola SIFA, Article 14:

Each Party shall, to the extent practicable, avoid requiring an applicant to approach more than one competent authority for each application for authorisation. If an activity for which authorisation is requested is within the jurisdiction of multiple competent authorities, multiple applications for authorisation may be required.

EU-Angola SIFA, Article 15:

If a Party requires authorization, it shall ensure that its competent authorities, to the extent practicable, permit the submission of an application at any time throughout the year. If a specific time period for applying for authorization exists, the Party shall ensure that the competent authorities allow a reasonable period of time for the submission of an application.

EU-Angola SIFA, Article 16:

If a Party requires authorisation, it shall ensure that its competent authorities:

a) to the extent possible, accept applications in electronic format; and

b) accept copies of documents, that are authenticated in accordance with the Party's laws, in place of original documents, unless the competent authorities require original documents to protect the integrity of the authorisation process.

Under Article 14, the Agreement encourages that Parties avoid requiring that applicants approach more than one competent authority for each authorisation application *"to the extent practicable"*, but also provides for instances where a single authorisation may require multiple applications from different competent authorities. The provision however falls short of suggesting that in such instances, and to the extent practicable, Parties may consider setting up a single window or OSS to coordinate multiple applications for single authorisations, among others, so as to further ensure the streamlining of authorisation procedures.[32] Rather, the Agreement envisages – in a provision featured under a separate Chapter – an "*investment facilitation focal point*", whose role is limited to an information-only portal, serving as *"first points of contact for investors regarding measures affecting investment"*, responsible for *"respond[ing] to inquiries from investors"* and redirecting investors in the event they are unable to respond to queries from investors, among others (EU-Angola SIFA, Article 22). In practice, the selected Southern Neighbourhood countries' respective IPAs go further than the measure suggested by the Agreement, as highlighted below.[33] Articles 15 and 16 encourage Parties' competent authorities to allow for the submission of applications free of time-bars, *"at any time throughout the year"*, but also considers the possibility that specific time periods may apply and recommends in such instances that Parties ensure that their competent authorities *"allow a reasonable period of time for the submission of an application"*. Separately, it requires that competent authorities, *"to the extent possible"*, accept applications in electronic format and copies of documents authenticated in accordance with domestic requirements, *"unless the competent authorities require original documents to protect the integrity of the authorisation process"*.

The selected Southern Neighbourhood countries deploy a variety of different measures to address the submission and handling of applications for authorisation, whether these authorisations involve single or multiple applications. In that regard, the mandates of their respective OSS vary, as well as the services offered under their banner. Broadly speaking, the OSS act as focal points, providing information to investors requiring guidance on authorisation applications. They may also – depending on the types of investment projects and economic activities contemplated, and the capital value of projected investments – operate as single windows, either directly issuing authorisations required by investors or ensuring the coordination between investors and relevant competent authorities with a view to ease investors' administrative burden.

The respective mandates of the OSS of four out of the five selected Southern Neighbourhood countries – i.e., all but for Tunisia – are defined by reference to their very membership, which includes representatives of relevant competent authorities that are either entrusted with processing and issuing authorisations that fall within their jurisdiction, *or* act as points of contact between investors and their relevant authorities for the granting of required authorisations. In **Algeria** and **Egypt**, the exact composition of the two countries' OSS is not publicly available, which blurs the effective mandate of the countries' respective OSS.[34] As such, while some authorisations can be issued directly by the countries' respective OSS – electronic applications are not available under these frameworks, and applications but therefore presumably be submitted in person at the physical OSS offices – others may fall within the jurisdictions of several competent authorities and could thus entail that investors contemplate multiple applications to obtain an authorisation for a single activity. In practice, it is likely that the countries' OSS coordinate any liaising between investors and different authorities.

In **Jordan**, the MoI's OSS – the CIS – processes applications and issues authorisations for some economic activities only, and as such only caters to investors operating in those economic sectors which fall within the scope of Jordan's 2022 Investment Environment Law. The Jordanian MoI recently announced in that regard that it had digitalised 95% of the services offered by it through its CIS portal. Outside of these, investors must address the relevant competent authorities to obtain authorisations that do not fall within the competence of the CIS. In parallel to authorisation applications, the Jordanian framework also requires pre-admission approvals in respect of a set number of economic activities; streamlining and centralisation of applications for these authorisations is also uneven.

Morocco's CRIs operate as OSS across the country's 12 regions and assist investors navigate through establishment and operation requirements and formalities, and its regional CRUIs are mandated with issuing certain investment-related administrative acts, identified by way of Decree.[35] Applications for such authorisations may be submitted via the country's centralised CRI-Platform. Investors must obtain other authorisations which they require for the realisation of their investment projects with the relevant competent authorities. Finally, in **Tunisia**, investment-related licences, authorisations and other administrative permits are processed and issued by a special commission attached to one of the country's main IPA – the TIA's *Commission for licences and approvals*, whose membership includes relevant ministries and other competent authorities. The *Commission* operates within the TIA and is directly responsible for reviewing, deciding upon and ultimately issuing investor applications for licences and authorisations necessary to carry out investment projects exceeding TND 15 million, in coordination with the relevant authorities. As such, the country's institutional arrangement features a streamlined, single portal mechanism to effectively address the question of multiple applications, but only in respect of a limited category of investments. Online services and electronic applications for these projects are envisaged but were at the time of writing in September 2023 not yet operational. Investors seeking to realise investment projects whose value falls under this threshold must submit applications to the relevant competent authorities, which could in practice entail multiple applications for single authorisations. Indeed, other IPAs and their OSS – such as the Tunisian APII – only operate as information focal points with respect to operation-related authorisations and procedures.

No specific provisions in the investment frameworks of any of the selected Southern Neighbourhood countries specifically define or otherwise limits the timeframes for the submission of authorisation applications. It can be presumed generally speaking that, unless provided otherwise for specific authorisations, applications may be submitted at any time throughout the year. Further, and save for Morocco's legislation adopted with a view to improve the efficiency of all administrative procedures and formalities (which stipulates that administrations may not require from the applicant to legalise documents nor to provide certified copies except in exceptional circumstances), none of the other countries' respective investment frameworks explicitly address matters related to the admissibility of authenticated copies in lieu of originals.

The somewhat fragmented single application services which are featured in the frameworks of each of the five selected Southern Neighbourhood countries, which vary depending on the investment projects and economic activities contemplated – e.g., in Jordan –, the types of authorisations and licences needed – e.g., in Morocco – and the breadth of projects envisaged – e.g., in Tunisia – may bring about burdensome authorisation – and multiple-application – procedures, and could thus ultimately result in delays in the implementation of investment projects. The selected countries have nevertheless introduced measures which seek to address these concerns. In **Morocco** and **Tunisia**, public administrations may only request from users documents required by laws and regulations in force and formally identified via the national portal for the simplification of administrative procedures and in **Morocco**, unless otherwise required by laws and regulations, public administrations are not to ask users for more than one copy of an application for an administrative document. Authorities in **Morocco, Jordan** and **Tunisia** must also refrain requesting from investors documents they may already have in their possession or which can be provided by other public administrations and/or coordinate and share among themselves documents relevant to processing investor applications. Measures that seek to cap procedural timelines may similarly palliate these concerns.

Processing of applications

Heavy administrative and bureaucratic procedures may result in cumbersome and time-intensive authorisation processes for investors. Investment projects call for a wide range of different types of authorisations for their realisation. These can significantly differ from one investment to another depending among others on the economic sector, activity and/or location of a project. As such, measures seeking to streamline authorisation processes have often been encouraged – as is witnessed in a number of the selected Southern Neighbourhood countries, such as Morocco and Tunisia for example – through a "*whole-of-government*" approach. These are complemented in practice by parallel measures that seek to simplify investment-specific procedures. The manner in which authorisation applications are processed, and the principles upon which these processes rest, directly impact the degree to which such processes are *streamlined* and their efficiency *enhanced*, and more generally, the overall predictability of an investment framework. Commitments to reduce and simplify administrative procedures have been recognised as *"contributing significantly to the objective of facilitating investment"* in the context of the WTO structured discussions on an investment facilitation for development agreement.[36] Earlier IIAs including investment facilitation provisions have at times featured general and broad-brushed requirements calling for the streamlining of application processes.[37] More recent international agreements – both IIAs as well as trade agreements – have featured similarly drafted and as ambitious streamlining provisions.[38]

EU-Angola SIFA, Article 17:

1. If a Party requires authorisation, it shall ensure that its competent authorities:
   a. to the extent practicable, provide an indicative timeframe for the processing of the application;
   b. upon request of the applicant, provide, without undue delay, information concerning the status of the application
   c. to the extent practicable, ascertain, without undue delay, the completeness of the application for processing under the Party's laws and regulations
   d. if they consider an application complete for the purposes of processing under the Party's laws and regulations[1], within a reasonable period of time after the submission of the application ensure that:
      i. the processing of the application is completed;
      ii. the applicant is informed of the decision concerning the application, to the extent possible, in writing[2];
   e. if they consider an application incomplete for the purposes of processing under the Parties' laws and regulations, within a reasonable period of time, to the extent practicable:
      i. inform the applicant that the application is incomplete
      ii. upon request of the applicant, identify the additional information required to complete the application, or otherwise provide guidance as to why the application is considered incomplete
      iii. provide the applicant with the opportunity to provide the additional information that is required to complete the application[3];

      if none of the actions referred to in points (i), (ii) and (iii) is practicable, and the application is rejected due to incompleteness, the competent authorities shall ensure that they inform the applicant within a reasonable period of time; and

f. if an application is rejected, inform the applicant, either upon their own initiative or upon request of the applicant, of the reasons for rejection and of the timeframe for an appeal, and, if applicable, the procedures for resubmission of an application; an applicant shall not be prevented from resubmitting another application solely on the basis of a previously rejected application.

2. Each Party shall ensure that its competent authorities grant an authorisation as soon as it is established, in light of an appropriate examination, that the applicant meets the conditions for obtaining it.
3. Each Party shall ensure that authorisation, once granted, enters into effect without undue delay, subject to the applicable terms and conditions.[9]

Notes
1. Competent authorities may require that all information is submitted in a specified format to consider it "complete for the purposes of processing".
2. Competent authorities may meet the requirement set out in point (i) by informing an applicant in advance in writing, including through a published measure, that a lack of response after a specified period of time from the date of submission of the application indicates acceptance of the application. The reference to "in writing" shall be understood as including electronic format.
3. Such "opportunity" does not require a competent authority to provide extensions of deadline.

Article 17 builds upon the overarching principles outlined at Articles 14 to 16. It outlines general administrative streamlining requirements relevant to the processing of applications for authorisations, from start – i.e., once an application is submitted – to finish – i.e., the granting of an authorisation, its refusal, and possible recourse against such refusal. By simplifying and rendering efficient, and ultimately speeding up authorisation application formalities and procedures, it seeks to promote transparency, and therefore legal certainty and predictability. Requirements related to informing investors of the status of their application – whether complete or incomplete – and allowing investors to provide additional information if competent authorities deem applications incomplete, and the introduction of a 'tacit approval' mechanism, are central tenets of investment facilitation, but also of good governance part of a broader, "*whole-of-government*" approach to administrative simplification and efficiency. The wording of the Article 17 leaves room for flexibility in *how* Parties should consider implementing these practical solutions, by underlining that several – but not all – requirements should be implemented *"to the extent practicable"*, thereby accommodating Parties' respective domestic regimes and legal systems, as well as their ability – practical and resource-based, among others – to implement some of the Agreement's requirements.

Comprehensive information on application processes is scarce in **Algeria**. While the country's OSS is mandated to play a role in facilitating the obtention of authorisations, no information is available as to the manner in which authorisation applications should be submitted, how they are processed, or the principles upon which these processes rest, neither via the country's framework for investment nor its Algeria's OSS. The remaining four countries features standardised streamlining principles which seek to establish a clear framework defining how authorisation applications are processed by their respective OSS and relevant competent authorities.

Morocco's legal framework requires that all investment-related authorisations be issued within a capped timeframe. Similarly, in **Jordan**, authorisation applications for those economic activities which fall within the scope of the country's 2022 Investment Environment law – and thus within the purview of its OSS, the CIS – also benefit from clearly set out and standardised processing timeframes. In **Egypt** and **Tunisia**, competent authorities have also established clear timeframes within which they are to issue authorisations further to receiving complete applications. Specific streamlining rules featured in the two countries' frameworks limit these timeframes in specific instances (e.g., in Tunisia, timeframes are capped by way of Decree when these are not defined by the competent authorities; in the case of

Egypt, GAFI is entrusted with the power to expedite pending authorisation applications if these are not granted within the established timeframes).

Further, investors in **Morocco** are able to follow-up on the status of their applications – and determine whether they have been deemed complete or incomplete by the OSS – via the online CRI-Invest Platform, for those applications that fall within the mandate of CRUIs; it is unclear whether this right is guaranteed for applications which fall within the purview of the competent authorities rather than the CRUIs. A formalised requirement to update investors as to the status of their applications is not featured in the **Egyptian**, **Jordan**, and **Tunisia** frameworks, but this may be observed in practice with the countries' respective OSS. In **Egypt**, in contrast to the other frameworks, competent authorities are nevertheless formally required to notify investors of the outcome of their application, in writing and within clear timeframes. All four frameworks also feature 'tacit approval' mechanisms, whereby complete authorisation applications that have not been explicitly denied by the competent authorities within a specified timeframe are deemed approved.

Each of the four countries have also introduced measures addressing incomplete authorisation applications. In **Egypt**, competent authorities – or competent authorities' representatives within the ISC –must request from investors any missing documents within a prescribed timeframe, beyond which application files are automatically deemed complete. Decisions which they render must be reasoned, justified and transparent, and investors may appeal negative decisions before GAFI's Grievance Committee, the procedures for which are set out in the 2017 Investment Law. The latter also prevents competent authorities from revoking or suspending authorisations without first providing users with prior notice and a prescribed "*grace period*" to rectify any notified breaches. In this scenario, it is GAFI that is entrusted with the authority to authorise revocations, where appropriate. Similar measures are available in **Morocco**, both in respect of applications for authorisations submitted to the CRUIs and those submitted directly to the relevant competent authorities. Rules on addressing incomplete applications have not been formalised in **Jordan** or **Tunisia**; while competent authorities must motivate any negative decisions they render and notify the outcome of the application process in writing, no recourse or appeal mechanisms are available to applicants. In that regard, **Jordan**'s 2022 Investment Environment Law explicitly prohibits some grounds for refusal to grant licences; further, it sets out that decisions to withdraw licences must follow a specific procedural framework: authorities need to notify the licence holder of the alleged violation of the licence terms and provide them with a timeframe for rectification or for providing evidence that no violation has occurred.

Fees

Administrative fees are another important feature of investment-related authorisation procedures. Along with delays, fees can become important impediments to business operations especially when administered in an untransparent, unpredictable or unreasonable way. At the same time, fees are often incumbent upon the authorisations requested and the administrative authorities under the jurisdictions of which they fall. As such, the fee-related governance differs significantly across competent authorities, and resultingly, the methods by which fees are devised and applicable rates, among others, vary considerably accordingly. The EU-Angola SIFA features several overarching principles that seek to enhance the transparency of administrative fees, to be considered and implemented by the Parties' competent authorities, with a view to mitigate discretionary concerns which the administration of fees could raise.

EU-Angola SIFA, Article 18:

1. For all economic activities other than financial services, each Party shall ensure that the authorisation fees charged by its competent authorities are reasonable and transparent and do not in themselves restrict the investment.
2. With regard to financial services, each Party shall ensure that its competent authorities, with respect to the authorisation fees they charge, provide applicants with a schedule of fees or information on how fee amounts are determined, and do not use the fees as a means of avoiding the Party's commitments or obligations.
3. Authorisation fees do not include fees for the use of natural resources, payments for auction, tendering or other non-discriminatory means of awarding concessions or mandated contributions to universal service provision.
4. Except in urgent circumstances, each Party shall allow adequate time between the publication and the entry into force of new or amended fees and charges related to authorisation procedures for investment, or information enabling investors to understand the calculation of those fees and charges. Those fees and charges shall not be applied until that information has been published.
5. Each Party shall, to the extent practicable, adopt or maintain procedures allowing the option of electronic payment for fees and charges collected by relevant competent authorities for the authorisation of investments.

Article 18 of the EU-Angola SIFA provides for general principles applicable to all administrative fees and special provisions concerning financial services fees:

- **General administrative fees** – excluding in respect of financial services – shall be *reasonable* and *transparent* so as to not restrict investments. **Fees for financial services** specifically shall either be set out in a schedule of fees or applicants should be provided information on how fee amounts are determined by administrative authorities.
- On the **administration** of all types of fees by licensing authorities, the EU-Angola SIFA reiterates some of the guiding regulatory predictability principles enshrined in its Article 8, including the requirement to allow for adequate time between the publication and entry into force of amended fees, or provide sufficient information to investors on how authorities calculate fees to enhance the transparency and predictability of authorisation procedures. Parties are also encouraged to provide for the electronic payment of fees.

As fees may vary significantly from one administrative authority to another, it is difficult to assess in practice the extent to which such fees are transparent and reasonable and whether they are administered in a way that does not restrict investment projects. Investment laws can nevertheless introduce overarching frameworks designed to rationalise administrative fees throughout government agencies, especially in respect of licensing authorities. Such practice is only featured – to some degree – in the **Tunisian** framework, which adopted an overarching framework to streamline all administrative processes in the country (beyond business and investment-related administrations). Under the 2019-47, authorities are required to make available and regularly update information on authorisation processes – which could include administrative fees – and to provide online electronic payment options for administrative fees.

Publication and information available

Information pertaining to *authorisations* and their procedures are central to enhancing the transparency and overall predictability of an investment framework. A requirement to make available such information is also the first building block to ensuring that authorisation procedures are streamlined and efficient. Regional IIAs with a facilitation focus have featured requirements to make available information relating to authorisations, and often so in the context of provisions requiring the establishment of single windows, for example.[39] The level of detail featured in Article 20 of the EU-Angola SIFA stands out, however.

In that regard, its bears noting that the matters covered by Article 20 of the EU-Angola SIFA could also have been considered in the scope of this Article 9, as indeed ensuring that information necessary for investors among others in the context of application procedures – such as licensing and qualification requirements and procedures, authorisation fees, contact information of the relevant competent authorities, and information on appeal procedures, among others – *also* enhances the transparency and predictability of the investment framework.

Lack of or absence of information necessary to investors – or persons seeking to invest – in a given economy are perceived as a considerable obstacle to business operations and can result in significant delays in the realisation of an investment project. In this regard, business surveys have highlighted concerns by investors in respect of obtaining business and investment-related authorisations – although it transpires that a higher proportion of domestic firms surveyed compared to foreign-invested ones identify business licensing and permits as a major constraint in the selected countries of the Southern Neighbourhood. Further, overall, delays in obtaining investment-related authorisations in Southern Neighbourhood countries are generally shorter than those observed on average in the MENA region, especially for operating licences and construction permits.

Indeed, in recent years, most of the selected countries of the Southern Neighbourhood introduced a series of measures seeking to enhance the transparency of their frameworks with respect to information relevant to authorisations and authorisation procedures, which has in turn contributed to significantly streamline such procedures in their respective frameworks. Algeria stands out as against the other four countries, however. While its AAPI plays a role in facilitating the obtention of approvals, licences and permits through its two OSS, the AAPI website does not provide comprehensive information on licensing and authorisation procedures applicable in Algeria.

Egypt's 2017 Investment Law – and its implementing decrees and other related legislation – does not specify or clarify specifically which investor "*approvals, permits and licences*" procedures the ISC facilitates and ultimately issues via the competent authorities representatives. However, competent authorities, together with the GAFI, have prepared and published in Arabic via a GAFI portal a number of sectoral licensing guides. These guides are not standardised and the information which each provides varies significantly in depth of detail; nevertheless, most broadly outline the relevant procedures for obtaining operation – and in some instances, establishment – authorisations, as well as their relevant eligibility conditions and requirements, the competent authorities to which applications must be submitted, and estimate timeframes for these procedures. These guides are reviewed and if and when necessary, updated, periodically every six months, and are legal binding.[40] It is unclear on the face of these guides whether the information provided therein is exhaustive or merely indicative. Appeal procedures, available under the Egyptian framework if authorisation applications are refused, are not outlined by way of these guides but rather in the Law itself and its 2017 Executive Regulations. A similar Arabic-language licensing guide was prepared and published by the **Jordanian** MoI with a view to enhance the transparency of the licensing framework. It provides detailed information on the conditions, procedures, documents, requirements, and timeframes for obtaining permits and licences, and features hyperlinks for e-services (when available).

In **Morocco**, the two sets of authorisations which investors require for the realisation of their investment projects are also identified by way of legislation. Information pertaining to CRUI-related authorisations – i.e., land authorisations, planning permissions and other permits – is set out via the CRI-Invest Platform, which provides comprehensive information on application requirements and procedures, competent authorities, fees and estimate timeframes. The portal also features online appeal services and connects investors with a relevant OSS officer to assist them throughout the application process. Other investment-related authorisations, which investor must directly submit to the relevant competent authorities, are outlined via the Idarati national platform, which provides standardised information on all formalities and requirements relevant to administrative acts issued by competent authorities, at national and regional level (procedural steps, relevant authorities, documents required, estimate timeframes, fees). A significant number of these authorisations have been identified by way of decree, adopted in May 2023.[41]

Finally, **Tunisia** stands out in its approach to make available information pertaining to authorisations and their procedures. It adopted Decree 2018-417, which comprehensively lists out in significant detail the administrative procedures relevant to obtaining all authorisations across all economic sectors. Activities within these controlled economic sectors which are not specifically cited in the instrument are in principle considered open to private investment activity. Each of these lists is organised on the basis of economic sectors. The lists set out in each of the Annexes define the pre-conditions and supporting documentation, competent authorities, indicative timeframes and legal frameworks relevant the authorisations. Recourse or appeal mechanisms are however not available to applicants on the face of this legislation; mechanisms may be available on a case-by-case basis with the relevant competent authorities.

Investment projects whose capital value exceeds TND 15 million are facilitated by the TIA, via its Commission for licences and approvals. Contact details of dedicated TIA liaison officers specifically mandated to assist this category of investors with authorisation procedures are available via the TIA Investor Guide portal. The portal also provides a general overview of the licensing requirements and their procedures. Procedural and institutional arrangements for authorisations for projects whose capital value falls below the TND 15 million threshold and outside of the TIA's mandate is limited, and investors are expected to submit their authorisation applications directly to the relevant competent authorities.

Investment and sustainable development

Investment facilitation allows host economies to create favourable conditions for businesses to operate and expand, increasing FDI flows. However, beyond its quantity, the quality of FDI matters. FDI can be an important contributor to enhance economic growth and innovation, create quality jobs and develop human capital, including for women, and raise living standards and environmental sustainability in host economies. By linking domestic firms to MNEs, it can also be a conduit for domestic firms to access international markets and integrate global value chains.

While more FDI resulting from broad facilitation efforts can *de facto* contribute to the sustainable development of a host economy, more tailored policy tools are required to specifically harness the positive benefits of FDI for the achievement of SDGs and promote *sustainable* investments, i.e., investments that have sustainable outcomes – whether it be in terms of boosting innovation, skills, labour market, gender equality or the environment.[42] The OECD (2022) Council Recommendation on Foreign Direct Investment Qualities for Sustainable Development is the first multilateral instrument of its kind that provides guidance to governments on how to leverage foreign investment to finance their SDGs, fulfil their commitments made in the Paris Agreement, and optimise the strength and quality of post-crisis recovery. The benefits of FDI to host economies can be assessed in several ways. As part of its 'FDI Qualities Initiative', the OECD has recently developed indicators to assess the positive benefits of FDI for host economies (Box 2.1).

Box 2.1. The OECD FDI Qualities Initiative

The Covid-19 pandemic and its devastating human, social and economic consequences have challenged efforts to achieve the Sustainable Development Goals (SDGs) and the commitments made in the 2016 Paris Agreement. This global crisis increased the risk of slowing down, or even reversing progress to make our societies and economies more resilient, inclusive and sustainable. Russia's war of aggression against Ukraine has thrown the trajectory of recovery into doubt, weakened economic prospects and generated further uncertainty. In this context, a key challenge for the international community is to mobilise significant financial resources to accelerate the implementation of the 2030 Agenda for Sustainable Development and to ensure that plans for a "decade of action" to advance the SDGs are not side-tracked.

The **OECD FDI Qualities Initiative** is about improving the impact of investment on sustainable development and focuses on four areas of the SDGs: productivity and innovation; employment, job quality and skills; gender equality; and low-carbon transition. The initiative comprises three components:

- The **FDI Qualities Indicators**, originally developed in 2019, seek to measure the sustainable development impacts of FDI in host countries across four SDG areas.
- The **FDI Qualities Policy Toolkit** helps governments identify priorities for policy and institutional reforms to enhance the impact of investment on sustainable development. For each area of sustainable development covered, it describes how to assess the impacts of FDI and policy recommendations related to governance, domestic and international regulation, financial and technical support, and information and facilitation services.
- The **OECD Council Recommendation on FDI Qualities** complements the Policy Toolkit by incorporating a concise set of key policy principles from the Policy Toolkit into a legal instrument. Adopted at the 2022 Meeting of the OECD Council at the Ministerial Level (MCM), it is the first government-backed standard on how to improve the positive contribution of international investment to the SDGs.

Based on the FDI Qualities Indicators, a recent OECD Report on FDI Qualities in the Middle East and North Africa (June 2023) found that while FDI has had generally positive benefits over all Southern Neighbourhood countries in the four SDG areas considered, they are harnessing these benefits unevenly, whether it be in terms of productivity and innovation, creating quality jobs, advancing gender equality principles or advancing decarbonisation goals:

- Foreign firms are more ***productive*** than domestic firms in nearly all Southern Neighbourhood countries, and the gap between the two is particularly large in **Morocco**, **Jordan** and **Egypt**. They also spend more on R&D activities, particularly in **Morocco** and **Tunisia**, and, as a result, are more likely to introduce new products or services. Linkages between local firms and foreign ones are uneven across the countries: while foreign firms are estimated to source more than 60% of their inputs domestically in **Egypt** and **Morocco**, that rate is smaller in **Jordan** and **Tunisia** and sits around 30%.
- FDI can be an important lever to ***create quality jobs***, but such effects can vary significantly depending on the sectors where investments are directed. In the Southern Neighbourhood, the highest intensity of job creation per million of USD in the past ten years was observed in **Tunisia** and **Morocco** where around 50% of FDI in the last years has been directed towards manufacturing industries which have a higher job-creating potential. FDI has less job-creating effects in countries where natural resources or other capital-intensive sectors dominate, including in **Algeria**, **Egypt** or **Jordan** for instance.

- While foreign firms operating in **Egypt** and **Tunisia** performed slightly better than domestic firms in terms of women employees, evidence for the general Southern Neighbourhood region that foreign firms perform better than their domestic peers on measures of ***gender equality*** appears to be inconclusive. Women employment may also be prevalent in the manufacturing sector of these countries. Such labour-intensive, low-value added sectors increases the risk of locking them in low-paid, low-skilled positions, perpetuating gender segregation in the labour market.
- The share of investment in **mining and fuels** in the selected Southern Neighbourhood countries increased substantially after the financial crisis of 2008 compared to the period before the last economic crisis, as investments in natural resources have shown to be relatively impervious to political instability (OECD, 2021[13]). However, there has been a positive shift of greenfield FDI towards more renewable energy projects across the MENA region (OECD, 2023[12]). The manufacturing industry has also received a growing share of FDI in recent years, although some countries have been more successful than others in expanding this sector (**Algeria**, **Morocco** and **Tunisia**).

To harness the positive benefits of FDI to SDGs, a comprehensive set of policies and tools is required. The EU-Angola SIFA goes in this direction by formulating policy recommendations for maximising such benefits. Most investment facilitation agreements have principally focused on enhancing regulatory predictability and transparency and streamlining of administrative processes to ease practical burdens faced by investors. Although they may have referenced sustainable development within their stated purpose, their provisions addressing specifically sustainable development were less comprehensive. In contrast, the EU-Angola SIFA's Chapter 5 demonstrates an ambitious approach to facilitation and sustainable development. It encourages Parties to implement reforms to maximise the positive benefits of all inward FDI to their sustainable development, in all of its 'dimensions' (labour and environmental notably);[43] but also, to use FDI itself as a lever to advance their SDGs (i.e., to promote and encourage investments with sustainable outcomes). The following sections provide a general outline of the types of provisions addressing investment and sustainable in the EU-Angola SIFA; and a broad overview of FDI policies and approaches in Southern Neighbourhood countries aimed at increasing FDI benefits to their sustainable development.[44]

Investment and sustainable development in Chapter 5 of the EU-Angola SIFA

EU-Angola SIFA, Article 28:

1. The Parties recognise that sustainable development encompasses economic development, social development and environmental protection, all three being interdependent and mutually reinforcing, and affirm their commitment to facilitate investment in a way that contributes to the objective of sustainable development.
2. The objective of this Chapter is to enhance the integration of sustainable development, notably in its labour and environmental dimensions, in the Parties' investment relationship in a manner that contributes to the achievement of the SDG's of the UN2030 Agenda.

Article 28 of the EU-Angola SIFA highlights and reiterates the Agreement's overarching objectives, in that it aims at "facilitating the attraction, expansion and retention of FDI between the Parties for the purposes of economic diversification and sustainable development" and notes that the contracting Parties reaffirm their commitment to "facilitate investment in a way that contributes to the objective of sustainable development".[45] The Agreement however goes beyond simply formulating recommendations to create favourable conditions for FDI to contribute to SDGs – which are principally the focus of its Chapters 2 to 4. It encourages Parties to implement reforms to align their legal frameworks with international labour and environmental standards and RBC principles to maximise the positive benefits of all inward FDI to their sustainable development, as well as to promote and facilitate specifically investment projects with sustainable outcomes.

The EU-Angola SIFA Chapter 5 on the relationship between investment and sustainable development directly reflects two of the five key high-level policy orientations of the OECD (2022) FDI Qualities Policy Toolkit, which relate specifically to *domestic policy and legal frameworks*, and *information and facilitation services*:

- On ***domestic policy and legal frameworks***: Chapter 5 of the SIFA features several key recommendations to ensure that contracting Parties align their domestic legal frameworks with international labour and environmental standards. As such, it reaffirms the Parties' right to regulate, as more recent investment treaty designs have increasingly done.[46] It also recommends that they shall maintain and enforce high levels of protection of environmental or labour standards in their domestic legal frameworks, and not weaken, waive or offer to waive them in order to encourage investment (Article 29). The Chapter explicitly identifies several standard-setting international agreements and instruments on labour,[47] the environment,[48] and RBC,[49] and encourages parties to cooperate – whether bilaterally or through intergovernmental fora[50] – on such matters.
- On ***information and facilitation services***: Article 11 of the EU-Angola SIFA in its Chapter 2 encourages Parties to make information on domestic suppliers available to investors to promote domestic linkages and enhance FDI spillovers. In addition, Article 33 of the EU-Angola SIFA's Chapter 5 reaffirms the Parties' commitment to facilitate and encourage investments that contribute to their SDGs, whether it be in sustainable production and consumption, in environmental goods and services or other investment of relevance for climate change mitigation and adaptation (Article 33(1)) and investments for the sustainable use of biological resources and conservation of biodiversity (Article 33(3)), and that facilitation of investments shall not impair their SDGs but rather shall contribute to them (Articles 33(5) and 33(6)). However, the Agreement does not lay out specifically what that such 'facilitation' efforts specifically tailored towards sustainable investments should entail in practice.

While Chapter 5 of the EU-Angola SIFA directly reflects these two key high-level policy directions of the recommendations laid out in the OECD FDI Qualities Policy Toolkit (2022) and represents a step in the right direction to encourage countries to attract and facilitate quality investments, the SIFA does not directly formulate measures in other key high-level policy directions of the Toolkit. The further inclusion of these sustainability elements within the Agreement could also be incorporated in Chapters 2 and 3 as they relate specifically to investment policy strategy and administration:

- On ***governance***: the EU-Angola SIFA could enshrine sustainability elements within the transparency and predictability requirements of Chapter 2, especially in relation to the recommendation for participative policy-making processes and the carrying out of stakeholder consultations for investment policymaking. Public-private consultations and social dialogue can promote collective and innovative solutions to emerging issues that can be, at least partly, driven by FDI. Stakeholder consultations also allow for feedback and build legitimacy and consensus around policy reforms and programmes at the intersection of investment and sustainable development. More open and inclusive policymaking processes help ensure that policies better match the needs and expectations of citizens, enterprises and sub-national regions and build consensus on policy reforms on investment and sustainable development specifically.
- ***Financial and technical support****:* Article 10 of the EU-Angola SIFA and other similar international investment facilitation agreements only require that information on incentives offered to investors shall be made available. While such requirement increases the transparency of a Party's investment incentives' framework, the Agreement falls short of addressing recommendations relating to the administration and design of their incentives offer,

as may be suggested by the FDI Qualities Policy Toolkit. Such recommendations could include prioritising sustainable development objectives or outcomes when providing financial and technical support to stimulate investment (OECD, 2022[9]); having clear eligibility criteria for incentives to reduce room for excessive discretion by implementing authorities or limiting the offer of undefined additional benefits to investors that meet unspecified criteria that is generally discouraged due to the increased risk of aggressive tax planning by firms and of corruption by administering authorities (OECD, 2021[13]). The inclusion of such substantial recommendations is not, on the face of it, inconsistent with the rationale of investment facilitation agreements, considering the practical solutions which they encourage in other investment policymaking areas.[51] While incentives are a common policy choice for countries to correct market failures and advance their SDG's, such as supporting renewable energy or skills and technology spillovers, the use of tax and financial incentives to promote FDI has to be carefully considered to prevent their costs – especially in terms of revenue foregone and potential market distortions – outweighing their benefits.

A new iteration of the SIFA with other key partners of the EU could consider directly reflecting these additional policy priorities within the Agreement's provisions. These recommendations are also only indicative of potential avenues for reform of the EU model of sustainable investment facilitation agreement, as reflected by the EU-Angola SIFA. Further research would thus be required to comprehensively identify avenues of improvement of the model agreement's approach to investment and sustainable development specifically.

Investment and sustainable development in the selected Southern Neighbourhood countries

All five selected countries of the Southern Neighbourhood have recently overhauled their legal frameworks for investment, and reaffirmed their commitments to promote investment projects with sustainable development outcomes, especially in their policy or strategy documents:

- The new **Algerian** Law on Investment (2022) aims at encouraging investment to ensure a sustainable and balanced territorial development, promote technology transfer, develop innovation and boost the creation of sustainable jobs, as set out by its Article 2.
- **Egypt**'s Sustainable Development Strategy ("*Egypt Vision 2030*") adopted in 2016 also underlines the important role of private investments in the achievement of the country's SDGs by 2030 and outlines key reforms to improve the country's investment policy. The strategy specifically mentions additional legislative reforms required to improve the Egyptian business environment to maximise the benefits of FDI for the economy.
- FDI is identified as an important lever to achieve the SDG's set out in **Jordan**'s Economic Modernisation Vision (2022-2025). The vision rests on two core pillars: enhancing economic growth and improving the quality of life for Jordanians. Both pillars are underpinned by sustainability goals which are expected to be achieved, in part, through investments in greener sectors such as renewable energies, ICT, and infrastructure development.
- One of the **Moroccan** Investment Charter's main goals is to spur regional investments which would aim at reducing disparities between the Kingdom's provinces in terms of investment attractiveness. The Charter also sets out priority sectors and activities for investment to contribute to the country's SDGs, in line with the country's nationwide Sustainable Development Strategy (the 'Stratégie Nationale de Développement Durable 2030' adopted by the Moroccan Council of Ministers in 2017) and the New Development Model ('Nouveau Modèle de Développement', April 2021). The strategy also underlines the pivotal role of the private sector in achieving the country's SDGs by 2030, including it consultative role in policy planning as well as in incorporating ESG principles within corporate practices.

- **Tunisia** plans on leveraging FDI to advance the priorities set out by its 'National Green Economy Strategy'. The Strategy rests on four strategic directions, including the need to develop strong dynamic, inclusive, innovative and supportive growth, reduce the sensitivity of natural resources and ecosystems which are subject to the effects of climate change, adopt a decentralised and participatory governance approach to encourage local initiatives and promote the quality of life of citizens and resistance to disruption. Orientation guides for investors in the green economy have been developed for four sectors (agroforestry, ecotourism, renewable energies and energy efficiency and waste management) to disseminate the Strategy, underlining support structures and the institutional framework, as well as financial and fiscal incentives for investment in the green economy sectors concerned.

All five countries of the Southern Neighbourhood resort to financial and fiscal incentives to encourage investments in certain economic sectors or activities that they consider being instrumental to the achievement of their SDG's or to projects with sustainable development outcomes:[52]

- To support ***productivity and innovation***: **Algeria** provides a VAT exemption and duties on equipment for R&D, while **Tunisia** provides an additional deduction of 50% of R&D expenses under corporate agreements concluded with public research establishments.
- To strengthen ***supplier linkages between foreign and domestic firms***: in **Jordan**, companies can receive a corporate income tax (CIT) reduction when they manufacture products with at least 30% domestic value added and purchase inputs by contracting with local suppliers. Similarly, **Egypt** applies a tax holiday in private SEZs if local inputs are at least 30%, while **Algeria** provides an extension of their tax holiday if an investment project uses inputs sourced locally.
- Most Southern Neighbourhood countries (except Tunisia and Morocco) have at least one existing tax incentive that aims at attracting FDI to ***foster job creation*** (particularly to hire local workers). For example, in **Jordan**, firms in the industrial sector can benefit from CIT incentives conditional on hiring a minimum number of Jordanian workers. **Algeria** provides a broad incentives regime across six key sectors, such as a five-to-ten-year CIT exception, for investments over 10 billion DZD that create 500 or more jobs. Some countries also provide direct financial incentives for job creation such as **Egypt** which offers IT companies an EGP 10,000 to 32,000 grant on each new hire for a period of three years.
- Tax incentives for ***skills development*** are less often used: only **Egypt** and **Morocco** have tax incentives with the objective to promote job quality and skills. Morocco offers a reduced CIT rate of 20% for vocational training, while Egypt offers a tax allowance to certain firms, provided employee wages exceed 30% of operating costs. Similarly, direct subsidies are less often used to improve job quality and skills, while being likelier to address employment, such as in **Tunisia**, which has several schemes, especially for younger workers and graduates.
- Most countries of the Southern Neighbourhood resort to incentives to ***support green investment***. These include mechanisms such as feed-in tariffs, as seen in **Algeria**, **Egypt**, **Jordan**, and **Morocco.** Fiscal incentive schemes are also implemented in **Jordan** which provide a ten-year CIT exemption for FDI in renewable energy infrastructure construction, while **Tunisia** offers a deduction of a portion of taxable profits during the exploitation phase, for up to the fourth year of activity, from 100% in the first year to 25% in the fourth and final year.

While offering financial and fiscal incentives to investments is a widespread policy choice to advance certain SDGs, these incentives should be carefully considered and designed to avoid their costs outweighing their benefits. Fiscal incentives especially could be costly for governments as they can represent important revenue foregone or could even create market distortions. Incentives that target specific investment expenditures (as opposed to profits), or certain, well-defined activities are also more likely to attract investment that would not otherwise have been made, can help achieve specific policy goals, and make it more difficult for firms to conduct aggressive tax planning (IMF-OECD-UN-World Bank, 2015[7]).

The five selected Southern Neighbourhood countries could also undertake additional efforts to promote and enable RBC, as recommended by the EU-Angola SIFA. Four of the five selected Southern Neighbourhood countries – **Egypt**, **Jordan**, **Morocco**, and **Tunisia** – have adhered to the OECD Declaration on International Investment and Multinational Enterprises, thus committing to promote the OECD Guidelines for Multinational Enterprises and to establish a National Contact Point (NCP) to further their effectiveness. However, except in Morocco where the NCP has taken an active role in the promotion of RBC, the mechanism in other Sothern Neighbourhood countries was often underutilised, especially in Egypt, Jordan and Tunisia (OECD, 2021[13]).

In terms of fundamental labour rights, none of the five selected Southern Neighbourhood countries have ratified all ten "*fundamental*" International Labour Organization (**ILO**) conventions – which cover fundamental principles and rights at work, such as the right to collective bargaining and elimination of forced labour – nor the four "*governance*" (or "*priority*") conventions for the exception of **Morocco** – which cover labour inspections, employment policy, and tripartite consultations (Table 2.1). There have been concerns about the application of these standards in practice in the Southern Mediterranean countries, including complaints raised to the ILO, primarily for alleged violations of Freedom of Association rights. The extent to which such labour standards are thus reflected in the countries individual legal frameworks and are effectively enforced is uncertain and would require a further analysis. However, the partial ratification of ILO conventions may, in part, show the selected Southern Neighbourhood governments' intent to work towards aligning their legal frameworks with international labour standards.

Table 2.1. Ratifications of ILO Conventions by the selected Southern Neighbourhood countries

Country (member since)	Fundamental (10)	Governance (4)	Technical (177)	Total (190)
Algeria (1962)	9	3	48	60
Egypt (1936)	8	3	53	64
Jordan (1956)	7	3	16	26
Morocco (1956)	8	4	53	65
Tunisia (1956)	9	3	52	64

Note: ILO conventions are all legally binding international treaties that may be ratified by ILO member states. If it is ratified, a Convention generally comes into force for that country one year after the date of ratification. The ILO Governing Body has identified ten "*fundamental*" conventions, covering subjects that are considered to be fundamental principles and rights at work, and has also designated another four conventions as "*governance*" (or "*priority*") instruments, thereby encouraging member states to ratify them because of their importance for the functioning of the international labour standards system. "*Technical*" conventions are also legally binding once ratified and encompass all of the other international labour standards in the ILO's scope of work.
Source: ILO (NORMLEX database).

Despite the five selected Neighbourhood countries having taken recent steps to promote the protection of the environment and natural resources, their environmental performance appears to be relatively poor in global comparison, evidenced by some of their low rankings in the latest iteration of the Yale Environmental Performance Index (2022). The Index ranks 180 economies on environmental health and ecosystem vitality and provides a gauge at a national scale of how close countries are to established environmental policy targets. While almost all of the selected Southern Neighbourhood countries have seen an increase in their environmental performance scores over the last ten years – with the exception of Algeria, these improvements have been relatively slow in comparison to what is observed globally.

Overall, while nearly all MENA governments have adopted measures to support sustainable development, more could be done to create an environment that advances human and labour rights, reduces opportunities for corruption, and improves environmental protection in business activities and their supply chains. The impetus to promote RBC among businesses in the region is also critical to ensure their integration in supply chain networks. Multinational companies may be deterred from investing in countries where RBC principles – especially in terms of labour standards – are poorly enforced due to reputational risks but also due to compliance requirements.

References

African Manager (2023), *En attendant le nouveau Code des investissements promis pour bientôt*, https://africanmanager.com/en-attendant-le-nouveau-code-des-investissements-promis-pour-bientot/ (accessed on 28 July 2023). [6]

Ampntel Chafiz, R. (2023), *Investment Tax Incentives in MENA: Design and Policy Goals*, https://www.oecd.org/mena/eu-oecd-mediterranean-investment/Investment%20tax%20incentives%20in%20MENA_insights%20from%20OECD%20ITID.pdf. [11]

IMF-OECD-UN-World Bank (2015), *Options for Low Income Countries' Effective and Efficient Use of Tax Incentives for Investment*, https://www.oecd.org/tax/options-for-low-income-countries-effective-and-efficient-use-of-tax-incentives-for-investment.pdf. [7]

Jedlicka, H. and Y. Sabha (2017), "Lessons from Five Years of Helping Governments Foster Incentives Transparency", *World Bank Blogs, "Private Sector Development" Blog*, https://blogs.worldbank.org/en/psd/lessons-five-years-helping-governments-foster-incentives-transparency. [14]

OECD (2023), *FDI Qualities in the Middle East and North Africa: A mapping of policies and institutions that can strengthen sustainable investment*, Background document for the regional seminar on sustainable investment in the MENA region, 19 and 20 June 2023, OECD Istanbul Centre, Türkiye, https://www.oecd.org/mena/eu-oecd-mediterranean-investment/FDI-Qualities-MENA.pdf. [12]

OECD (2023), "Improving transparency of incentives for investment facilitation", *OECD Business and Finance Policy Papers, No. 35*, https://doi.org/10.1787/ab40a2f1-en. [10]

OECD (2022), *FDI Qualities Policy Toolkit*, OECD Publishing, Paris, https://doi.org/10.1787/7ba74100-en. [9]

OECD (2021), *Improving the Legal Environment for Business and Investment in Central Asia: Policy Insights*, OECD Publishing, Paris, https://www.oecd.org/eurasia/Improving-LEB-CA-ENG%2020%20April.pdf. [4]

OECD (2021), *Middle East and North Africa Investment Policy Perspectives*, OECD Publishing, Paris, https://doi.org/10.1787/6d84ee94-en. [13]

OECD (2021), *Regulatory Policy Outlook 2021*, OECD Publishing, Paris, https://doi.org/10.1787/38b0fdb1-en. [3]

OECD (2015), *Policy Framework for Investment*, OECD Publishing, Paris, https://doi.org/10.1787/9789264208667-en. [2]

OECD (2013), *Principles to Enhance the Transparency and Governance of Tax Incentives for Investment in Developing Countries*, https://web-archive.oecd.org/2015-10-22/221727-transparency-and-governance-principles.pdf. [8]

OECD (2012), *Recommendation of the Council on Regulatory Policy and Governance*, OECD Publishing, Paris, https://doi.org/10.1787/9789264209022-en. [5]

World Bank Group (2017), *Global Investment Competitiveness Report 2017/2018: Foreign Investor Perspectives and Policy Implications*, https://doi.org/10.1596/978-1-4648-1175-3. [1]

Notes

[1] The survey was based on interviews with 754 executives of multinational corporations with investments in developing countries. The legal and regulatory framework is the second most cited factor for investment decisions by surveyed investors, after "*political stability and security*".

[2] A fourth principle ('independence') governs the administration of measures related to investment authorisations specifically (EU-Angola SIFA, Article 19). See page 21 on how 'independence' may relate to these three principles – specifically with 'impartiality' – on the administration of investment-related measures of general application.

[3] The EU-Angola SIFA is silent as to the meaning of "*administration of measures*", specifically in the context of its Article 6. The scope of application of GATS Article VI:1, which uses similar wording, was also never clarified. The dispute settlement Panel in the *US – Gambling* case only specified that the principles of reasonableness, objectivity and impartiality enshrined in GATS VI:1 applied to the *administration* of measures rather than to the measures themselves – i.e., rather than to their substantive content, and therefore encompassed "*disciplines of a procedural nature*" (*United States – Measures Affecting the Cross-Border Supply of Gambling and Betting Services*, WT/DS285, Panel Report, 10 November 2004 (adopted on 20 April 2005), para. 6.432). The absence of specific language on the meaning of *administration* of measures in the context of regulatory transparency and predictability commitments within trade or investment facilitation agreements leaves room for interpretation as to their scope of application. The broad interpretation used in this Report is only illustrative as it constitutes one approach among others that could be narrower, and does not necessarily reflect the Parties' intent as to the meaning of Article 6 of the EU-Angola SIFA, or more generally, of any other agreements with similar wording.

[4] This interpretation is directly inspired by Article X:3 of the GATT which requires that "*Each contracting party shall administer [trade-related measures] in a uniform, impartial and reasonable manner*". The meaning of a *reasonable* administration of trade-related measures in the context of GATT X:3 was specified by the WTO DSB Appellate Body to include basic fairness and due process requirements – the essential implication being that relevant stakeholders that are affected or that are likely to be affected by governmental measures "*should have a reasonable opportunity to acquire authentic information about such measures and accordingly to protect and adjust their activities or alternatively to seek modification of such measures*" (*United States – Restrictions on Imports of Cotton and Man-Made Fibre Underwear*, WT/DS24, Report of the Appellate Body, 10 February 1997 (adopted on 25 February 1997), p. 21; see also, *United States – Import Prohibition of Certain Shrimp and Shrimp*

Products, WT/DS58, Report of the Appellate Body, 12 October 1998 (adopted on 6 November 1998), para. 181).

[5] The notions of 'impartiality' and 'independence' are often used as synonyms in natural language, but they are nevertheless commonly distinguished conceptually as encompassing two distinct aspects of procedural fairness. While the former refers primarily to an individual or an entity's capacity not to be biased in relation to parties involved in decision making processes so as to not cloud their judgment, the latter ore specifically refers to their ability to resist to 'external' pressures and undue influence in the context of decision-making processes. 'Independence' is explicitly included in Article 19 of the EU-Angola SIFA relating to the administration of investment authorisation measures specifically.

[6] See, the WJP Rule of Law Index website for a list and explanation of all factors covered by the WJP Rule of Law Index (2022).

[7] See e.g., GATS, Article III; WTO Trade Facilitation Agreement (section 1, Article 1) also uses similar wording by encouraging Parties to publish regulatory material in a "*non-discriminatory and easily accessible manner in order to enable governments, traders, and other interested parties to become acquainted with them*".

[8] See e.g., the US Model BIT (1984), Article XII ('Transparency').

[9] See e.g., the United States Model BIT (2012), Article 10; the Australia-Uruguay BIT (2019), Article 6; the Brazil-Morocco BIT (2019), Article 8; and the Canada Model BIT (2021).

[10] In this vein, Article 9(3) of the EU-Angola SIFA states that "*No fee shall be imposed on any investor in a Party's territory for access to the information provided under this Article or under Article 7.*"

[11] See e.g., the WTO Trade Facilitation Agreement, Article 2; the UK-Moldova Strategic Partnership, Trade and Cooperation Agreement (2021), Article 324; the EU-Vietnam FTA (2019), Article 14.3.

[12] See e.g., the Burkina Faso-Canada BIT (2015), Article 12.3(1); Brazil-Angola CFIA (2015), Article 13.3; Japan-Jordan BIT (2018), Article 8; Brazil-India CFIA (2020), Article 8.2; Japan-Morocco BIT (2020), Article 2.8. See also, the Canada Model BIT (2021), Article 15.2(a).

[13] Tunisia has in recent years undertaken a number of commitments via the Open Government Partnership. Notably, Tunisia has undertaken a *Right to Information* commitment in 2018, which sought to strengthen the right of access to information; the action plan seemingly yielded overall moderate results based on publicly available information. Tunisia had also committed, between 2016 and 2018, to reform its open data legal and regulatory framework at national level (*The completion of the legal and regulatory framework of open data at the national level*) with the establishment of an online open data portal, as well as a commitment to *Modernizing the regulatory framework to enforce the right to access to information*. The objectives underlying these two commitments were not fully achieved based on publicly available information.

[14] These considerations are disconnected from the requirement under Chapter IV relating to periodic reviews of measures of general application affecting investment with a view to determine whether specific measure implemented should be modified, streamlined, expanded or repealed for more effectiveness in achieving its policy objectives. In this context, Parties are also required to consider stakeholder feedback, among others (EU-Angola SIFA, Article 26).

[15] Jordan is currently engaged in a program to develop an electronic portal for public participation, with a view to unify and institutionalise e-participation with government institutions to enhance civic participation, including with respect to government projects and legislative proposals. Separately, Morocco has undertaken a series of commitments together with the Open Government Partnership, with a view to further public participation in the legislative process ("*Open Parliament*"), as part of the country's Action Plan Review 2021-2023. These include among others, a *Commitment to enhance dialogue with and the participation of societal actors in parliamentary consultations, including in the legislative process*, a *Commitment to implement a legal framework on public consultation* and a *Commitment for citizen involvement in parliamentary action*, among others. Morocco's Action Plan Review also refers to a Commitment to develop an *e-Parliament platform for participatory democracy*, to further enhance participation and legislative transparency. Morocco has already achieved considerable progress in this regard, in the backdrop of the 2011 Constitution which establishes the right of public participation, among others. Finally, Tunisia's National E-Participation Portal seeks to enhance the involvement of citizen's in the country's public affairs via public consultations, public dialogue and forums, among others, remains limited (see, Open Government Partnership, Tunisia Action Plan Review 2021-2023, *Promoting the use of national portals for public participation*.

[16] Building upon the initial transparency requirements of the GATT (1947) for trade-related measures, such regulatory predictability requirements were also included in subsequent multilateral trade agreements adopted following the Uruguay Round of negotiations (see for e.g., the Agreement on the Application of Sanitary and Phytosanitary Measures, Annex B, para. 2; Agreement on Technical Barriers to Trade, Article 2.12 on technical regulations and Article 5.9 on conformity assessment procedures).

[17] See e.g., the ASEAN Investment Facilitation Framework (2021), Article 4, which provides that Member States shall *"4.3 Encourage the publication of measures adopted or maintained by Member States related to investments through a single digital platform [...] 4.4 Encourage the provision of information on the single digital platform that is sufficiently clear, precise and up-to-date so as to enable an investor to be informed of– 4.4.1. the agencies or regulatory bodies involved in the applications for admission, establishment, acquisition and expansion of any specific investment [...]"*.

[18] Jordan's MoI appears to be planning the publication of 'instructions' on its website as well, although no such instrument has been published yet at the time of writing in September 2023.

[19] See, Open Government Partnership, Tunisia Action Plan Review 2021-2023, *Developing a range of online administrative services at the sectoral level* (last accessed on 11 September 2023).

[20] See, the second revised Decision of the Council on International Investment Incentives and Disincentives (the "*Instrument on International Investment Incentives and Disincentives*") adopted in 1984 which currently forms part of the Declaration, alongside three other components: the Guidelines for Multinational Enterprises which formulate recommendations on RBC addressed by governments to MNE's operating in or from adhering countries, the Third Revised Decision of the Council concerning National Treatment ("*National Treatment Instrument*") and the Decision of the OECD Council on conflicting requirements. All OECD Members as well as 12 non-OECD countries – including some of the Southern Neighborhood (Egypt, Jordan, Morocco, Tunisia) – have adhered to the Declaration, and further countries are currently undergoing reviews to join this growing group. The Recommendation of the OECD Council on Foreign Direct Investment Qualities for Sustainable Development (2022) also recommends that countries "*take steps to ensure that financial and technical support is transparent and*

subject to regular reviews" in order to prioritise sustainable development objectives when providing financial and technical support to stimulate investment.

[21] The scope of information to be made available as set out under Article 10 of the EU-Angola SIFA is aligned with international recognised practice in this regard. The World Bank has also recommended similar measures in the context of country programmes. Such recommendations have included mandating by law, and maintaining in practice, a database and inventory of incentives available to investors, listing in the inventory all aspects of key relevance to stakeholders (specific incentive provided, the eligibility criteria, the awarding and administration process, the legal reference and the awarded amounts), and making the inventory public in a user-friendly format (Jedlicka and Sabha, 2017[14]).

[22] The inventory was available on the Jordan Investment Commission (JIC)'s website and appeared to be updated annually by a dedicated team within the JIC. Due to recent institutional reshufflings and the absorption of the JIC by the newly created MoI in 2021, the inventory is no longer available and a new inventory reflecting incentives offered under the recent Investment Environment Law (2022) hasn't been developed yet.

[23] The Investment Promotion Strategy (2023-2026) states that the MoI "*will completely revamp its website drawing from multiple examples of good practice IPA websites around the world"* and is expected to launch an electronic platform entitled 'Invest in Jordan' (*Invest.Jo*) which shall, among others, highlight the advantages and incentives granted according to the Investment Environment Law, alongside other relevant information on the country's investment framework (p. 21).

[24] See e.g., the ASEAN Investment Facilitation Framework (2021), Article 8, Facilitation of Investment Supporting Factors, *"Assist investors in identifying investment supporting factors such as labour force, funding sources, domestic suppliers and business matchmaking opportunities"*; see also, Protocol on Investment to the Agreement establishing the African Continental Free Trade Area, Zero Draft (November 2021), Article 23, Pursuit of Development Goals, *"Notwithstanding the provisions of this Protocol, State Parties may introduce measures to promote domestic development and local content. Measures covered by this paragraph include among others: [...] b. measures to support the development of local entrepreneurs and to establish linkages with local firms, industries and institutions towards assisting the development of local capabilities [...]"*.

[25] E.g., the CRI Oriental and CRI Marrakech both feature affiliated portal (Intaj Oriental and MarrakechB2B) which meets the requirements of Article 11. Similarly, CRI RSK features a form titled Business matchmaking; it is unclear at the time of writing in September 2023 whether this feature is operational. The CRI Béni Mellal provides a directorate of operating businesses in the region; resources provided are limited and it is unclear at the time of writing in September 2023 whether this feature is operational.

[26] See e.g., the Regional Comprehensive Economic Partnership (RCEP) (2020).

[27] See e.g., the Investment Agreement of the China-Hong Kong (China) CEPA (2017); ASEAN Investment Facilitation Framework (2021); Canada Model BIT (2021).

[28] This section focuses mainly on post-establishment licensing procedures as they are the most common type of authorisations found in the Southern Mediterranean countries. Other investment procedures, such as company registration, are dealt with for each Southern Neighbourhood countries

in the individual country fiches of Annex A. Domestic legal frameworks for investment in selected Southern Neighbourhood countries.

[29] The EU-Angola SIFA covers measures against corruption and other illicit activity in its general provisions (Chapter 1, Article 5) in which the Parties recognise the negative impact of such practices in discouraging investment and confirm their commitments to adopt adequate measures to tackle and fight corruption in accordance with internationally agreed standards. While Chapter 2 does not make explicit reference to corruption or undue influence at the level of policymaking or implementation of policies, Chapter 3 covers such scenarios in cases of investment authorisations specifically (Article 19).

[30] As defined under the EU-Angola SIFA, Article 3, *"a central, regional or local government or authority or non-governmental body exercising powers delegated by central, regional or local governments or authorities, which is entitled to take a decision concerning an authorization"*.

[31] See e.g., the ASEAN Investment Facilitation Framework (2021).

[32] In that regard, see e.g., the WTO Trade Facilitation Agreement (2017), Article 10(4), as well as the ASEAN Investment Facilitation Framework (2021), Article 4. See also, UNECE Trade Facilitation Recommendations, Recommendation no. 33; and Calamita, N. J. and S. Schacherer (2022), *Investment facilitation for sustainable development within the context of the Regional Comprehensive Economic Partnership, the ASEAN Investment Facilitation Framework and the WTO Draft Investment Facilitation Framework for Development*, United Nations Economic and Social Commission for Asia and the Pacific (ESCAP), Studies in Trade, Investment and Innovation No. 96, p. 25.

[33] See, paras. 0 *et seq*. In that regard, see, OECD (2018), *Mapping of Investment Promotion Agencies in OECD Countries,* OECD Publishing, Paris and OECD (2019), *Mapping of Investment Promotion Agencies: Middle East and North Africa*, OECD Publishing, Paris which outline the core functions, main objectives and activities of IPAs across OECD countries and the MENA region, respectively. A wide array of activities falls under the umbrella of one of the four core functions of IPAs, investment facilitation and retention, including but not limited to e.g., the provision of information, site visits, MNE-SME linkages programmes, as well as administrative support (such as OSS services).

[34] The APII in Algeria does not provide a publicly available and exhaustive list of the competent authorities represented within it. That is similarly the case in Egypt. GAFI publishes Guides on permits, approvals and licences procedures and applications to be considered with different authorities, Ministries and public administrations. It is likely that investors consider obtaining such authorities either via the OSS route or via the competent authorities' route.

[35] The operation authorisations which CRUIs are mandated to consider, as listed in Law 47-18, fall within three general categories: land-related authorisations, planning permissions and discretionary exemptions, and operating licences and permits. Investors submit their investment file applications directly via the Platform, with the assistance of their allocated CRI advisor, based on the CRI-Invest platform User Guide.

[36] See, WTO, *Structured discussions on investment facilitation for development, meeting of 31 October 2019 – Summary of discussions by the Coordinator*, INF/IFD/R/8, 21 November 2019 (last accessed on 13 September 2023). See, WTO, *Structured discussions on investment facilitation for development, meeting of 31 October 2019 – Summary of discussions by the Coordinator*, INF/IFD/R/8, 21 November 2019 (last accessed on 13 September 2023).

[37] See e.g., the Agreement on Investment of the ASEAN-China Framework Agreement (2009), Article 21(b) provides that the Parties shall cooperate to facilitate investments among ASEAN and the People's Republic of China among others through *"simplifying procedures for investment applications and approvals"*.

[38] See e.g., Canada-EU Trade Agreement (CETA) (2016), Chapter 12, Article 12.3 pertaining to *Licensing and qualification requirements and procedures*; see, the ASEAN Investment Facilitation Framework (2021), Article 2 pertaining to *Streamlining and speeding up administrative procedures and requirements*. The Canada Model BIT (2021) in its Section C dedicated to *Investment Promotion and Facilitation*, features a provision on the *Processing of Applications for an Authorization* (Article 21), the scope of which is similar to that of the EU-Angola SIFA's Article 17.

[39] See e.g., the ASEAN Investment Facilitation Framework (2021), Article 4; the Regional Comprehensive Economic Partnership (2020) (RCEP), Article 10.17.

[40] Information provided further to consultations with GAFI, August 2023.

[41] Launched further to Law 55-19 to streamline administrative procedures and formalities. See also, Guide prepared relative to the streamlining of administrative procedures and formalities (*Simplification des procedures et des formalités administratives*) prepared by *Secretariat de la Commission de la simplification des procedures et des formalités administratives*,

[42] These four clusters are also used in the OECD FDI Qualities Indicators to assess the contribution of FDI to SDGs.

[43] The tri-dimensional presentation of sustainable development in the EU-Angola SIFA (economic, social and environment) reflects the standard understanding of the concept of 'sustainable development' as framed by the United Nations, especially since the Rio Summit in 1992. See, the United Nations Conference on Environment and Development, "*Agenda 21*" adopted in Rio de Janeiro (1992).

[44] This section provides a broad overview of the EU-Angola SIFA's provisions on investment and sustainable development and the implementation of domestic policies within Southern Neighbourhood countries aimed at boosting FDI contribution to their SDGs. An ongoing parallel project carried out by the OECD in collaboration the EU Commission's DG TRADE aims specifically at mapping out comprehensively the EU-Angola SIFA's Chapter 5 to support the incorporation of a wider spectrum and more ambitious sustainability considerations into future SIFA iterations as well as to offer guidance to governments for the implementation of domestic reforms and measures to maximise the impact of such treaty provisions on the quality of FDI.

[45] See e.g., for comparison, the ASEAN Investment Facilitation Framework (2021), which does not reference sustainable investment within its provisions.

[46] See, for e.g., the EU-Canada CETA (2016), Article 8.9(1); the USMCA (2018), Article 14.16; the EU-Viet Nam Investment Protection Agreement (2019), Article 2.2(1).

[47] In this regard, Article 30 of the EU-Angola SIFA refers to the ILO Declaration on Social Justice for a Fair Globalization (2008), the ILO Constitution and the ILO Declaration on Fundamental Principles and Rights at Work and its follow-up.

[48] See e.g., Articles 32(1) which refers to the United Nations Framework Convention on Climate Change (1992), the Paris Agreement (2015) and other multilateral environment agreements and multilateral

instruments in the area of climate change; Article 32, which mentions the Montreal Protocol on Substances that Deplete the Ozone Layer (1987); Article 33(2) which refers to the Convention on Biological Diversity (1992) and its protocols; and the Convention on International Trade in Endangered Species of Wild Fauna and Flora (1973).

[49] See e.g., Article 34 referring to the United Nations Guiding Principles on business and Human Rights, the United Nations Global Compact; the ILO Tripartite Declaration of Principles Concerning Multinational Enterprises and Social Policy; and the OECD Guidelines for Multinational Enterprises and related due diligence guidance.

[50] See e.g., EU-Angola SIFA, Article 31(1) which refers to the United Nations Environment Assembly, the United Nations Environment Programme, the United Nations High-level Political Forum for Sustainable Development etc.

[51] See, for example Article 21 of the EU-Angola SIFA which encourages Parties to adopt *"clear, objective and transparent criteria*" for investment authorisation procedures and to ensure that such procedures are administered impartially and independently.

[52] This paragraph offers an overview of financial and tax incentives based on sustainability criteria in Southern Neighbourhood countries. For a more in-depth analysis of different incentives schemes across the MENA region, see OECD (2023[12]), *FDI Qualities in the Middle East and North Africa: A mapping of policies and institutions than can strengthen sustainable investment*, July 2023.

3 The opportunity for SIFA negotiations between the EU and Southern Neighbourhood countries

All five Southern Neighbourhood countries have made impressive efforts in recent years to improve the transparency and predictability of their legal frameworks for investment, and for the streamlining of investment applications procedures by their relevant administrative bodies. Despite these important efforts, all countries fare differently in terms of investment facilitation and have, to varying degrees, incorporated key SIFA provisions relating to within their domestic frameworks. Based on the benchmarking assessment carried out in Chapter 1, this Chapter aims at identifying potential room for improvement in the five countries of the Southern Neighbourhood, to guide the EU Commission on potential future SIFA negotiations.

Algeria

The Algerian investment framework: the 2022 Investment Law

Algeria recently modified its institutional framework for investment facilitation with the establishment of the Algerian Investment Promotion Agency (*Agence algérienne de promotion de l'investissement,* **AAPI**), which succeeds the National Investment Development Agency. The AAPI's establishment was part of broader legislative reforms aimed at enhancing the country's legal framework for investment. The new 2022 Investment Law seeks to promote investment in priority sectors and sectors with high added value to ensure sustainable development and to develop natural resources and local raw materials. It covers acquisition and ownership operations, extensions of capacity, and greenfield investments in the production of goods and services and provides for a general principle of 'transparent' and 'equal' treatment of foreign investors.

Addressing a number of transparency and predictability priorities

Algeria features several core principles enshrined in the EU-Angola SIFA with regards to the transparency and predictability of its legal framework for investment. Regulatory material is readily available via the Secretariat General's website, allowing users to consult laws alongside all of their related and implementing instruments. Information relevant to the country's investment framework is also centralised on the AAPI website, especially relating to business establishment. Dissemination of proposed or expected regulatory changes is a pivotal element of regulatory transparency and predictability, as reflected by the EU-Angola SIFA. Algeria has shown significant strides in recent years to enhance the transparency of its policymaking process. Some drafts of regulatory changes are features on the People's National Assembly and the Council of the Nation websites.

Further, the newly launched AAPI website features some information on Algeria's investment framework, especially on steps to invest in the country. It also provides an extensive overview of the country's incentives framework, which is also available via the country's nation-wide investor-platform. These sources provide an overview of the country's investment framework, including information on eligible activities and types of incentives available.

Recent institutional rearrangements aim at further streamlining administrative procedures

Burdensome investment authorisation procedures have in past years often been highlighted by investors as a shortcoming to Algeria's business and investment framework (World Bank Group, 2020[1]; U.S. Department of State, 2022[2]).[1] Such bottlenecks may have stemmed, in part, from the absence of an overarching framework to streamline investment authorisation procedures across different regulatory authorities. Delays for the processing of applications would ultimately depend on sector-specific legislation governing licensing procedures and may vary across competent authorities.

Most of Algeria's recent regulatory changes have principally focused on measures to streamline investment-related authorisations and processes. Such efforts have led to the creation of two OSS operating within the AAPI mandated with overseeing investment-related procedures specifically: one dedicated to foreign investments and "*large projects*" (i.e., investments having a capital equal or greater than DZD 2 billion), and the other one caters to domestic investments that do not qualify as "*large projects*".

Both OSS share the same structure and perform similar duties under the Law with regards to investments falling within their competence. They serve as a single interlocutor for investors, offer an information desk, and facilitate licencing and authorisations procedures via competent and sectoral authorities' representatives. These are either mandated with directly issuing authorisations, decisions and documents on behalf of their respective authorities, while others serve as points of contact to ensure smooth communication lines between investors and their respective authorities. The implementation of these institutional arrangements should, in time, ensure streamlined business establishment and operation procedures.

Looking forward: continued implementation of the Law and enhanced transparency and streamlining efforts

The publication of translations of legal instruments as well as of further aspects of the investment framework (e.g., relating to FDI restrictions, and separately, the administration of investment incentives) could increase the accessibility of legal information by investors and thereby enhance the predictability of the Algerian investment framework. Published material could also include information on application procedures, documents, and institutional settings for incentives. Information on activities subject to licensing or admission-related authorisations could also be centralised with a view to ensure ease-of-access to investors. In that regard, several sector-specific executive decrees adopted over the years have nevertheless defined the regime for controlled activities in oil and gas distribution, wholesale and retail trade, manufacturing activities, scientific activities (testing laboratories), or even public utilities.

The Law has sought to address regulatory predictability concerns by incorporating a "*stabilisation clause*" within its provisions. While this mechanism – adopted in other Southern Neighbourhood countries as well – seeks to address predictability objectives, it also carries the potential of creating a fragmented legal landscape and could also hamper the effective implementation of reforms on labour or environmental standards and responsible business conduct principles. Formalising requirements relating to the provision of an opportunity to comment on proposed measures (and considering such comments in the proposed measures' elaboration process), providing explanations as to the objective of a measure once published, and finally, allowing a reasonable time between a measure's publication and its application to investors, could be more effective in tackling regulatory predictability concerns. For instance, it appears that limited stakeholder involvement was considered in the adoption of the Law (Algérie Eco, 2022[3]). Fostering inclusive and participative policymaking further enhances the legitimacy of regulatory activity among stakeholders and ensures that the changes yield their intended results.

While the establishment of two OSS with clearly delineated mandates highlights Algeria's strong intent to further facilitate authorisation procedures, it is unclear at the time of writing in September 2023 whether these institutional reforms have effectively been implemented, or whether the single OSS under the previous IPA's mandate – the ANDI – continues to operate during a transitional period. Algerian officials have recently restated their intent to introduce reforms aimed at tackling bureaucracy and corruption in administrative agencies, and to establish a legal framework to simplify administrative procedures, guarantee their transparency and improve the overall quality of public services (Algérie Presse Service, 2022[4]). Overall, a strong procedural framework to streamline administrative procedures and to address information gaps would bolster the country's recent efforts that aim at enhancing the transparency and predictability of its investment framework.

Egypt

The Egyptian investment framework: the 2017 Investment Law

Egypt has in recent years reformed its investment promotion and facilitation architecture. In 2017, Egypt introduced a new Investment Law – complemented by a series of Executive Regulations and implementing Decrees – thereby repealing its previous 1997 Investment Guarantees and Incentives

Law. The new investment framework has sought to enhance the clarity of the investment regime via the consolidation of investment rules which had until 2017 been fragmented under various laws and regulations, and by streamlining procedures through the strengthening of GAFI's mandate (OECD, 2020[5]). The Law applies to greenfield investment and acquisition and ownership operations and defines the legal regime for domestic and foreign "*investment projects*" in a wide range of sectors, identified therein. It sets out the principles and guarantees offered to investors, including fair and just treatment, national treatment to foreign investors, non-discrimination, protection against unlawful expropriation, and free transfer of capital in foreign currency. The Law also establishes Egypt's new approach to investment promotion, via the establishment of several investment regimes, governed by different authorities, incentives regimes and at times, operation procedures and requirements.

Important advances in enhancing regulatory transparency and predictability

Egypt has made important advances in infusing its legislative and regulatory framework for investment with transparency principles. The Egyptian Official gazette is restricted by a paywall, but several governmental platforms provide access to the Law and its accompanying Executive Regulations, including a dedicated GAFI portal, although access to investment instruments is at times fragmented and/or not consolidated. The GAFI portal also features additional laws and regulations relevant to investment and investors, including company, environmental, fiscal, labour, finance, and protection of intellectual property rights legislation.

Egypt has also introduced a number of measures and taken steps that seek to enhance the overall transparency of its investment framework, including with respect to establishment formalities, operation authorisations, and incentives. The website of the Egyptian OSS, the ISC, and the ISC Investor Guide provide information and assistance to investors with respect to company incorporation formalities. Incorporation formalities may also be carried out online, with GAFI's e-incorporation portal (these e-services were as at September 2023 not fully operational and/or digitalised). GAFI and the ISC must complete company legal incorporation within one business day of receipt of an application file. Separately, GAFI's website features several sectoral licensing guides (available for the most part only in Arabic), elaborated by ministries. Most guides broadly outline the relevant procedures for obtaining permits, approvals and licenses, eligibility conditions and requirements, the competent authorities to which applications must be submitted, and estimate timeframes of these procedures. These guides are reviewed and if and when necessary, updated, periodically every six months, and are legally binding. The ISC Investor Guide also outlines some of the formalities, documents required, applicable pre-conditions, and applicable fees for some of these procedures.

Further, the Law partly outlines some of the investment incentives schemes' eligibility conditions; the conditions and benefits granted under some specific schemes – namely, Special and Additional Incentives Schemes – are fragmented in separate instruments. GAFI's website also features some information about the incentives schemes available under the main "Inland" investment regime. A GAFI-developed *"Golden Licence Guidebook"* provide investors information on eligibility conditions and application procedures under this separate scheme. The Law does not explicitly and comprehensively outline in a readily accessible way the formalities which investors must comply to benefit from Special and Additional Incentives. In contrast, Golden Licence incentives applications may be submitted online via the Egyptian Cabinet's official website.

New streamlining mechanisms introduced, and additional forthcoming measures

Only a small share of foreign-invested enterprises identified business licensing and permits as a "major constraint hampering their operations", although some business surveys have pointed to bureaucratic red tape as impacting Egypt's investment climate. In that regard, the Egyptian ISC – headquartered in Cairo, with regional branches across governorates – is mandated under the Law to receive investor applications for approvals, permits and allocation of real estate and licences required for the realisation of investment projects, with a view to centralise the processing of investment-related authorisations. ISC membership consists of representatives ranging a large number of competent authorities that are either vested with the authority to directly issue authorisations, or alternatively, that act as liaison officers between the competent authorities they represent and investors. Investors were at the time of writing in September 2023 expected to carry out authorisation applications and formalities at the relevant physical ISC offices and/or directly with the competent authorities.

The Law has also introduced structural investment framework-specific streamlining measures which bind GAFI, the ISC and the competent authorities represented therein to streamline authorisation procedures and enhance investors' confidence in the Egyptian investment framework. These establish clear timeframes within which the ISC and competent authorities must decide upon investor authorisation applications. They also require that competent authorities notify investors of the outcome of their applications in writing and within clear timeframes. GAFI is entrusted with the power to expedite pending authorisation applications if these are not granted within the established timeframes. Further, a 'tacit approval' mechanism is available if competent authorities do not issue a decision within a defined timeframe. In the event of incomplete applications, competent authorities and their ISC representatives must request missing documents from investors within a prescribed timeframe, beyond which application files must be considered complete. ISC and competent authorities' decisions on investor application for operation authorisations and licences must be reasoned, justified and transparent, and investors may appeal negative decisions before GAFI's Grievance Committee, the procedures for which are set out in the Law. The Law also prevents competent authorities from revoking or suspending authorisations without first providing the user with prior notice and a prescribed "*grace period*" to rectify any notified breaches. In this scenario, it is GAFI that is entrusted with the authority to authorise revocations, where appropriate.

Looking forward: expected streamlining reforms for investment authorisation procedures and enhanced transparency

Egypt remains engaged in continued reforms to further improve its investment facilitation framework, specifically with regards to enhanced streamlining of authorisation procedures. Consultations with GAFI have indicated that a system for license automation and was currently under development, which would allow investors to electronically submit and follow up on their applications for approvals, permits and licenses, as well as submit inquiries and complaints online. The Egyptian Supreme Council for Investment has also recently approved a number of decisions and proposed amendments to the current investment framework with a view to reduce the costs and timeframes for company incorporation and lift restrictions linked to foreign ownership of land (Ahram Online, 2023[6]).

The Law has sought to alleviate regulatory predictability concerns via a "*stabilisation clause*". While this mechanism – adopted in other Southern Neighbourhood countries as well – seeks to address predictability objectives, such clauses also carry the potential of creating a fragmented legal landscape and could also hamper the effective implementation of reforms on labour and environmental standards, and responsible business conduct principles. Other measures could be considered to further enhance the transparency and predictability of the Egyptian framework. This could include the introduction of participative policymaking measures, either via a whole-of-government approach or investment framework-specific (e.g., relating the publication of drafts of proposed measures in advance of their adoption, arrangements that afford the public with a reasonable opportunity to comment during the elaboration of proposed measures). Ensuring easy and free access to relevant and applicable consolidated and up-to-date legislation (e.g., via a centralised searchable and regularly updated multilingual database)[2] could also further enhance the transparency, and in turn, predictability, of the Egyptian investment and overall regulatory framework. Further, measures to enhance the ease of access to comprehensive and consolidated information, e.g. via an online single portal, on: investment incentives schemes (specifically with respect to Special and Additional Incentives Schemes, currently fragmented across several instruments, in line with Single-Approval Scheme procedures, which have been centralised via a recently launched online platform), on FDI restrictions, and on practical steps relevant to investors (connection to essential infrastructure, acquisition and registration of property) as well as domestic suppliers with a view to strengthen local economy linkages, could similarly improve the Egyptian investment framework's overall predictability.

Jordan

The Jordanian investment framework: the 2022 Investment Environment Law

Jordan recently overhauled its legal framework for investment with the adoption of the Investment Environment Law in October 2022, which entered into force on 14 January 2023. The Law reflects Jordan's investment policy strategy aimed at enhancing its investment environment and encouraging sustainable investments. It applies to greenfield investments as well as acquisitions and ownership operations by Jordanian or non-Jordanian natural or legal persons in a defined number of sectors, including industrial, commercial, agricultural activities, services, tourism, information technology or creative industries. The Law sets out a principle of national treatment of foreign investors, and enshrines the principle of fair, equitable and transparent treatment within Jordan's regulatory framework. It also limits the possibility of partial or total expropriation of an investment to circumstances where a "*public, specific and legitimate purpose*" may warrant it and if carried out in a non-discriminatory manner and subject to fair compensation. Against common institutional arrangements observed in the Southern Neighbourhood countries and beyond, investment facilitation is not entrusted to a separate IPA in Jordan; rather, investment facilitation is overseen by the MoI, which was established in October 2021 to address the shortcomings of the previous IPA in operation since 2014.

Significant strides towards a transparent and predictable legislative framework

Jordan has in recent years made significant strides to enhance the transparency and predictability of its legal framework for investment. New measures pertaining to participative policymaking processes have been introduced, whereby ministries and regulatory authorities are strongly encouraged to publish texts of proposed regulations before their adoption. Draft legislation is available for consultation on relevant ministry websites, often accompanied by explanatory notes on proposed changes, and stakeholders are often provided with an opportunity to comment on draft bills. The Law's development itself closely involved stakeholders: a draft of the law was made public several months prior to its adoption, along with an explanatory note underlining the rationale of the proposed changes and what these might entail in practice for potential and established investors, and the draft also appears to have been subject to extensive consultations with public and private sector representatives prior to its adoption in October 2022. The Law entered into force nearly three months further to its publication in the Official Gazette, which also provided investors with sufficient time to familiarise themselves with the new instrument.

Legislation is available in Jordan in Arabic via the country's Official Journal website. Translations are in some instances featured for business-related legislation via the MoI website, which was still under construction at the time of writing in September 2023. The website provides English translations of the Law and the 2020 Public-Private Partnership Projects Law, along with their implementing regulations. Other pieces of legislation can be found in English on the Companies Control Department's (**CDD**) website. Further, and in accordance with the Law, a licensing guide was made available in September 2023 in Arabic only; it provides detailed information as to the conditions, procedures, documents, requirements, and timeframes relevant to obtaining permits and licences.

Important streamlining measures introduced to simplify authorisation procedures

Investors' perceptions of the Jordanian investment climate have improved significantly in recent years (World Bank Group, 2019[7]). The MoI's OSS – the Comprehensive Investment Services Unit (**CIS**) – has been mandated under the Law with providing guidance to foreign investors on licensing conditions applicable to their intended projects, and in some cases, even facilitate the obtention oof these licences in the 12 economic sectors falling within its competence as defined by the Decree 7 of 2023. These include permits in the health sector, agricultural permits, tourism, environmental permits etc. The CIS thus comprises fully authorised competent authority representatives entrusted with the authority to directly issue approvals and licences for investment projects on behalf of their respective authorities, including tax authorities and several relevant ministries, including the Ministry of Tourism or the Ministry of Agriculture (for sectoral licences), the Ministry of Environment (for environmental approvals), and the Ministry of Labour (for work permits).

Outside of CIS services for licensing, investors need to address relevant authorities to obtain licences that do not fall within the competence of the CIS. The Law provides for an overarching framework for the processing of applications by authorities in the country. It enshrines procedural principles to significantly reduce authorities' discretion in appreciating authorisation applications: authorities are required to publish the conditions relevant to obtaining licences, negative decisions must be reasoned and motivated, and the Law explicitly prohibits a number of grounds for refusals of licences. Decisions to withdraw licences *ex post* must follow a specific procedural framework under the Law, as authorities are required to notify the licence holder of the alleged violation of the licence terms and provide them with a timeframe for responding with evidence that no violation has occurred or for rectification of the violation.

The Law foresees the creation of a joint electronic platform operated by the MoI to ease communications between different licensing authorities assessing applications. It also introduces several guiding principles for the streamlining of administrative processes, similar to those introduced by other selected Southern Neighbourhood countries. These pertain to the types of documents authorities may request from users and applicants, and on what basis; the timeframes for the processing of applications are also within the general framework; as well as a 'tacit approval' mechanism.

Finally, certain controlled activities – about 360 in total – also require prior authorisation for company incorporation, based on sector-specific legislations. These authorisations fall within the competence of 35 distinct public authorities, including the Energy and Minerals Regulatory Commission, the Ministry of Interior, the Ministry of Public Works and Housing, the Telecommunications Regulatory Commission, and the Jordan Central Bank. The CDD's website publishes a list of pre-registration approval requirements, creating transparency as to the regimes applicable to these authorisations. Jordan has also recently simplified the application procedures for some of these pre-registration approvals with the launch of a single CIS portal for pre-registration approvals. These relate to approvals granted by authorities that have partnered with the CCD for the provision of these pre-registration approvals. At the time of writing in September 2023, only 6 out of the 35 competent public authorities have partnered with the CCD to facilitate the obtention of these approvals and authorisations. Aside of the authorisations granted by these agencies, investors must apply for pre-registration approvals directly with the competent authorities prior to registering an enterprise with the CCD.

Looking forward: progressive implementation of the Law to enhance transparency and further efforts to streamline authorisation procedures

Although the Law has sought to alleviate regulatory predictability concerns via a *"stabilisation clause"* – adopted in other Southern Neighbourhood countries as well – such mechanisms carry the potential of creating a fragmented legal landscape, and could also hamper the effective implementation of reforms on labour and environmental standards and responsible business conduct principles. Additional reforms to further enhance the transparency of the investment framework could rather focus on enhancing information on the country's legal framework for investment and facilitating access to it. The MoI's website for instance provides little information on FDI restrictions, which are nevertheless consolidated in negative lists within the implementing decree of the Law. Similarly, information on practical steps and their procedures relevant to investors, such as connection to essential infrastructure, acquisition and registration of property, among others, do not appear to be available on the MoI's website. Jordan is the only country in the Southern Neighbourhood that does not currently provide a comprehensive information portal on the country's incentives offer despite its previous IPA having developed and launched an 'incentives inventory' under the previous regime. This gap is expected to be palliated in the near future, as underlined by the country's priorities enshrined in the Investment Promotion Strategy (2023-2026).[3]

While the Law contains important provisions to rationalise administrative procedures in the country, streamlining efforts appear to be uneven across administration. The MoI's CIS has a limited mandate, and the latter could be expanded to cover investment projects falling outside of the Law's scope. Similarly, pre-incorporation approvals required in certain sectors could be further streamlined by expanding the CCD's partnerships beyond the 6 authorities it currently cooperates with.

Morocco

The Moroccan investment framework: ongoing institutional and regulatory reforms since 2019 and the 2022 Investment Charter

Morocco's institutional approach to investment promotion and facilitation is unique among the selected Southern Neighbourhood, as it is primarily undertaken at regional level by regional CRIs and CRUIs, rather than entrusted to the country's nation-wide IPA, the AMDIE. The governance structure of CRIs was reformed in 2019, and their mandates harmonised across the country's regions, which significantly enhanced the efficiency of the country's institutional framework for investment. CRIs, together with CRUIs – a complementary investment facilitation entity operating at regional entity – among others centralise investment-related applications, procedures and decision-making. Following these institutional reforms, Morocco overhauled its legal framework for investment with its new Investment Charter in 2022, adopted against the backdrop of broader structural reforms which the country has set in motion since 2019 to improve administrative efficiency, specifically decentralisation. The Charter and its implementing decrees together define the legal regime for domestic and foreign investors across economic sectors, except for agricultural activities which are subject to sector-specific policies. It sets out general principles and rights enjoyed by investors, including freedom of enterprise, free competition, equal treatment irrespective of the nationality of the investor, the right to transfer funds related to investment projects, and legal predictability and good governance.

Significant strides in enhancing regulatory transparency and predictability

Investors' assessments of the Moroccan investment climate have been fairly positive, partly owing to the country's recent efforts to enhance the transparency of its investment framework (World Bank Group, 2022[8]; U.S. Department of Commerce, 2023[9]). Investment legislation is publicly accessible and free of charge in both Arabic and French through the website of Morocco's Official Journal, and the principal investment instruments are also accessible through most regional CRIs' online portals. Some CRIs have also yielded efforts to provide information via their online portals on domestic suppliers and investment opportunities relevant to foreign investors. The development of a freely accessible centralised searchable and regularly updated multilingual database would significantly enhance the transparency and accessibility of the investment – and overall regulatory – framework, and Morocco is currently working towards developing and launching an online comprehensive platform to that effect. From the perspective of participative policymaking, the Moroccan legislative framework requires that public authorities undertake public consultations in their decision- and policy-making processes, and the Moroccan House of Representatives and House of Councillors are both expected to publish drafts of laws and regulations.

The country's regional CRIs feature considerable information and assistance on company incorporation and establishment formalities and information on Morocco's newly enacted investment incentives regime (e.g., eligibility criteria, legal basis of available incentives, forms of incentives, documents required for applications and an outline of the application process). Separately, the country's unified CRI-Invest Platform outlines relevant investment-related authorisations, as well as the formalities and documents required to successfully complete them, the regulatory frameworks relevant to them, and an estimate timeframe for their successful completion. A manual outlining these procedures is also expected to be prepared by the relevant authorities as per legislation in force.

Important whole-of-government and investment-specific streamlining reforms

While investors perceptions of the Moroccan investment climate are fairly positive, some have occasionally reported facing bottlenecks in terms of administrative processes, including with respect to business licensing and permits (World Bank Group, 2023[10]). In the light of these constraints, Morocco has made strides towards to simplify administrative processes and improve the efficiency of the country's two sets of investment authorisation procedures specifically. Further to institutional reforms introduced throughout the years, CRUIs have been mandated with considering applications for and issuing a defined list of investment authorisations ("*administrative acts*"), which include land authorisation, planning permissions and other permits. CRIs facilitate these procedures by liaising between investors and CRUIs. Investors may submit their applications electronically via the centralised CRI-Invest Platform, and are kept informed in real time of the status of their applications. The platform also provides comprehensive information on application requirements and procedures, competent authorities, and estimate timeframes (which are prescribed clearly by way of decree and may be extended only in certain defined circumstances). Investors are also afforded the opportunity to provide additional information required to complete their applications. Denied applications must be reasoned and communicated to investors, and investors may appeal CRUIs' negative decisions; appeal procedures are in that regard prescribed by defined timeframes and may be submitted and managed via the same Platform.

Other permits, licenses and authorisations which may be required by investors for the realisation of their investment projects are issued by the relevant competent authorities. A considerable number of these authorisations have been identified by way of decree, and the processes by which these applications are streamlined have in large part been laid out by way of legislation enacted in 2020, which among others prescribes information requirements with a view to simplify application-related documentary procedures. Several online governmental platforms have been launched to provide information on application procedures and formalities, competent authorities, estimate timeframe and fees relevant to these authorisations, but only one of these operated as an application portal at the time of writing in September 2023. Investors are currently required to submit their applications directly to the relevant authorities, which may require the submission of several applications to more than one authority for a single authorisation, and thus generally impact the overall ease by which investors obtain authorisations required for the realisation of their investment projects. unified and national digital platform for authorisation procedures and formalities, which is expected to be launched by 2025, is likely to further ensure that application procedures are efficient, streamlined and predictable for investors. A tacit approval mechanism may operate when prescribed timeframes have elapsed, and public administrations are also bound by the same facilitation arrangements that seek to ensure streamlined procedures as those applicable to CRUI-processed applications outlined above.

Looking forward: forthcoming measures to further enhance streamlining investment authorisations

Reforms introduced by Morocco in recent years – the overhaul of the institutional architecture for investment facilitation, "whole-of-government" measures to simplify administrative procedures, the enactment of the new 2022 Charter – have enhanced the overall predictability of the country's investment framework and also significantly streamlined all investment-related authorisations and procedures. Additional reforms are also currently being considered to continue improving the country's investment climate, including facilitating access to property for investment projects and the development of special economic zones; facilitating access to finance; and advancing ongoing reforms for the streamlining of investment-related administrative procedures and formalities at the regional level.

From a policymaking perspective, ensuring that existing formal requirements (e.g., publication of drafts of proposed measures in advance of their adoption, arrangements that afford the public with a reasonable opportunity to comment during the elaboration of proposed measures) are effectively implemented could further enhance the transparency and predictability of the Moroccan investment framework and create a more investment-friendly business climate. The overall transparency of the framework could also be enhanced by facilitating access to comprehensive and consolidated information on FDI restrictions across sectors, and similarly, to information on practical steps and their procedures relevant to investors, such as connection to essential infrastructure, acquisition and registration of property, among others, e.g., via an online single portal.

Tunisia

The Tunisian investment framework: the 2016 Investment Law and more recent whole-of-government reforms

Tunisia overhauled its investment framework in 2016 with the adoption of a new Investment Law, repealing and replacing the Investment Incentives Code of 1993. The Law and its implementing decrees rest on three main pillars: the reform of the country's investment governance architecture, with the establishment among others of a new IPA that carries a core facilitation role; the adoption of a new, reformed investment incentives regime; and the introduction of core standards intended to significantly streamline authorisation procedures. It defines the legal regime for domestic and foreign investors across economic sectors and applies to greenfield investments as well as acquisition and ownership operations in Tunisia. It also establishes a general principle of freedom of investment and guarantees treatment of foreign investors no less favourable than that enjoyed by domestic investors and protection of investor assets against unlawful expropriation, among others.

More recently, Tunisia also adopted whole-of-government legislation with a view to enhance the transparency and predictability of its investment framework and further streamline investment-specific and other authorisation procedures. The country operates more than one IPA, as two principal agencies feature complementary investment facilitation mandates: the Tunisian Investment Authority (**TIA**), established further to the 2016 Investment Law coexists together with a network of smaller agencies, including the Agency for the Promotion of Industry and Innovation (**APII**). The TIA was originally established with the objective of integrating and replacing investment facilitation functions carried out by APII among others, but the latter still operates to date. This architecture directly impacts how investment facilitation is conceived and implemented in the country.

Substantial transparency-enhancing measures to enhance the predictability of the investment framework

The Tunisian investment frameworks features important pillars of transparency. Regulatory material, including investment-related measures, are published in Tunisia's Official Journal and are freely accessible online, in Arabic and French. The websites of the TIA and the APII feature the principal legal and regulatory instruments of Tunisia's investment framework, as well as a number of 'Fact Sheets' – available in Arabic, French and English – which shed light on specific features of the investment framework. Both IPA portals also make available information destined to foreign investors on domestic suppliers and the local economy with a view to encourage linkages. Establishment and legal incorporation formalities are outlined via both the TIA's and the APII's portals, in accordance with their respective mandates, and investors can in great part carry out these procedures online.

In relation to investment authorisations, Tunisia adopted some regulations that set out comprehensive lists of all economic activities subject to authorisations. This regulation also identifies the pre-conditions, formalities and requirements, competent authorities, indicative timeframes and legal frameworks relevant these authorisations. The TIA Investor Guide also provides a general overview of the licensing requirements, the relevant procedures to obtain them and the contact details of dedicated TIA staff and liaison officers. Finally, implementing decrees and orders adopted further to the Law have clarified the eligibility conditions, procedural requirements, estimate timeframes and institutional arrangements relevant to the new Tunisian investment incentives schemes; these also establish that incentives-related decisions be motivated, and provides investors with a right of appeal for negative decision. To complement this, the TIA Investor Guide features an interactive portal which provides an overview of the different types of available incentives, as well as information pertaining to the value of incentives, relevant procedures, and contact details of dedicated TIA liaison officers. It does not however specify the conditions for obtaining incentives or provide practical information on any post-approval processes, which may negatively impact the transparency of the investment framework insofar as investment incentives are concerned.

Significant measures introduced to streamline the investment framework against the backdrop of whole-of-government reforms

Foreign investors have at times pointed out to processes and procedures relating to business licensing and permits as representing an obstacle in the Tunisian investment climate (World Bank Group, 2020[11]). To tackle such concerns, Tunisia has, between 2019 and 2020, introduced a series of facilitation measures and standards which seek to create streamline authorisation procedures throughout the country's administrative authorities. These include specific rules which prescribe the types of documents competent authorities may request from users and applicants, and on what basis, what information competent authorities should make publicly available, and a requirement to develop a general framework for the digitalisation of application procedures. To complement these overarching streamlining measures, investment-specific streamlining standards have been introduced by way of regulation with a view to simplify the processing of operation authorisations. These among others define binding and capped timeframes for the issuance of authorisations when these are not clearly set out by competent authorities, and requires that negative decisions be motivated and grounds for refusal notified in writing (recourse or appeal mechanisms are however not available to applicants). The framework also features a 'tacit approval' mechanism, whereby complete authorisation applications which competent authorities have not expressly denied within the defined timeframe are deemed approved.

Further streamlining services are available in respect of authorisations required for the realisation of investment projects whose capital value exceeds TND 15 million, which are processed through the TIA's Commission for licences and approvals. The Commission, whose membership includes relevant ministries and public bodies, is directly responsible for reviewing, deciding upon and ultimately issuing applications for these authorisations, in coordination with the relevant competent authorities, with whom it is required to liaise according to defined procedures and within specified timeframes. The TIA also provides general assistance to qualifying investors; in that regard, the TIA Investor Guide provides a general overview of licensing requirements, relevant procedures and contact details of dedicated TIA staff and liaison officers. The TIA's dedicated investor portal is also expected to offer online services for investment incentive and authorisation applications. It is not clear whether this feature was operational at the time of writing in September 2023. In contrast, procedural and institutional arrangements for authorisations for projects whose capital value falls under the TND 15 million threshold and outside of the TIA's mandate is limited, and investors are expected to submit their authorisation applications directly to the relevant competent authorities, which may prove administratively burdensome and time inefficient.

Looking forward: reform projects underway to further improve the Tunisian business climate

Tunisia's recent "whole-of-government" reforms have significantly enhanced the overall predictability of the country's investment framework and contributed to the streamlining of investment-related authorisations and procedures. Tunisia is currently considering further reform to enhance its investment facilitation framework: it has launched, in the context of its 2023-2025 National Reform Programme, a "National Strategy for the Improvement of the Business Climate", accompanied by a nation-wide public e-consultation process and a wider public-private dialogue with the aim of addressing perceived obstacles to an improved business climate and to identify relevant structural reforms, ultimately with a view to stimulate foreign investment. This process may bring about additional reforms to address constraints and difficulties flagged by investors. Reforms envisaged in the context of this National Strategy currently include establishing a database providing easy access to applicable legislation relevant to sectoral conditions applying to FDI, further cuts in the number of required authorisations to carry out economic activities and implement investment projects, and enhanced simplification of authorisation processes (Government of Tunisia, 2023[12]). The introduction of measures seeing to achieve these objectives would significantly enhance the Tunisian investment facilitation framework.

Additional transparency and accessibility measures could also be considered to further strengthen the predictability of the Tunisian investment framework, including with respect to policymaking: ensuring that existing formal requirements (e.g., publication of drafts of proposed measures in advance of their adoption, arrangements that afford the public with a reasonable opportunity to comment during the elaboration of proposed measures) are effectively implemented could contribute to creating a more investment-friendly business climate. Further, boosting facilitation services, especially as regards to operation authorisations, destined to smaller-scale projects, and in that context clarifying the role of the TIA vis-à-vis other entities that carry a facilitation mandate, such as the APII, would also contribute to strengthening Tunisia's investment framework (Government of Tunisia, 2023[12]). The overall transparency of the framework could also be enhanced by facilitating access to comprehensive and consolidated information on practical steps and their procedures relevant to investors, such as connection to essential infrastructure, acquisition and registration of property, among others, e.g., via an online single portal. In that regard, Tunisia is currently working towards developing a range of online administrative services at sectoral level, including services specifically intended for investors; these would include among others the filing and processing of administrative permits, social security affiliation, customs, and tax formalities.[4]

The Tunisian local press reported in May 2023 that a new investment law was currently under elaboration; this development had not at the time of writing in September 2023 been reported via official government channels, nor had any drafts of measures have been shared with the public (African Manager, 2023[13]).

References

African Manager (2023), *En attendant le nouveau Code des investissements promis pour bientôt*, https://africanmanager.com/en-attendant-le-nouveau-code-des-investissements-promis-pour-bientot/ (accessed on 28 July 2023). [13]

Ahram Online (2023), *Egypt announces new single-approval system to facilitate investment*, https://english.ahram.org.eg/NewsContent/3/12/506166/Business/Economy/Egypt-announces-new-singleapproval-system-to-facil.aspx (accessed on 15 September 2023). [6]

Algérie Eco (2022), *Le nouveau code de l'investissement va libérer et booster les investisseurs*. [3]

Algérie Presse Service (2022), *Le Gouvernement déterminé à lutter contre la bureaucratie et la corruption*, https://www.aps.dz/algerie/146136-benabderrahmane-reaffirme-la-determination-du-gouvernement-a-lutter-contre-la-bureaucratie-et-la-corruption (accessed on 16 September 2023). [4]

Government of Tunisia (2023), *Programme National des Reformes – Stratégie Nationale pour l'amélioration du climat des affaires – Feuille de route (2023-2025)*, http://www.mdici.gov.tn/wp-content/uploads/2023/01/Strategie_nationale_pour_l_amelioration_du_climat_des_affaires-1.pdf. [12]

OECD (2020), *OECD Investment Policy Reviews: Egypt 2020*, OECD Investment Policy Reviews, OECD Publishing, Paris, https://doi.org/10.1787/9f9c589a-en. [5]

U.S. Department of Commerce (2023), "Morocco (2023)", *Investment Climate Statements*, https://www.state.gov/reports/2023-investment-climate-statements/morocco/. [9]

U.S. Department of State (2022), "Algeria (2022)", *Investment Climate Statement*, https://www.state.gov/reports/2022-investment-climate-statements/algeria/. [2]

World Bank Group (2023), *Enterprise Surveys: Morocco (2023)*, https://www.enterprisesurveys.org/en/data/exploreeconomies/2023/morocco. [10]

World Bank Group (2022), "Economy Profile: Morocco", *Doing Business*, https://archive.doingbusiness.org/en/data/exploreeconomies/morocco. [8]

World Bank Group (2020), "Economy Profile: Algeria", *Doing Business*, https://archive.doingbusiness.org/en/data/exploreeconomies/algeria#DB_gc. [1]

World Bank Group (2020), *Enterprise Surveys: Tunisia (2020)*, https://www.enterprisesurveys.org/en/data/exploreeconomies/2020/tunisia. [11]

World Bank Group (2019), *Enterprise Surveys: Jordan (2019)*, https://www.enterprisesurveys.org/en/data/exploreeconomies/2019/jordan. [7]

Notes

[1]. In June 2020, after data irregularities on Doing Business 2018 and 2020 were reported internally, the World Bank management paused the next Doing Business report and initiated a series of reviews and audits of the report and its methodology. Data irregularities were subsequently corrected. The World Bank Group is currently working on a new project (Business Ready, B-READY) to assess the business and investment environment worldwide annually (forthcoming). World Bank Doing Business data was used in this Report only for illustrative purposes, and corresponds to corrected data by the World Bank Group. For more information, see: Doing Business.

[2] Egypt has been working on a regulatory reform program for a number of years, including in respect of the development of an Egyptian Legislation Register. It remained unclear at the time of writing in September 2023 whether this platform is operational.

[3] The Investment Promotion Strategy (2023-2026), published in June 2023, provides that the MoI *"will completely revamp its website drawing from multiple examples of good practice IPA websites around the world"* and is expected to launch an electronic platform entitled 'Invest in Jordan' (*Invest.Jo*) which, among others, will highlight the advantages and incentives granted according to the Investment Environment Law, alongside other relevant information on the country's investment framework (p. 21).

[4] See, Open Government Partnership, Tunisia Action Plan Review 2021-2023, *Developing a range of online administrative services at the sectoral level* (last accessed on 11 September 2023).

Annex A. Domestic legal and institutional frameworks for investment in Southern Neighbourhood countries

Algeria

Investment climate in Algeria: a practical overview

Foreign investments truly accelerated in Algeria in the mid-1990s, with the macroeconomic reforms and the country's efforts to liberalise its economy. In 1993, the country adopted its first Investment Code which offered a variety of incentives to foreign investments and supported investors institutionally through the Algerian Agency of Promotion, Support and Follow-up of Investment (*Agence de Promotion, de Soutien et de Suivi de l'Investissement*, **APSI**) established the same year.

The country later enhanced its investment incentives offer in the early 2000s and refurbished its institutional framework by replacing the APSI with the Algerian National Investment Development Agency *(Agence Nationale de Développement des Investissements*, **ANDI***)* entrusted with a reshaped mandate and a distinct legal status (OECD, 2019[1]). FDI inflows grew increasingly as a result and peaked at USD 2.7 billion in 2009 – representing 2% of the country's GDP.

Despite its positive FDI performance between the mid-1990s to the late-2000s, FDI inflows in Algeria have somewhat been volatile since the global financial crisis and the political upheavals affecting the whole MENA region in 2011. FDI inflows to the country ultimately plummeted in 2015. Although they have recovered significantly since, they have been generally on the decrease, a trend accentuated by the economic shocks induced by the COVID-19 pandemic in 2020. In 2022, FDI inflows to Algeria were at a record low since the mid 1990s – beside in 2015 – at barely USD 75 million (Figure A A.1).

Figure A A.1. FDI inflows in Algeria (1990-2022)

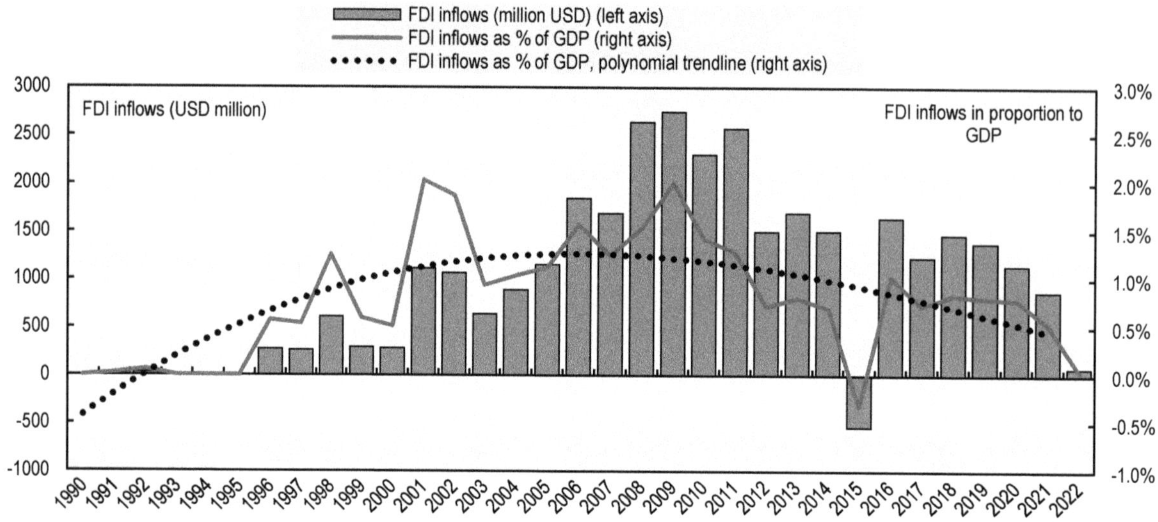

Source: OECD elaboration from IMF (Balance of Payments and International Investment Position Statistics) and World Bank (GDP data).

The geographic origins of inward FDI stock in Algeria have been stable in the last years. Investors from the **EU** (37%) – mainly from Italy (11.2%), France (10.4%) and Spain (6.7%) – the **United States** (29%), the **MENA region** (15%) and the **United Kingdom** (6%) held more than 85% of the total USD 23.1 billion inward FDI stock in the country in 2022 (Figure A A.2).

Figure A A.2. Origins and total value of inward FDI stock in Algeria (2018-22)

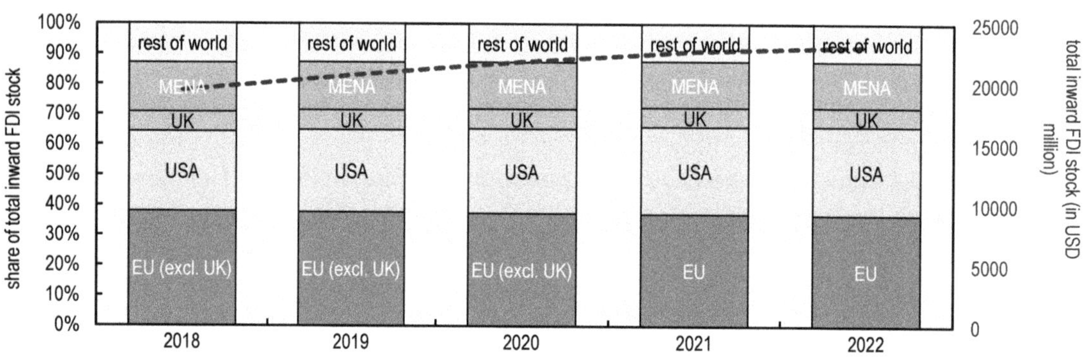

Note: Inward direct investment positions calculated based on data reported by Algeria to the IMF since 2018.
Source: OECD calculations based on IMF Coordinated Direct Investment Survey (CDIS) data.

As other countries of the MENA region, foreign investments in Algeria have historically been concentrated in the oil and gas sector, a sector with limited job-creating potential due to its relatively low labour-intensity. Although the oil and gas sector remain an important driver of FDI in the country to this day, the sectoral coverage of FDI has diversified since, in line with the priorities flagged in the 2020 governmental Action Plan.

In global indicators developed to assess local business environments, Algeria fared rather poorly in comparison to its regional peers (World Bank Group, 2020[2]). Investors report facing important hurdles in carrying out their business activity in the country. Bottlenecks identified by relevant stakeholders relate to bureaucratic red taping, which render administrative procedures relatively cumbersome for investors. Procedures to obtain licences, getting electricity, registering a property, paying taxes, etc. are reportedly lengthier in Algeria than the regional average – even twice as high to register a company, and appear to be costlier for businesses and individuals. Foreign-invested firms have also pointed towards the country's unpredictable business climate, with laws and regulations appearing to be volatile and applied inconsistently (U.S. Department of State, 2022[3]). Recent legislative and institutional reforms aim at improving the country's investment climate.

General institutional framework for investment in Algeria

Algeria's efforts to promote and facilitate investment in the country are undertaken by the Algerian Investment Promotion Agency (**AAPI**). The AAPI operates two OSS: one geared towards foreign investments and high-stakes investment projects; and a second tailored to domestic investments.

Agence Algérienne de promotion de l'investissement (AAPI). The AAPI succeeds the National Investment Development Agency (*Agence nationale de développement de l'investissement*, **ANDI**), Algeria's previous IPA. Its mandate is set out in the new Investment Law (**2022 Investment Law**), and was formally established by Executive Decree 22-298 (2022) (**Decree 22-298**). Two additional ministerial orders dated 28 September 2022[1] and 24 November 2022[2] outline its governance and organisation.

AAPI's main mandates, as established by Decree 22-298, include:[3]

- Elaborating an investment promotion strategy at the national and regional levels, in coordination with the private and public sector.
- Providing information to investors on investment legislation, procedures, relevant authorities to obtain authorisations and permits required for the implementation of projects and investment opportunities in the country.
- Registering investment projects through an online "*investor portal*" to benefit from incentives. The investor portal also allows investors to directly recommend improvements for the business environment that can be directly transferred by AAPI to the Cabinet.[4]
- Accompanying investors when dealing with other authorities for the obtention of licences, authorisations and permits.
- Monitoring investors' compliance with commitments and processing investor complaints.

Two separate OSS operate within the AAPI to facilitate investment into the country. The first OSS is specifically dedicated to foreign investments and "*large projects*" (i.e., investments having a capital equal or greater than DZD 2 billion)[5]; while the second one deals with domestic investments that do not qualify as "*large projects*". It was unclear at the time of writing as at September 2023 whether two structurally independent OSS are effectively established, as envisaged initially by the 2022 Investment Law, or if the previous single OSS under ANDI's mandate is still operating during a transitional period.[6]

Both OSS share the same structure and perform similar duties with regards to investments falling within their competence.[7] They serve as a single interlocutor for investors: they offer an information desk to investors, register investments required to benefit from incentives,[8] and facilitate licencing and authorisations procedures.[9]

The AAPI's OSS host representatives from several administrative authorities that facilitate setting up and operating a business in the country:

- Some representatives from authorities as listed in Decree 22-298, including tax authorities, the customs authority, and the national centre for commercial registration,[10] which may directly issue authorisations, decisions and documents on behalf of their respective authorities and within the limits set by Decree 22-298 (Article 26).

- Additional representatives may also be hosted by AAPI, although they are not vested with the powers to render decisions and authorisations on behalf of their respective licensing authorities.[11] Rather, they act as points of contacts for investors relying on OSS services to liaise with their relevant authorities with regards to the applications and formalities required for their investment projects.[12]

Other relevant authorities. The Investment Law refers to two additional "*bodies in charge of investment*", namely the National Investment Council (*Conseil national de l'investissement,* **CNI**) and the High National Commission for Appeals related to Investment (*Haute commission nationale des recours liés à l'investissement*, **HCNRLI**).[13] The CNI – established by Decree 22-297 of 8 September 2022[14] – is mandated with putting forward a Government investment strategy, overseeing its overall coherence and evaluating its outcomes by way of an annual report submitted to the President of the Republic.[15] The HCNRLI – established by Decree 22-296 of 8 September 2022[16] – is a special commission affiliated to the Presidency of the Republic. It issues decisions regarding investor complaints and grievances in relation to the withdrawal or refusal of incentives, or the refusal by administrative authorities to issue decisions, documents and authorisations for the implementation of projects.[17]

Transparency and predictability of the Algerian legal framework for investment

This section considers Algeria's investment framework and those measures which the country has adopted for facilitating investment, including with respect to accessibility to and transparency of the country's legal and regulatory framework for investment, establishment restrictions and conditions, and operation authorisations; and the manner in which investment-related procedures are streamlined.

Legal and regulatory framework. Algeria recently overhauled its regulatory framework for investment by adopting a new Investment Law 2022.[18] The 2022 Investment Law seeks to promote investments in priority sectors and sectors with high added value to ensure sustainable development and to develop natural resources and local raw materials.[19] The 2022 Investment Law covers acquisition and ownership operations, extensions of capacity, and greenfield investments in the production of goods and services,[20] and provides for a principle of 'transparent' and 'equal' treatment for foreign investors.[21]

Several Decrees have been adopted to complete the investment framework. These Decrees concern the institutional setting of investment-related agencies operating in the country,[22] investment incentives[23], and investment-related procedures.[24] The Algerian government's Secretariat General's website provides for a platform to consult Algerian legislation extracted from the Official Journal in Arabic and in French. It outlines the instruments alongside all of their related and implementing instruments, which allows for a comprehensive and easy-to-access overview of the different legal instruments. Investors may also consult legislation in Arabic via the Algerian Law Portal.

Transparency and predictability. Ministries and regulatory authorities are not required to publish proposed regulations before their adoption or the rationale behind regulatory amendments, nor are they required to solicit comments on them. In practice however, the People's National Assembly (APN) and the Council of the Nation (CN) both have dedicated web pages where draft legal texts prior to their adoption are published. Neither offer an opportunity to comment. With regards to the Investment Law 2022 specifically, the proposed legislation's rationale was explained in a press release of the Council of ministers published on 19 May 2022. News clippings also seem to indicate that consultations had taken place prior to the adoption of the Law in July 2022,[25] although it is unclear if these consultations were based on informal exchanges between regulatory authorities and selected stakeholders or if all potential stakeholders were provided a reasonable opportunity to comment on the draft legislation. The legislation was subsequently published in the Algerian Official Gazette on 28 July 2022, four days after its adoption.

Streamlining of investment-related administrative and other procedures.

At the time of writing in September 2023, measures adopted within the Algerian legal and regulatory framework for investment which seek to enhance transparency and predictability and streamline relevant administrative procedures are not overarching but rather apply to specific pre- or post-establishment procedures.

Facilitation of business establishment by foreign investors.

- Restrictions to foreign investment

Algeria applies several restrictions to foreign investment in the country. Restrictions – which may include foreign equity caps, limitations on the appointment of key personnel and prior authorisation procedures – apply in a variety of sectors, including agriculture, electricity, transport and distribution, media, finance, real estate, mining and manufacturing.[26] Information related to restrictions applicable to foreign investments does not appear to be consolidated in a negative list, which negatively impacts the transparency of the investment framework.[27] Instead, the Ministry of Commerce provides some information on its website with regards to restrictions applying to foreign investors specifically in commercial activities. Information on restrictions applying in non-commercial activities does not seem to be readily available on Algerian official websites.

Algeria recently alleviated some restrictions to foreign investment activity through the adoption of the latest Finance Law 2020. The country lifted the 49% equity cap in enterprises carrying out manufacturing activities and services, for the exception of activities relating to the import of raw materials, to products and goods intended for domestic re-sale, and to strategic sectors.[28] Separately, some controlled activities require temporary authorisation by the competent authorities[29] prior to legal incorporation *(activité ou profession réglementée soumise à inscription au registre du commerce)*.[30] The conditions of operation of such controlled activities are defined by sector-specific laws or regulations,[31] and are currently governed by Decree 15-234 (modified by Decree 20-355). Under Decree 20-355 (Article 4), pre-approval seems to be mandated only if required explicitly by the sector-specific legislation.

- Pre-admission formalities and legal incorporation of companies

Foreign investors may register an enterprise in Algeria through the same commercial forms available to Algerian nationals: partnerships (les *sociétés en nom collectif*), limited partnerships (les *sociétés en commandite*), limited liability corporations (*sociétés à responsabilité limitée*), joint-stock companies (*sociétés par actions*) and simplified joint-stock corporations (*sociétés par actions simplifiées*).[32] These are governed by the provisions of the Algerian Commercial Code.

The conditions for the operation of commercial activities are governed by Law 04-08, as amended.[33] Legal incorporation in the Commercial Register is required for all natural or legal persons to operate a commercial activity.[34] Once incorporated, investors may freely operate their activity unless subject to licensing or authorisation conditions.

With respect to company legal incorporation specifically, Law 18-08 has amended Law 04-08 to include a provision on the creation of an online portal to facilitate the registration of enterprises.[35] The portal is managed by the National Centre of the Commercial Registry (*Centre National du Registre du Commerce*, **NCCR**). Investors may directly fill out registration forms on the portal, which are then validated by the NCCR. Once validated, investors may complete other mandatory establishment formalities with the tax authorities, and the social security authority.[36] The company legal incorporation process is facilitated by the presence of representatives from the NCCR within AAPI's two OSS which can directly issue decisions and authorisations on behalf of their respective authorities.

Facilitation of business operations by foreign investors.

Licensing requirements to carry out specific activities apply generally to domestic and foreign investors alike. Information on activities subject to licensing or prior authorisations is scattered throughout various legal sources. Several sector-specific executive decrees adopted over the years specify the regime for controlled activities in oil and gas distribution,[37] wholesale and retail trade,[38] manufacturing activities,[39] scientific activities (testing laboratories),[40] or even public utilities.[41] There exists no comprehensive list of controlled activities, although the Ministry of Commerce's website provides an illustrative list of activities that require its authorisation.

The AAPI's website does not provide comprehensive information on licensing and authorisation procedures applicable in Algeria. It contains a description of both of its OSS and their missions, as well as a description of the nine representatives working within the OSS. AAPI plays a role in facilitating the obtention of approvals, licences and permits through its OSS. Representatives within the OSS may either issue these authorisations directly where they are competent or facilitate the liaison with their relevant authorities.[42]

The 2022 Investment Law does not provide any procedural framework for the streamlining of licensing formalities and the processing of investment-related applications. Delays for the processing of applications also depend on sector-specific legislations governing licensing procedures.[43]

Transparency and predictability of the Algerian Investment Incentives Regime

Incentives play a pivotal role in the 2022 Investment Law's goals to encourage investment in priority industries and promoting the country's sustainable development.[44] The new incentives' schemes (together the **Investment Incentives Regime**) are available to both domestic and foreign investors, provided their investments are covered by the scope of the 2022 Investment Law.[45] The Law provides a procedural framework to facilitate and streamline the processing of applications, their evaluation, and the granting of incentives.

Three distinct incentives schemes are available under the Investment Law (2022):[46]

- Incentives for "*priority sectors*";
- Incentives for "*zones of particular interest*"; and
- Incentives for high-stakes investment projects ("*structuring investments*").

Information pertaining to Algeria's Investment Incentives Regime is available through various sources. The 2022 Investment Law alongside its implementing decrees are published in Arabic and French on the Official Gazette's website as a bundled package under the same issue. The AAPI's official website (available in Arabic, English, and French) and its investor's digital platform (available in Arabic and French) also publish measures, but do not provide practical details beyond the Law.

Types of available incentives and eligibility requirements.

Incentives available under the 2022 Investment Law include exemptions from tax, customs duties, and certain corporate and real estate administrative fees. Promoted "*structuring investments*" could also benefit from the State's participation in the infrastructure works required for their implementation. All incentives schemes may also benefit of State-owned lands, subject to conditions.

Incentives under the Investment Law may generally be cumulated with other incentives offered under other Algerian legislation,[47] provided they do not overlap and are not of the same nature.[48]

Incentives are implemented for promoted investments in two separate phases:

- During the implementation phase, all schemes give access to identical incentives.

- During the operational phase, for which periods for benefiting from incentives may be higher for zones and "*structuring investments*" (five to ten years) than for priority sectors (three to five years). The exact period is determined following the investment registration with AAPI's OSS.[49]

Eligibility conditions to incentives are clearly detailed in the 2022 Investment Law, as well as by Decree 22-300. These are framed by positive and/or negative lists:

- "*Priority sectors*" eligible to sectoral incentives are listed out. These include mining activities, agriculture, fishing, industry, services and tourism, new and renewable energies, and information and communication technologies (**ICT**) amongst others. Economic activities ineligible to sectoral incentives are also set out in Annexes I and II of Decree 22-300.[50]
- Incentives for "*zones of particular interes*t" are broader in scope than sectoral incentives: eligible zones are framed by positive lists annexed to Decree 22-301,[51] as well as a negative list enshrined in Annex I of Decree 22-300.[52]
- Additional negative lists limit the scope of incentives for priority sectors and for zones (mainly activities governed by a special tax regime or that fall out of the scope of the Investment Law or specific goods that are ineligible to incentives).[53]

The incentives scheme for "structuring investments" appears to be the broadest in scope. "Structuring investments" refer to investments that have a "high potential to generate wealth and employment and could increase the attractiveness of the territory and create a ripple effect over the economic activity pursuant to a sustainable, economic, social, and territorial development" and which contribute to the essential goals set out by the 2022 Investment Law.[54] As such, eligibility to the scheme is not assessed by reference to a list of economic sectors specifically, but rather, is subject to two cumulative conditions as set out by Decree 22-302: the creation of a minimum of 500 direct employments, and a minimum investment amount of DZD 10 billion.[55]

Procedural requirements and processing of applications.

Algeria's investment incentives regime falls under the main supervision of AAPI.[56] Investment registration with AAPI is required to obtain incentives under the Algerian framework.[57] Such registration to obtain investment incentives is undertaken by APII's OSS: one for foreign investors and projects with a capital beyond DZD 2 billion, and one for domestic investments below DZD 2 billion.[58] The registration process may be fully undertaken online on the investor platform.

The process to register investment projects or to amend registration certificates already issued is mainly governed by Decree 22-299.[59] The Decree sets out the required documents to support the registration request, the list of goods and services to be filled by applying investors for all incentive schemes, as well as application fees. Supporting documents vary depending on the nature of the investment – whether greenfield, acquisitions or other.[60]

AAPI reviews registration applications with a view to assess investor eligibility to incentives and lists out its findings in the registration certificate along with the list of goods and services qualified for the incentives.[61] Issuance of the registration certificate is done "*immediately*", but a specific timeframe is not defined.[62] The registration certificate and its attached list of goods and services are enforceable vis-à-vis the concerned authorities (tax, customs etc.).[63]

Following the delivery of the registration certificate and the list, a second evaluation is undertaken to determine the period during which incentives are granted during the operational phase. These periods vary depending on the specific incentives scheme, ranging between three to ten years.[64] Decisions must be notified to the investor within seven days.[65]

Decisions of refusal to grant incentives must be motivated, and cannot be based on incompleteness or errors in the application, as the APII OSS is required to contact the concerned investor to complete its application.[66] Furthermore, investors may file appeals before the AAPI in the face of a refusal or negative decision, and ultimately before the HCNRLI.[67]

Structuring investments are effective upon the conclusion of an agreement between the investor and the state. The request to conclude such an agreement is submitted to AAPI by the investor, based on a detailed and descriptive quotation of the needed works.[68] This request must be approved by the Algerian government.[69]

Promoted investments must start operations within a maximum period of five years (three years for the investment benefiting of the "*priority sectors*" regime),[70] which could be extended twice, each time for twelve months only[71] by submitting a request to the AAPI's OSS.[72] Furthermore, Decree 22-303 sets out how the monitoring of the investment is undertaken, along with the investor's obligation to report to AAPI of all the necessary information concerning its investment.[73] In case of the investor's persistent default to meet its obligations to report, AAPI may proceed with the revocation of the registration certificate and the incentives, while demanding the investor to reimburse all the advantages it got, along with any possible sanctions.[74] Revocation decisions may also be subject to appeal before the AAPI or the HCNRLI.[75]

Egypt

Investment climate in Egypt: a practical overview

FDI in Egypt surged in several waves over the last three decades. Foreign investments began to emerge with the progressive opening of the Egyptian economy to the private sector initiated in the 1970s with the *infitah* ('open door') policy. The policy led to the adoption of the Law on Arab Capital Investment and Free Zones adopted in 1971, the first ever legislation dedicated to investment in Egypt (OECD, 2020[4]). The General Authority for Investment and Free Zones (**GAFI**) was also subsequently established, making it one of the oldest IPAs operating in the region.

Macroeconomic stabilisation, the country accession to the WTO in 1995 and further liberalisation of cross border investment in the early 2000s further paved the way for a sustained wave of FDI increase between 2000 and 2007, reaching its peak at almost USD 12 billion. However, the global financial crisis and the post-2011 instability in the region had a negative effect on the country's FDI performance. Egypt was one of the most affected countries of the selected Southern Neighbourhood countries following the Arab Spring movements, with investors having massively suspended their operations, downscaled their commitments, or withdrawn their investments altogether (Figure A A.3). Between 2012 and 2016, FDI inflows had been on a positive upward trend representing around 2% of GDP, yet below the pre-2007 crisis levels of 8%. The COVID-19 pandemic further slowed Egypt's post-2011 recovery, although FDI inflows in 2022 appear to be the highest they've ever been since 2007.

Figure A A.3. FDI inflows in Egypt (1990-2022)

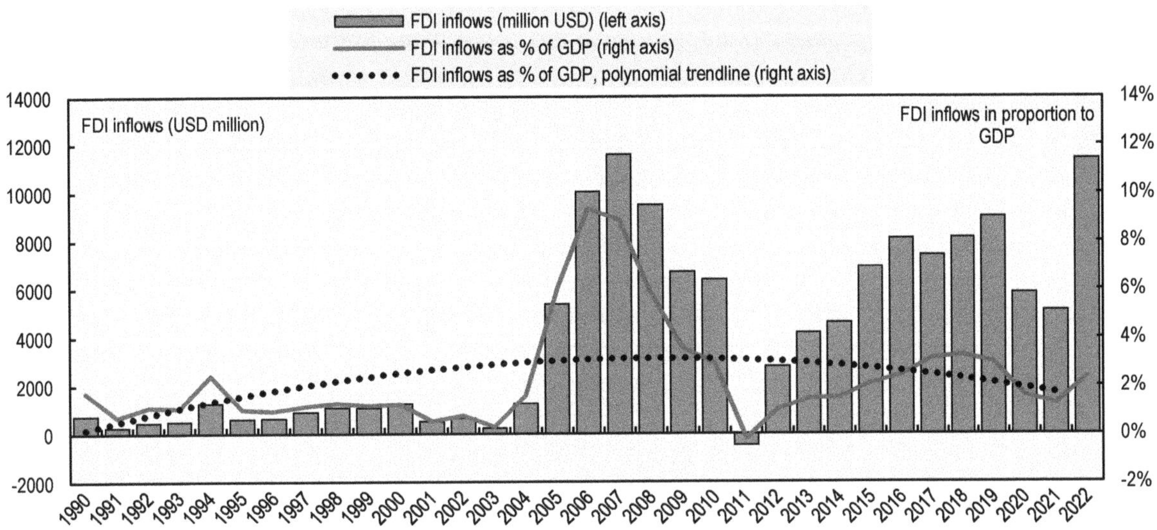

Source: OECD elaboration from IMF (BOP/IIP statistics) and World Bank (GDP data).

The share of FDI stock in Egypt held by European investors and those from the MENA region has increased in the last years. In 2021, more than 90% of Egypt's inward FDI stock was held by investors from the **United Kingdom** (29%), the **EU** (24%) – mainly from Italy, Belgium, the Netherlands and France, the **MENA region** (19%) – especially from the United Arab Emirates and Saudi Arabia, and the **United States** (19%) (Figure A A.4).

Figure A A.4. Origins and total value of inward FDI stock in Egypt (2018-2021)

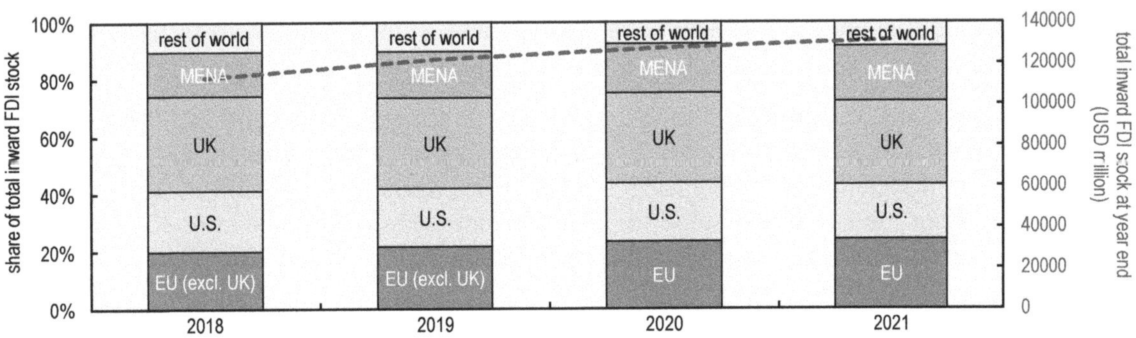

Note: Due to data availability issues, FDI stock origins were estimated based on FDI inflows data published by the Central Bank of Egypt covering the 2002 to 2021 period. Total volume of FDI stock based on reported international investment positions.
Source: OECD estimations based on FDI inflows data of the Central Bank of Egypt and the IMF Balance of Payments and International Investment Position Statistics (BOP/IIP).

In Egypt, as in most of the MENA region, FDI is concentrated in natural resources, real estate, construction, and light manufacturing (e.g., textiles). Most of these sectors have limited job-creating potential due to their relatively low labour-intensity. Since 2010, instability in the region has further skewed the sectoral composition of FDI towards the natural resources sector, which has been more immune to political shocks (OECD, 2014[5]). FDI inflows in non-oil manufacturing and services sectors have stagnated, while these sectors have a higher propensity to create jobs and promote transfers of technology and managerial knowledge, making it more challenging for Egypt to participate in global value chains.

Comparative surveys reveal sensible differences in the perceptions of the Egyptian investment climate between domestic and foreign-invested firms. Over 65% of foreign invested enterprises surveyed by the World Bank in 2020 identified corruption (23.6%), political instability (26.5%) and customs and trade regulations (16.8%) as being their biggest obstacle in the country, whereas tax rates and fiscal administration appear to affect more domestic businesses than foreign-invested firms (World Bank Group, 2020[6]). Bottlenecks reported by investors include excessive bureaucracy, lack of transparency, uneven enforcement of laws and regulations, difficulties accessing foreign currency to repatriate profits or import goods, a shortage of skilled labour, cumbersome customs procedures, corruption, and intellectual property issues (U.S. Department of State, 2023[7]). In recent years, Egypt revised its investment promotion and facilitation structure and enacted legislative changes to address these obstacles identified by investors. In 2017, a new Investment Law was introduced significantly improving the clarity of the investment regime by consolidating the so far scattered investment rules and by streamlining procedures through GAFI's mandate (OECD, 2020[4]).

General institutional framework for investment in Egypt

The role of Egypt's nation-wide IPA, the General Authority for Investment and Free Zones (**GAFI**), was significantly enhanced further to the 2017 Investment Law, with the establishment of Investor Services Centres (**ISCs**). ISCs are institutional units operating within GAFI and through its regional branches. The ISCs feature a core investment establishment mandate and facilitate operation formalities by hosting representatives of relevant authorities. The Board of Directors of investment, free and technical zones offer additional facilitation services.

General Authority for Investment and Free Zones (GAFI). GAFI was established in 1971 as an autonomous agency and currently operates under the authority of the Prime Minister. The 2017 Investment Law details GAFI's governance structure as well as its broad investment promotion, generation, and to a more limited extent, facilitation mandate. GAFI is broadly responsible for developing and implementing investment facilitation measures, including by overseeing the operation of ISCs.

The Investor Service Centre (ISC). The ISC entity was established under the 2017 Investment Law, which outlines its mandate and structure. It is described as an "*administrative unit*" operating within GAFI – both in its headquarters and via GAFI's regional branches – and effectively acts as the latter's OSS. ISCs fall under the supervision of GAFI Board of Directors, which is missioned with developing and fully implementing the entity and its two-fold mandate:

- A core establishment mandate, which pertains to the provision of corporate services, including company incorporation, establishment of company branches, formalities relating to company administration meetings, share allotments, change of activity and liquidation procedures.
- An operation mandate, which is not *de jure* carried out by the ISC itself, but via the Competent Authorities represented within the ISC and that are mandated with receiving investor applications for approvals, permits, licences and allocation of real estate properties required for the realisation of Investment Projects, as well as deciding upon such applications as per the laws and regulations in force.

The ISC does not enjoy a dedicated website; rather, its mandate and functions are listed via the GAFI website, which outlines the different categories of services it offers, namely: company incorporation and establishment services; and a wide range of what are labelled as "*after establishment services*", including corporate-related legal services (e.g., ratifying minutes of ordinary and extraordinary general assemblies, ratifying board minutes, and changing the legal form of companies), technical services (e.g., establishment formalities relating to custom duties), governmental services (e.g., residence and work permits related formalities), private incentives unit services, and publication services (e.g., publication of company Articles of association). In that regard, an ISC Investor Guide outlines the relevant procedures and formalities, documents required, applicable pre-conditions, and fees for each of these categories of services.

Competent authorities are represented in ISCs in one of two capacities: as "*delegates*", vested with the power to directly issue those approvals, permits and licences that fall within their Authority's jurisdiction; or as "*liaison* officers", which may not directly issue authorisations and act as points of contact between the competent authorities they represent and investors. As neither the GAFI Board of Directors' resolutions nor the outcomes of the underlying decision-making process are publicly available, it is unclear which authorities are represented within GAFI through delegates or liaison officers. Further, evidence suggests that authorities are not equally represented throughout all of the ISC regional branches, which could effectively hamper the transparency and predictability of authorisation procedures for investors, and suggests that facilitation services – including services seeking to streamline authorisation procedures – may be uneven across the country's governorates.

A number of physical ISCs currently operate across the country.[76] It is unclear if the composition of ISCs across the country is harmonised and if the same Competent Authorities are represented across all ISCs. While that may be the 2017 Investment Law's intention, existing evidence suggests that it is not the case in practice, which could suggest uneven investment facilitation services across governorates. As at the time of writing in September 2023, the ISC Investor Guide listed the "*Services/Scope of Functions Carried out by each Ministry/Body Represented at the ISC*"; these include a number of Ministries, the Egyptian Exchange, the Investment Taxes Office and the Egyptian Customs Authority Office. On the face of the ISC Investor Guide, each of these representative offices are mandated with providing "*investment services relating to [their] scope of work*" as well as licenses and other required certificates and authorisations that fall within their respective jurisdictions, among others.

"Accreditation" or "Approval Offices". The 2017 Investment Law provides for the establishment of private-sector Accreditation Offices. Such Offices are licensed and registered by GAFI on the basis of a number of conditions and are subject to GAFI's scrutiny.[77] Their envisaged mandate seeks to expedite the licensing and related processes. It remained unclear at the time of writing in September 2023 whether such Offices have been registered in practice.[78]

Transparency and predictability of the Egyptian legal framework for investment

This section considers Egypt's investment framework and those measures which the country has adopted for facilitating establishment and operation for foreign investment, including with respect to accessibility to and transparency of the country's legal and regulatory framework for investment, establishment restrictions and conditions, and operation authorisations; and the manner in which investment-related procedures are facilitated.

Legal and regulatory framework. Egypt adopted a new investment framework in 2017 (**2017 Investment Law** or the **Law**), which repeals the previous 1997 Investment Guarantees and Incentives Law.[79] The Law was complemented by the Prime Minister Decree 2310 of 2017 adopting Executive Regulations to the Investment Law as amended (**2017 Executive Regulations**).[80] Separate decrees were subsequently adopted to implement additional provisions of the 2017 Executive Regulations concerning certain aspects of the Egyptian incentives' regime and the constitution of the Supreme Council for Investment among others.[81]

The 2017 Investment Law defines the legal regime for domestic and foreign "*Investment Projects*" in a wide-ranging list of sectors. The Law applies equally to greenfield investment and acquisition and ownership operations.[82] The Law sets out the principles and guarantees offered to investors, including fair and just treatment, national treatment to foreign investors, non-discrimination, protection against unlawful expropriation, and free transfer of capital in foreign currency, among others.[83] It also sets out Egypt's investment promotion policy, which consists of a 'general investment framework', the "**Inland Investment Regime**", as well as three additional special investment regimes, namely, free zones, investment zones, and technical zones. Special economic zones are governed by a stand-alone legislation. Different competent authorities, incentives regimes and at times, operation procedures and requirements apply with respect to each of these different regimes. The present section will exclusively consider the Inland Investment Regime as Egypt's general investment regime.[84] The Law also introduces a new investment promotion tool, the "*Investment Map*", elaborated by GAFI in coordination with relevant authorities, including the Supreme Council for Investment. It defines the investment opportunities, regimes, State- or public sector-owned real estate property available for investment on a geographic basis, and the manners in which the latter may be granted for investment under the Law.[85]

Transparency and predictability. Egypt's legislation is published in Arabic in the Official Gazette and its supplement (*Al-Jarida Al-Rasmiya* and *Al-Waqae Al-Misriyya,* respectively) by the Government Printing Office (*Al Amiria*). The latter's website does not however provide free access to the Official Gazette. Other online governmental sources such as the Egyptian Legislation Portal and the Legal Encyclopaedia of the Ministry of Justice are equally fee-based.[86] Consolidated official Arabic versions of the 2017 Investment Law and the 2017 Executive Regulations are available via the website of the Court of Cassation of Egypt; however, these are not updated with the implementing decrees relevant to the 2017 Investment Law. The country's legal and regulatory framework of investment is also available in part through a dedicated portal on the GAFI website: the Law – both its official Arabic version and its English translation – is up to date and reflects its 2019 amendment; the 2017 Executive Regulations, on the other hand only reflects two of the six amendments introduced thereto, in both languages.[87] The same GAFI portal lists additional laws and regulation relevant to investment and investors, including companies', environmental, fiscal, labour, finance, and protection of intellectual property rights legislation. Fragmented and at times, partial only, access to the investment framework may in practice negatively impact the latter's transparency.

Ministries and regulatory authorities are not required to publish proposed regulations before their adoption or the rationale behind regulatory amendments, nor are they required to solicit comments on them. The draft investment law was thus not published by government or regulatory authorities before its adoption and entry into force.[88] Little time was arranged between the adoption of the 2017 Investment Law and its entry into force, as the law was officially approved on 31 May 2017, and entered into force on 1 June 2017 (however, while the Law repeals and replaces the previous 1997 Investment Guarantees and Incentives Law, it specifies that it "*does not prejudice the tax privileges and exemptions and other guarantees and incentives*" granted to investors existing at the date of its entry into force, who shall keep such benefits until their term expires).[89] Further, and based on unofficial sources, public consultations were carried out further to the media sharing a draft of the investment law, in December 2016, principally with stakeholders hailing from the business and investor community. These appear to have been limited to informal exchanges between regulatory authorities and select stakeholders. Information as to the identity of these investors – and whether they were domestic and/or foreign – the outcomes of this consultation process, its specific duration and its impact on the adoption of the 2017 Investment Law is not publicly available.[90]

Streamlining of investment-related administrative and other procedures. At the time of writing in September 2023, measures adopted within the Egyptian legal and regulatory framework for investment which seek to enhance transparency and predictability and streamline relevant administrative procedures are not overarching but rather apply to establishment and operation procedures specifically. These are considered in turn.

Facilitation of business establishment by foreign investors.

- Restrictions to foreign investment

Restrictions on foreign investment apply in several sectors, and are set out by sector-specific legislation, among others, rather than being consolidated in a negative list, which negatively impacts the transparency of the investment framework.[91] These include, among others, foreign equity limits in the construction, distribution (retail), maritime and air transport, media, and professional services (namely legal, audit and accounting) sectors.[92] A number of horizontal, cross-sectoral restrictions also apply, namely in respect of land and real estate ownership by foreigners.

- Pre-admission formalities and legal incorporation of companies

There exist no cross-sectoral or horizontal requirements or pre-conditions applying to foreign investors and/or investments in relation to the making of new investments in Egypt. Some specific formalities may be required in relation to certain types of activities; these would be governed by specific sectoral legislation. Nevertheless, foreign investors must obtain a Government background check, carried out by the "*Central Security Department at the Investment Services Sector*", which may in practice delay the company legal incorporation process.[93]

Legal incorporation of companies. GAFI enjoys exclusive jurisdiction over the legal incorporation of companies via the ISC, save for company incorporation under the Financial Regulatory Authority and Special Economic Zones regimes[94] and company incorporation in respect of certain economic activities that require other competent authorities' establishment authorisations, e.g., sector-related approvals from other sectoral competent authorities.[95] Investors may incorporate their business vehicles under one of two available governing laws, namely, Companies Law 159 of 1981,[96] or the 2017 Investment Law.[97] Incorporation under the 2017 Investment Law requires that the company's economic activity falls within the scope of the Law,[98] and provides access to the Investment Incentives Regime thereunder.[99] Incorporation under the Companies Law regime is primarily available for those companies whose economic activities fall outside of the scope of the Law. Irrespective of the choice of governing law, all companies incorporated in Egypt are subject to the provisions of the Companies Law. In that regard, different legal commercial entities are available to both Egyptian owned-businesses and foreign-invested enterprises, joint-stock companies (general and limited by shares), limited liability companies, and single member companies.

Company legal incorporation formalities and procedures fall within the mandate of the ISC.[100] The ISC Investor Guide outlines the relevant procedures and formalities which can be carried out at the Cairo ISC branch,[101] which enhances the investment framework's transparency and predictability insofar as establishment conditions are concerned, as well as the documents, pre-conditions, and fees relevant to the incorporation of all types of commercial forms. In theory, incorporation formalities may also be carried out online, with GAFI's e-incorporation portal, as required by the Law.[102] E-services were however as at September 2023 not fully operational and/or not fully digitalised (e.g., formalities relating to company general assembly meetings). A separate GAFI page features separate "*easier and faster*" facilitation services for the incorporation of limited liability companies. It is unclear whether the procedure envisaged thereunder differs from the formalities undertaken by the ISC as outlined in the ISC Investor Guide. The limited availability of electronic applications for the legal incorporation of companies generally hinders the streamlining of authorisation procedures with respect to establishment procedures.

GAFI and/or the ISC are required to complete company legal incorporation applications within one business day of receipt of an application file,[103] and streamline all formalities relating to company administration meetings (e.g., approval of general assembly and board of directors' meetings).[104] It is unclear as at the time of writing in September 2023 whether the entirety of these facilitation measures have been adopted and implemented.[105] The portal provides information as to the formalities relevant to the incorporation of single member companies, joint stock companies (partnerships limited by shares), partnership companies (general and limited partnerships), limited liability companies, and sole proprietorships. It outlines step-by-step breakdowns of incorporation formalities, including relevant prerequisites and requirements, fees, estimate timeframes and competent authorities (namely, the ISC). Applications may be submitted at any time throughout the year. These considerations enhance the streamlining of the incorporation processes.

Facilitation of business operations by foreign investors.

The ISC is mandated under the 2017 Investment Law to receive investor applications for approvals, permits and allocation of real estate and licences required for set up or management of Investment Projects. The Competent Authorities represented within ISCs that are vested with the authority to issue approvals, permits and licenses, as well as real estate allocations, in line with the conditions and requirements set out in the relevant laws and regulations in force.[106] This mandate seeks to centralise operation authorisations at ISC-level, thereby implying both that Competent Authorities representatives within the ISC are entrusted with the powers to directly issue such licences, approvals, permits and other authorisations; and that ISC membership is harmonised across each of the governorates' ISCs. ISC membership is determined by way of GAFI Board of Resolutions, which are not publicly available. The lack of transparency as to ISC membership and the decision-making powers of Competent Authorities representatives within ISCs generates legal uncertainty as to the mandate of the ISC as a OSS. Further, existing evidence suggests that Competent Authorities representation is not harmonised and consistent across the country's ISCs,[107] which could also point to uneven authorisation procedures' streamlining services across governorates.

The Law does not specify or clarify specifically which investor "*approvals, permits and licences*" procedures the ISC facilitates and ultimately issues via the Competent authorities representatives. However, GAFI is under the 2017 Investment Law mandated with preparing – in coordination with the "*Competent Authorities*" – and regularly updating a guidebook outlining the relevant bodies, procedures, indicative timeframes, fees, applicable regulatory frameworks, required documents and forms relevant to the issuance of approvals, permits and licences and the allocation of real estate for the realisation of investment activities as defined under the Law.[108] Several such sectoral licensing guides elaborated by ministries are available via the Arabic version of the GAFI website.[109] These are not standardised, and the information which each provides varies significantly in depth of detail. Nevertheless, most guides broadly outline the relevant procedures for obtaining operation – and in some instances, establishment – permits, approvals and licenses, eligibility conditions and requirements, the competent authorities to which applications must be submitted, and estimate timeframes of these procedures. These guides are reviewed and if and when necessary, updated, periodically every six months, and are legal binding.[110] It is unclear on the face of these guides whether the information provided therein is exhaustive or merely indicative. In parallel, investors may also carry out the necessary formalities and procedures for operation licences, approvals, permits and other authorisations in person directly with the ISC.[111] At the time of writing in September 2023, the ISC's automated e-services were limited to establishment procedures, but consultations with GAFI have confirmed that a system for license automation was currently being developed, and representatives of the entities are being trained for trial operation of such system in preparation for its official launch. This system is expected to allow investors to electronically submit and follow up on their applications for approvals, permits and licenses, as well as electronically submit inquiries and complaints.[112]

GAFI, the ISC and the Competent Authorities represented therein are bound by a number of facilitation measures introduced by the 2017 Investment Law. These contribute to enhancing both the predictability of the investment framework with respect to licensing and other authorisations, as well as the streamlining of authorisation in that respect – as follows:[113]

- ISC Competent Authorities representatives are bound by general obligations of due process and diligence;[114]

- Competent Authorities representatives within the ISC must decide upon investor applications for approvals, licences or permits within 20 days business of receipt of a complete application;[115]
- Competent Authorities representatives must notify investors of the outcome of the application review by way of registered letter or agreed upon electronic means within five business days from the date of the elapse of the above-cited term;[116]
- GAFI shall follow up on investor applications which have not been settled within the above-cited timeframe, and coordinate with the relevant Competent Authorities with a view to expedite the decision-making process;[117]
- In the event of an incomplete application file, Competent Authorities representatives and the Competent Authorities themselves must request from investors any missing documents within two business days of receipt of the application; the application file is deemed complete beyond that timeframe;[118]
- Decisions rendered further to approvals, permits and/or licences requests must be justified, reasoned and transparent,[119] and investors may appeal refusals or negative decisions before a GAFI's *Grievances Committee*, the procedure for which is set out in the Law;[120]
- Competent Authorities may not revoke or suspend issued licenses or reclaim allocated real estate property without providing the investor with prior notice and a "*grace period*" not exceeding 60 days to rectify any notified breaches; GAFI must authorise any revocation where appropriate, within seven days of a Competent Authority's notification;[121]
- A 'tacit approval' mechanism also applies if, within 60 days of receipt of a complete application, the relevant Competent Authority has not issued a decision in respect of a licence, approval or permit request, GAFI's Chief Executive Officer will issue the decision directly. This decision must be communicated to the investor by way of registered letter within seven days of expiry of the above-cited term.[122]

As outlined above, "*Accreditation*" or "*Approval*" Offices are also envisaged under the 2017 Investment Law with a view to further facilitate the approvals, permits and licences review and issuance process. Their mission concerns the review of investor applications for approvals, permits and licences for establishing, developing and expanding an Investment Project, with a view to ascertain whether they meet the technical and financial conditions required under the applicable laws and regulations.[123] The outcome of this review process is the delivery to the investor, the ISC, the Competent Authorities and other relevant administrative authorities of an "*accreditation certificate*" valid for one year, that attests that a given Investment Project has "*satisfied all or part of the conditions in accordance with the laws and regulations which regulate the issuance of approvals, permits, and licences*". The Competent Authority – or its representative via the ISC – may object to the accreditation certificate within 10 business days of receipt. If no objections are raised in respect of the certificate, the latter will be deemed accepted, and the Competent Authorities – either directly and/or via the ISC – are required to decide on the application for licences, approvals and/or permits within 60 days of receipt; no response within this timeframe will be deemed a tacit approval.[124] It is nevertheless unclear at the time of writing in September 2023 whether any such Offices have been effectively implemented in practice.

Investors may also under the 2017 Investment Law access real estate property which they may require for pursuing or expanding Investment Projects, in accordance with the Investment Map and applicable laws and regulations.[125] The rules pertaining to real estate property allocation to investors are set out in detail in the Law.[126] In parallel to the ISC mandate for operation approvals, permits and licences, GAFI is mandated with reviewing and issuing approvals, permits and licences required in the context of activities on real estate allocated for investment.[127]

Transparency and predictability of the Egyptian investment incentives regime

The 2017 Investment Law introduced three incentives schemes under the general investment framework, which repeal and replace the investment incentives provided under Law 8 of 1997 on Investment Guarantees and Incentives.[128] They include general incentives, special incentives,[129] and additional incentives for projects in Investment zones and Technological Zones.

Specific eligibility conditions as well as application processes and procedures apply with respect to each incentives regime. While information pertaining to the General Incentives Scheme is clearly detailed in the 2017 Investment Law, the eligibility conditions as well as the benefits granted under the Special and Additional Incentives Schemes are fragmented in several instruments. Some information about the incentives schemes available under the Inland Investment Regime is provided via the GAFI website, but it is unclear as to whether this information is up-to-date and/or regularly updated.

Types of available incentives and eligibility conditions.

General Incentives Scheme. All "*Investment Projects*" as defined under the 2017 Investment Law enjoy the benefits granted under the General Incentives Scheme, save for those projects established under the Free Zone Regime.[130] General incentives include a number of benefits and discounts, such as stamp duty and notary fees exemptions for company incorporation documents among others; a standardised custom duty rate for the import of certain equipment and custom duty exemptions.

Special Incentives Scheme. The Scheme is available to two categories of investments. First, greenfield investments which meet certain eligibility conditions set out under the 2017 Investment Law, including a timeframe requirement during which an investor seeking to benefit from advantages under the Scheme should have incorporated their company.[131] The Law also provides that establishment in accordance with the Investment Map is a pre-condition to obtaining Special Incentives; this requirement is not outlined in further detail in the Law. Second, Investment Projects that seek to extend capacity and which meet additional conditions.[132]

This Scheme effectively grants a discount off of the eligible Investment Projects' taxable net profits, calculated on the basis of "*investment costs*" as defined under the relevant instruments.[133] Different discounts apply to different territorial "*sectors*", which are defined by reference to three criteria (geographic location, type of investment, and economic sector). Additional eligibility requirements apply with respect to each of these sectors. The applicable discount rates, the sectors to which they apply, the sectors' eligibility requirements, and the determination of these sectors, are set out in the 2017 Investment Law, the 2017 Executive Regulations, as well as subsequent decrees which further specify and amend the Scheme's implementation.[134] Benefits granted under the Scheme may not exceed seven years as of the start date of the "*activity*" and are capped to 80% of the paid up capital at the time of the start date, and can only be granted for a period not exceeding from that time.[135] The process by which an activity's "*start date*" is ascertained by procedures established and carried out by GAFI.[136] Beneficiaries may cumulate different discount rates in the Schemes' two separate sectors, when applicable, provided that separate accounts are kept for each of the companies operating in the different zones.[137]

Additional Incentives Scheme. The Scheme is available to those Investment Projects that fulfil the eligibility conditions of the Special Incentives Scheme,[138] as well as the additional requirements set out in the 2017 Executive Regulations, namely having commenced operations – as per criteria and a procedure defined by GAFI – and satisfying one of a number of requirements, including but not limited to Egypt being the principal place of production or a minimum 50% of local contents involved in the Investment Project's production.[139] Benefits are granted under this Scheme by way of Cabinet Decree, and are set out in the 2017 Investment Law. Some of the notions relevant to the granting of those benefits (e.g., the definition of an "*industrial project*", which can benefit of a 50% refund of the value of the land allocated for an industrial project under certain conditions) are either not defined in the 2017

Investment Law and related instruments, or those definitions are not readily available. The Cabinet may also define further non-tax incentives under the Additional Incentives Scheme by way of decree.

Single-Approval Mechanism. Joint stock companies and limited liability companies may benefit from a single-approval mechanism if they are undertaking *strategic* or *national projects*.[140] The mechanism seeks to facilitate licencing procedures and the allocation of real estate property for the establishment, operation and management of investment projects.[141] Investment projects qualifying for the Single-Approval Mechanism may also benefit from incentives provided under the Schemes outlined above.[142] Eligibility conditions were initially defined under the 2017 Investment Law and the 2017 Executive Regulations. These were subsequently amended and supplemented more recently by Cabinet Decree 56 of 2022.[143] These are currently as follows:[144]

- The Investment project must qualify as a *strategic* or *national project* as per Cabinet Decree 56 of 2022, *i.e.,* (i) operate within a priority sector listed in the Decree (electricity, renewable energy, oil and mineral resources, transportation, industry, telecommunications and information technology, housing, tourism, youth and sports, environment, and agriculture sectors);[145] and (ii) meet two out of the eight economic performance criteria listed therein, relating among other to its planned contribution to sustainable development and employment of Egyptian nationals.[146]
- The Investment Project must meet the conditions as set out under supplemental Decrees amending the 2017 Executive Regulations; these concern limited liability companies specifically, which are required to provide a proof of solvency and have incorporated in Egypt after the entry into force of the 2017 Investment Law.[147]

A *"Golden Licence Guidebook"*, prepared and published by GAFI, provides investors information on eligibility conditions and application procedures. It was recently updated, in April 2023, and an Arabic version of the Guidebook is now publicly available, reflecting the mechanism's latest implementing decrees.

Procedural requirements and processing of applications.

The 2017 Investment Law does not outline the formalities and procedures which investors must comply with a view to benefit from Special and Additional Incentive, which negatively impacts the transparency and hinders the predictability of these schemes for investors. In that regard, the 2017 Investment Law notes that Additional Incentives are granted by way of Cabinet Decree.[148] Incentives under the General Scheme are in contrast automatically granted to investors further to legal incorporation under the regime of the 2017 Investment Law.[149] Separately, Single-Approval applications are submitted to and processed by a special unit within GAFI created for this purpose.[150] The application is reviewed before submission to the competent Minister, and is ultimately approved by the Cabinet.[151] This application may be submitted online via the Cabinet's official website, operational at the time of writing in September 2023.

GAFI must, with respect to all three schemes, issue a certificate allowing investors to benefit from incentives thereunder. It is described under the Law as being *"final and self-executory without the need for the approval of other authorities"*.[152] While the 2017 Investment Law provides some information as to requirements regarding some of the schemes,[153] the process and practical procedures by which such a certificate is obtained, or what steps investors must engage with further to obtaining this certificate, is not clarified in the Law or the relevant implementing Decrees.[154]

GAFI is required under the 2017 Investment Law to publish the list of companies which benefit from incentives under the 2017 Investment Law in an annual report freely accessible online, so as to enhance the transparency of the Investment Incentives Regime.[155] At the time of writing in September 2023, this list was not readily available via the GAFI website. Companies benefiting from incentives under any of the Investment Incentives Regime's Schemes are bound by an annual reporting obligation.[156] The scope of these reporting obligations is unclear.

Further, GAFI may revoke incentives, in whole or in part, and adopt sanctions in case of violation of the 2017 Investment Law.[157] It is unclear whether investors may appeal such decisions, as the GAFI *Grievances* Committee's competence is limited to matters related to approvals, permits and licences.[158]

Jordan

Investment climate in Jordan: a practical overview

Jordan truly advanced its attractivity to foreign investment after a series of reforms launched in the mid-1990s reducing the state's participation in the economy and after its accession to the WTO in April 2000. The country issued its first law regulating investment in 1987, amended it in 1992 and replaced it by the Investment Promotion Law 16 of 1995 which established the Jordan Investment Board (JIB),[159] the first IPA operating in the country.

As a result, FDI inflows grew rapidly and reached their peak at USD 3.5 billion in 2006, representing almost a quarter of the country's GDP recorded at the time. Following their initial contraction in the aftermath of the Global Financial Crisis and the political upheavals in the country between 2011 and 2012, FDI inflows stabilised relatively until 2017. Followingly, they have systematically been declining, a trend further accentuated by the shocks induced by the Covid-19 pandemic (Figure A A.5).

Figure A A.5. FDI inflows in Jordan (1990-2021)

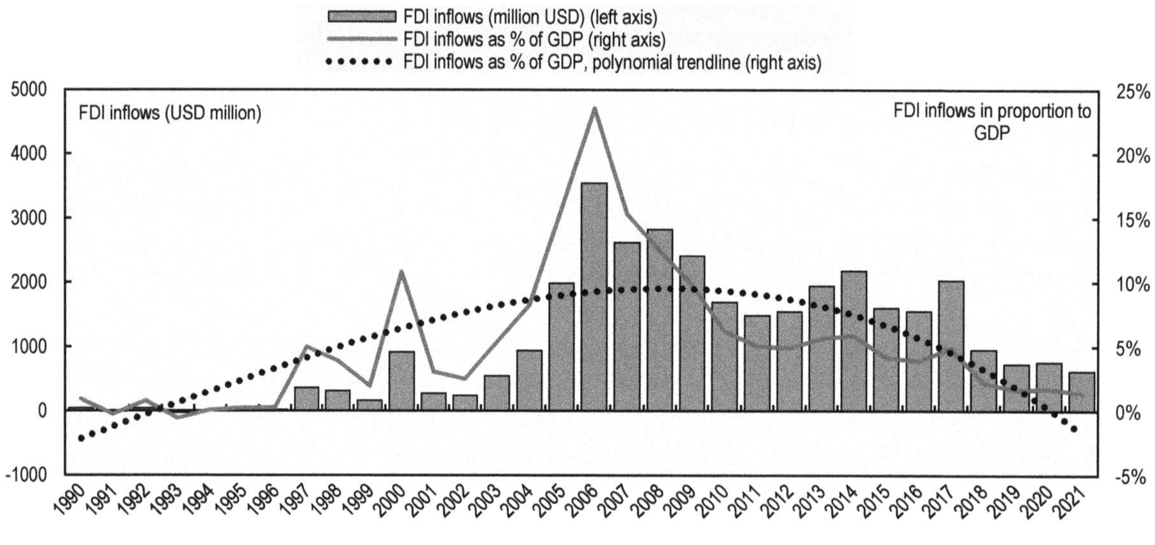

Source: OECD elaboration from IMF (Balance of Payments and International Investment Position Statistics) and World Bank (GDP data).

Jordan's inward FDI stock is principally held by investors from the **MENA region** (42%) UAE, Kuwait, and Saudi Arabia; from the **EU** (17%, mainly from Belgium, Italy, the Netherlands), the **United Kingdom** and People's Republic of **China** (hereafter 'China') (Figure A A.6).

Figure A A.6. Origins and value of inward FDI stock in Jordan (2019-2020)

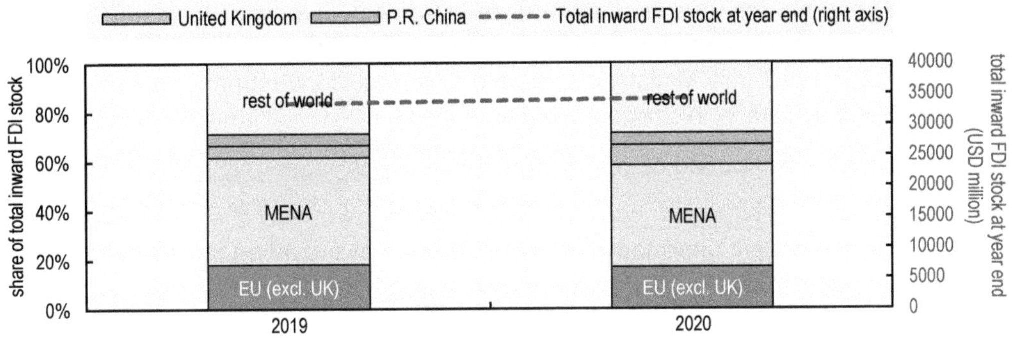

Note: Total volume of inward FDI stocks at year-end estimated by accumulation of inward FDI flows.
Source: OECD calculations based on Central Bank of Jordan, Foreign Investment Survey (geographical origins of inward FDI stock) and World Bank (total volume of inward FDI stock).

Jordan has historically seen significant FDI flowing into industries like real estate, construction, and oil and gas-related energy, despite not necessarily being the primary contributors to the creation of high-quality jobs or the fostering of innovation. There has been a notable shift in the sectoral composition of FDI in recent years from traditional sectors such as manufacturing or construction towards industries with the potential to generate more high-quality employment opportunities and foster the transfer of knowledge. These emerging sectors include renewable energy, business, financial, and health services, transport and logistics, and the field of information and communication technology.[160]

In global reports developed to assess local business environments, Jordan has demonstrated favourable performances when compared to its regional peers.[161] This success may be attributed to the country's repeated efforts to rearrange its regulatory framework for investment, primarily motivated by its eagerness to improve the general business climate. Despite notable advancements, numerous investors still voice concerns about persistent challenges. Obstacles include excessive red tape or bureaucratic hurdles, shifting interpretations of laws and regulations, difficulties in both starting and exiting businesses[162] and various other factors including elevated operational expenses of doing business – in particular in terms of energy costs – limited access to financial resources, burdensome procedures for talent hiring, and obstacles related to land acquisition.[163] Moreover, almost half of the firms – whether domestic or foreign-invested – surveyed by the World Bank identified the Jordanian tax administration as a major constraint in doing business in the country.[164]

Recent positive developments in terms of improved co-ordination and streamlining of licensing procedures are the country's effort to overhaul its regulatory and institutional framework for investment by creating an MoI in October 2021[165], the adoption of a new Investment Environment Law in 2022, and the MOI's announcement to digitalise most of the ministry's investment services.[166] FDI is identified as an important lever to achieve the SDGs set out in the country's Economic Modernisation Vision (2022-2025), especially in renewable energies, ICT, and infrastructure development.

General institutional framework for investment in Jordan

Under its current framework, Jordan does not operate an IPA as a separate administrative agency in charge of promoting and facilitating investment in the country. Rather, investment facilitation is overseen by the MoI, which was established in October 2021 to address the shortcomings of the previous IPA – the Jordan Investment Commission.[167] The Ministry absorbed the JIC's missions, which was the IPA operating previously in the country since 2014, as well as the Private-Public Partnership Unit which used to be under the Prime Minister's jurisdiction.[168]

The Ministry of Investment (MoI). According to the Investment Environment Law (2022), the MoI is "*the main reference authority for investment in the Kingdom*", and shall aim to "*attract, encourage and promote investment, ensure the sustainability of an attractive investment climate, and enhance confidence in, develop and organise the investment environment*" (Article 7). To the extent that the MoI absorbed the duties of the JIC, the Ministry's mandate in terms of investment facilitation mirrors the Commission's previous mandate in this regard.

The Ministry's Secretariat is composed of several functional directorates and units, including:

- A "*Comprehensive Investment Service*" (CIS) which oversees the Jordanian "*investment window*" (**OSS**) previously operated by the JIC. It aims at providing information and technical assistance to investors by simplifying the registration of companies and licensing procedures for investors. However, the scope of its facilitation services is limited to 12 economic sectors as defined by Schedule 1 of the Decree 7 of 2023 on the Investment Environment Law. A list of its facilitation services for establishment and operation matters is provided under Schedule 2 of the Decree.[169] To fulfil its facilitation mandate, the CIS includes fully authorised representatives of public agencies who have the authority to issue directly approvals and licences for investment projects, such as representatives of tax authorities (for company registration procedures), of the Ministry of Tourism or the Ministry of Agriculture (for sectoral licences), of the Ministry of Environment (for environmental approvals) or even of the Ministry of Labour (for work permits).
- The Ministry also comprises a "Follow-Up and After Care" section which aims at resolving all obstacles faced by investors with central or local authorities for the implementation of their projects. The section was established initially as a JIC department in 2018. The section may also receive suggestions by investors or relevant stakeholders to improve the Jordanian business environment.
- Finally, the Ministry operates a grievance mechanism which was introduced in 2019 to address investors' complaints. The grievance mechanism aims at avoiding investment disputes arising from investment procedures or decisions by official bodies related to a given investment in the country. As such, the mechanism is available to investors that have not yet formally filed complaints in domestic courts or initiated arbitration proceedings against the State.[170]. The grievance committee may issue recommendations to the official body of which a decision is subject of the investor's grievance, although its recommendations are not binding upon the authorities concerned.

The Investment Council. Chaired by the Prime Minister, and comprising ministers with economic portfolios, and representatives from the private sector, the Investment Council oversees the management and development of national investment policy and proposes legislative and economic reforms to facilitate and promote investment in the country.[171] The Investment Council also acts as a grievance mechanism in case investors face administrative hurdles in the implementation of their projects.[172]

The Incentives and Exemptions Committee (IEC). An Incentives and Exemptions Committee (**IEC**) was created pursuant to Article 12 of the Investment Environment Law (2022). The IEC is an inter-ministerial committee which plays an important role in the granting of incentives to eligible investors, especially for the additional incentives scheme and the single approval mechanism which it supervises in conjunction with the Council of ministers.

Transparency and predictability of the Jordanian legal framework for investment

Legal and regulatory framework. Jordan recently overhauled its legal framework for investment by adopting the Investment Environment Law in October 2022 which entered into force on 14 January 2023.[173] The Law applies to greenfield investments as well as acquisitions and ownership operations by Jordanian or non-Jordanian natural or legal persons. It has a limited material scope as its provisions apply to industrial, commercial, agricultural activities, services, tourism, information technology or creative industries and exclude banking or money exchange, or any professional activities governed by sector-specific regulations.[174]

The Law reflects Jordan's investment policy strategy aimed at enhancing its business environment and encouraging sustainable investment in the country. Article 3, which frames the purpose of the Law, mentions the country's willingness to:

- Create an appropriate environment for the development of small and medium enterprises;
- Digitalise and automate all procedures and services provided to investors; and
- Protect the environment and encourage the transition to a green economy, safety and public health, according to social standards, among others.

The Law sets out a principle of national treatment of foreign investors, and enshrines the principle of fair, equitable and transparent treatment within Jordan's regulatory framework.[175] It also limits the possibility of partial or total expropriation of an investment to circumstances where a "*public, specific and legitimate purpose"* may warrant it and if carried out in a non-discriminatory manner and subject to fair compensation.

Transparency and predictability. Some business- and investment-related legislations and regulations can be found on the Companies Control Department (CCD)'s website. English translations are provided for three main legislations (Investment Environment Law, Insolvency Law and Commercial Code) whereas regulations are only available in Arabic. The MoI's website only provides an English translation of the Investment Environment Law (2022) and of the Public-Private Partnership Projects Law (2020). Other implementing instruments are available in Arabic through the Official Journal's website. The official government portal also provides an overview of several business-related procedures in Jordan (company registration, obtaining licences, loans, permits, electricity, water etc).

There exist no legal or regulatory requirement which requires regulatory bodies to publish draft laws and other instruments. Ministries and regulatory authorities are nevertheless encouraged to publish texts of proposed regulations before their adoption, especially those related to investment, to enhance regulatory transparency and predictability.[176] Proposed legislation and regulations are readily available for consultation on the relevant ministries' websites, often completed by explanatory notes on the proposed regulatory changes. More specifically, investment-related amendments are available on the MoI's website, where stakeholders are provided with an opportunity to comment on the drafts within a timeframe, as specified by the drafts' explanatory notes. The House of Representatives also provides a dedicated section on its website to receive comments from relevant stakeholders. It appears that the draft Investment Environment Law (2022) was made public several months prior to its adoption. It was first published by Petra, the government's news agency, in June 2022, followed by the Prime Minister's office in July 2022, along with an explanatory note to the Law. It also appears from publicly available information that the draft was subject to extensive consultations with public and private sector representatives prior to its adoption in October 2022. The Law entered into force 90 days after its publication in the Official Gazette on 10 October 2022.

Facilitation of business establishment by foreign investors.

Restrictions to foreign investment

Jordan maintains limited restrictions to foreign investment in the country. Besides in a handful of sectors in which foreign ownership caps apply, wholly foreign-owned enterprises may operate in the country.[177] The Decree 7 of 2023[178] adopted pursuant to the new Investment Environment Law sets out two negative lists of restricted sectors: a list of activities in which foreign investments are prohibited; and a list of activities in which a foreign ownership cap of 50% applies. Restricted sectors to foreign investments include financial activities, commercial activities, transport, and engineering services among others.[179]

Pre-admission formalities and legal incorporation of companies

Outside of controlled or restricted activities, investors may register their enterprises freely to carry out their businesses. The Law shifts Jordan's investment policy from a system of "*prior control*" to a system of "*post control*", in accordance with the previously announced business practice requirements.[180] As such, the registration of enterprises is generally not subject to review by the relevant authorities and no prior authorisation is required for enterprise registration except for certain controlled activities according to sector-specific legislations.[181] Around 360 economic activities require prior approvals in Jordan, which fall within the competence of 35 distinct official bodies, including the Energy and Minerals Regulatory Commission, the Ministry of Interior, the Ministry of Public Works and Housing, the Telecommunications Regulatory Commission, the Jordan Central Bank etc. A list of pre-registration approval requirements is provided by the Companies Control Department (CCD) in charge of company registration in Jordan.

Only a handful of pre-registration approvals required for certain economic activities may be directly obtained through the CCD's online portal for enterprise registration. These concern approvals granted by authorities having partnered with the CCD specifically for the provision of the pre-registration approvals falling within their jurisdiction. At the time of writing in September 2023, there seems to be only 6 agencies out of the 35 competent authorities that have partnered with the CCD to facilitate the obtention of these approvals and authorisations: the Ministry of Industry and Commerce's Insurance Department; the Jordan Securities Commission; the Central Bank of Jordan; the Ministry of Public Works and Housing; the Ministry of Interior; and the National Committee for Demining and Rehabilitation. Besides those granted by these six agencies, pre-registration approvals need to be obtained directly from the competent authorities prior to registering an enterprise with the CCD, which may pose additional administrative hurdles to investors in controlled activities.

The MoI's Comprehensive Investment Service, which acts as a OSS for investors, facilitates the registration of enterprises in the economic sectors subject to the provisions of the Investment Environment Law (2022).[182] Schedule 1 of Decree 7 of 2023 defines more precisely a list of 12 sectors in which investors may benefit from the CIS' services. Beyond these 12 sectors, investors are required to carry out the registration of their enterprises by liaising directly with the CCD and obtaining pre-registration approvals from the relevant authorities as required by sectoral policies. The OSS' limited material scope creates an imbalance in its facilitative services which are not equally available to all investors throughout all economic activities in the country.

Company registration follows the process set out by the Companies Law 1997, as amended. Specific guidance for company registration in Jordan is provided in Arabic on the CCD's website. Foreign-registered enterprises may either register "*non-operational companies*" (representative or liaison offices or branches), or "*operational companies*" (subsidiaries) in Jordan. The conditions and supporting documentation are set out in detail in Article 240 (for offices) and Article 241 (for subsidiaries) of the Companies Law (1997).

Other commercial forms available to investors in Jordan include limited liability companies, joint liability companies and single partnerships. The registration of companies may be undertaken through the CCD's online portal, developed with the support of the United States Agency for International Development (**USAID**) through the Jordan Local Enterprise Support Project (**LENS**).[183] Fees are publicly accessible through the CCD's website.

Facilitation of business operations by foreign investors.

After having registered their enterprises, investors are required to obtain operational licences to carry out some controlled activities in Jordan. There appears to be no aggregate information on activities subject to licensing conditions, which hinders the overall transparency and accessibility of Jordan's legal framework for investment. The 2022 Investment Environment Law refers to *"professional activities governed by sector-specific regulations"* to exclude them from its provisions, without mentioning which activities are concerned specifically. The MoI's OSS may however provide some guidance to foreign investors with regards to the licensing conditions applicable to their intended projects, and in some cases, may even facilitate the obtention of these licences in the 12 economic sectors falling within its competence as defined by the Decree 7 of 2023.[184] These include permits in the health sector, agricultural permits, tourism, environmental permits etc. Outside of CIS services for licensing, investors need to address relevant authorities to obtain licences that do not fall within the competence of the CIS which may cause delays in the implementation of their investment projects.

The 2022 Investment Environment Law, which aims specifically at improving the Jordanian business climate, incorporates specific provisions for the facilitation of licensing and authorisations procedures by the MoI. It provides for the creation of a joint electronic platform between the MoI and the competent licensing authorities. It also provides for several guiding principles for administrative practices with regards to licensing, to streamline approval procedures:

- Authorities shall not request a document that has been delivered by another administrative body if they already have access to it.[185]
- The delays for the processing of applications are set within the general framework: authorities have 15 days to process complete applications for licences, unless specified otherwise by the relevant authorities. The Law enshrines a principle of 'tacit approval' if no answer has been received by the investors following their complete application to the relevant authorities within this timeframe.[186]
- The Investment Environment Law organises a process for following-up with the implementation of projects by nominating an official to issue additional licences as required and on behalf of the authority they represent.[187]

The Law also enshrines principles of transparency and stability to ensure legal security and procedural fairness to investors regarding licensing procedures:

- Authorities may not impose additional requirements for the approval of a licence beyond what is provided by sector-specific legislations.[188]
- The list of conditions to obtain licences as well as the licences' validity periods need to be provided by the relevant authorities.[189]
- Decisions refusing to grant licences need to be clearly motivated and the Law explicitly prohibits some grounds for refusal to grant licences.[190]
- Decisions to withdraw licences must follow a specific procedural framework under the Law: authorities need to notify the licence holder of the alleged violation of the licence terms and provide them with a timeframe for rectification or for responding with evidence that no violation has occurred.

To enhance the transparency of the licensing framework, the Law requires that a "*licensing guide*" be published, which should include the conditions, procedures, requirements, and legal periods for issuing licences in accordance with sector-specific legislations and that these guidelines shall be regularly updated.[191] The new licensing guide was published by the MoI in April 2023. The guide, available in Arabic, provides detailed information on the conditions, procedures, documents, requirements, and timeframes for obtaining permits and licences. It covers incorporation, pre-approvals, operating permits and licences, construction permits, FDI restrictions, environmental assessment, services offered by the OSS, and the single approval, amongst other topics. It also provides hyperlinks for the available online services. In that regard, the Jordanian MoI recently announced that it had digitalised 95% of the services offered by it through its CIS portal. Outside of these, investors must address the relevant competent authorities to obtain authorisations that do not fall within the competence of the CIS.

Transparency and predictability of the Jordanian Investment Incentives Regime

Two sets of investment incentives are available under the Investment Environment Law (2022): incentives for investments in "*free and development zones*", and those outside of zones. The Law does not specify nationality requirements for the obtention of investment incentives: all incentives schemes are available to domestic and foreign investors alike.[192]

The Council of Ministers and the Minister of Investment, each within their respective jurisdictions, are mandated to issue the executive instruments of the Law's provisions.[193] Some of these provisions were fully complemented by the Council of Ministers' Regulation 7 of 2023, while additional instruments are yet to be adopted to complete the incentives' framework (e.g., rules on monitoring economic activities benefiting of the additional incentives,[194] the required documents to apply to the additional incentives,[195] the required fees for applying to the single approval[196]).

Jordan is also the only country among the selected Southern Neighbourhood countries that does not currently maintain a webpage centralising information on the country's investment incentives, despite its previous IPA successfully developing and launching an 'incentives inventory' in 2016, relevant to the previous investment framework.[197] The country's current priorities, as outlined in its Investment Promotion Strategy (2023-2026), include addressing such shortcomings through a dedicated online investor portal.[198]

Types of available incentives and eligibility conditions. The Jordanian incentives regime is comprised of "*basic incentives*" for promoted investors that may be cumulated with "*additional incentives*" on a case-by-case basis:[199]

- *Basic incentives* include exemptions from customs duties, a zero-rate general sales' tax, and a waiver, in whole or in part, from income tax for a maximum period of five years;
- *Additional incentives* include tax and non-tax advantages (e.g., preferential sale and rental of State-owned lands, subsidising energy,[200] water, deducting the costs of infrastructure works from their due accounts).[201] Additional incentives also include a "*single approval*" scheme, which replaces "*any licence, permit or permission required by any legislation*" for eligible investors.[202]

Incentives under the Law may be granted to investments in the sectors covered by its provisions.[203] Eligibility to incentives is assessed based on a variety of criteria including the economic sector of the investment, the region of the investment, capital thresholds, and even performance requirements in terms of employment of Jordanian nationals and exportation. The eligibility criteria are clearly detailed by the Law and its Regulation:

- **Exemptions from customs duties** or **zero-rate general sales tax** may be granted for fixed assets, "*production requirements*" and "*production inputs*" as defined by the Regulation[204] and spare parts that are necessary to implement the investment project. The economic activity, provided that the economic activity falls within the scope of the Law. A schedule approved by the Council of Ministers also frames the eligibility of goods to the zero-rate general sales tax.[205]
- **Partial or total waivers of income tax** for a maximum period of five years, are offered only to projects that have not yet started operations nor benefited from any tax incentives under the previous regime.[206] These projects must operate within a positive list of eligible sectors and activities, set out under Regulation 7 of 2023, which includes industrial activities, agriculture,

hospitals, hotels, entertainment cities, call centres, information technology, media production among others.[207] A negative list of sectors is also set out under the Regulation to exclude activities or investment projects from the benefits of the income tax waiver (electricity generation, some mining activities, and activities undertaken by enterprises established in a free or development zone).[208] Additional eligibility criteria include the geographic zone of the investment or performance requirements in terms of employment of Jordanian nationals.[209] Eligible zones are classified into three categories,[210] each unlocking a different rate of waiver.[211]

- Eligibility to **additional incentives** is assessed by reference to eight alternative criteria to assess the "*strategic*" nature of the economic activity,[212] including the employment of Jordanian nationals, activities that export 50% of their production, transfer of knowledge and technology, private-public partnerships, and activities that target poverty areas,[213] accompanied by a negative list of ineligible activities (e.g., activities undertaken by enterprises established in a free or development zone, and some mining activities).[214] The amount and types of additional incentives depend on the specific fulfilment of cumulative criteria by the investors.[215] Although additional incentives are capped at 20% of the investment amount, the cap may be increased by increments on a case-by-case basis depending on the fulfilment of individual criterion.[216]

Procedural requirements and processing of applications. The procedural framework to apply for incentives under the Investment Environment Law is mainly detailed by the Regulation 7 (2023) and is expected to be completed by a series of additional regulations pertaining to the monitoring of promoted investments, required documentation to apply for incentives and fees for the single approval scheme.[217]

Several authorities are involved in the process of assessing investors' eligibility to incentives and deciding upon incentives applications. Access to information on incentives is unequal as the process, timeframes and required supporting documentation for each scheme are set out with varying degrees of detail within the Law and implementing regulations:

- **Customs duties exemptions** and **zero rate sales tax** are assessed by the MoI and granted by a decision of the Minister to be issued within 15 business days following a complete application. The Regulation does not seem to mention the documents required to support investors' applications. It only specifies the elements to be included in such a decision.[218]
- **Partial or total income tax waiver** applications are assessed by a special committee formed by the Minister of Investment, which shall issue its recommendations to the Minister within 15 business days for final decision.[219] Neither the Law nor the Regulation sets out a specific timeframe for the decision to grant such incentives following the assessment by the special committee. The Regulation hints at supporting documentation to be submitted to support investors applications.[220]
- The process to apply for **additional incentives** (besides the single approval) is yet to be fully determined by the Minister of Investment.[221] Applications are assessed by the Incentives and Exemptions Committee (IEC), which issues its recommendations directly to the Council of Ministers[222] within 15 business days.[223] The Law and implementing regulations do not specify a timeframe for the Council of Ministers' decision or supporting documentation to be submitted.
- The process for applying for the **single approval** scheme seems to be the most elaborate yet under the current regulations, which list the required documents,[224] timeframes, as well as the evaluation method by relevant authorities. Applications for the single approval scheme follow a three-fold process: (*i*) a committee formed by the Minister of Investment would first assess the applications and submit its recommendations to the Minister if the investments are deemed eligible; (*ii*) applications would then be transferred to the IEC for a second assessment; [225] and (*iii*) in case the latter has a favourable opinion, it would submit its recommendation to the Council of Ministers for final decision.[226] The decision to grant the single approval takes the form of a decree containing the timeline for the implementation of promoted projects, which may be

extended by the Council of Ministers.[227] The evaluation process by the IEC and the decision-making process at the Council of Ministers level do not seem to be subject to specified timeframes. Fees for the processing of single approval applications are also expected to be set in the coming months, as required by the Regulation 7 of 2023.[228] The process to apply for single approvals may be facilitated by the MoI's OSS as it is the only incentive scheme falling within its facilitation services.[229]

The granting of incentives may entail specific obligations and requirements for promoted investors to avoid their misuse or abuse.[230] As such, promoted investors may be subject to the scrutiny of authorities following the granting of incentives, which may lead to revoking their promotion status. Investors are required in some instances to provide regular updates to the MoI on the effective implementation of their projects, as well as to the tax or customs authorities, as required.[231] The Regulation sets in detail the rules governing this administrative scrutiny regarding the exemption from customs duties and the zero-rate general sales' tax.[232] It does not however contain similar provisions for the waiver of income tax, despite being subject to post-approval scrutiny as stated by the Law.[233] As for the additional incentives and the single approval, such process is yet to be determined in detail by the IEC,[234] and the Minister of Investment,[235] respectively. The Regulation only sets an obligation to submit annually the necessary documents proving that the investor remains eligible to the advantages it was granted.[236]

The Investment Environment Law and its implementing instruments contain provisions on the exceptional revocation of incentives or sanctions that could arise if an investor or investment does not meet the requirements for their benefit. Tax amounts may be reclaimed and additional fines may apply if the goods and services benefiting of basic incentives (exemption from customs duties or general sales' tax, or a full or partial waiver of income tax) were sold, transferred, disposed of, or used in activities other than those for which they were granted.[237] The single approval may also be revoked, although the rules governing such a process are yet to be determined by the IEC.[238]

Morocco

Investment climate in Morocco: practical overview

Privatisation programmes and the progressive liberalisation of the economy in the mid-1990s[239] opened up opportunities for foreign investors in Morocco, leading to it becoming one of the largest investment destinations in the MENA region. As part of its commitment to fostering private sector growth, Morocco enacted a first major investment legislation in 1995, being – with some provisions revised – the foundation for investment activities until its replacement by the new Investment Charter in 2022.

While FDI flows have been rather volatile over the past two decades, the overall trend has remained positive even following the 2008 economic crisis or the upheavals caused by political instability in the MENA region in the early 2010s. In 2018, FDI flows reached an all-time high of USD 3.6 billion, representing almost 3% of the country's GDP (Figure A A.1). Despite the global Covid-19 pandemic and its resulting negative effects on investor confidence, FDI flows in the country did not plummet and have fairly recovered and stabilised since.

Figure A A.1. FDI inflows in Morocco (1990-2022)

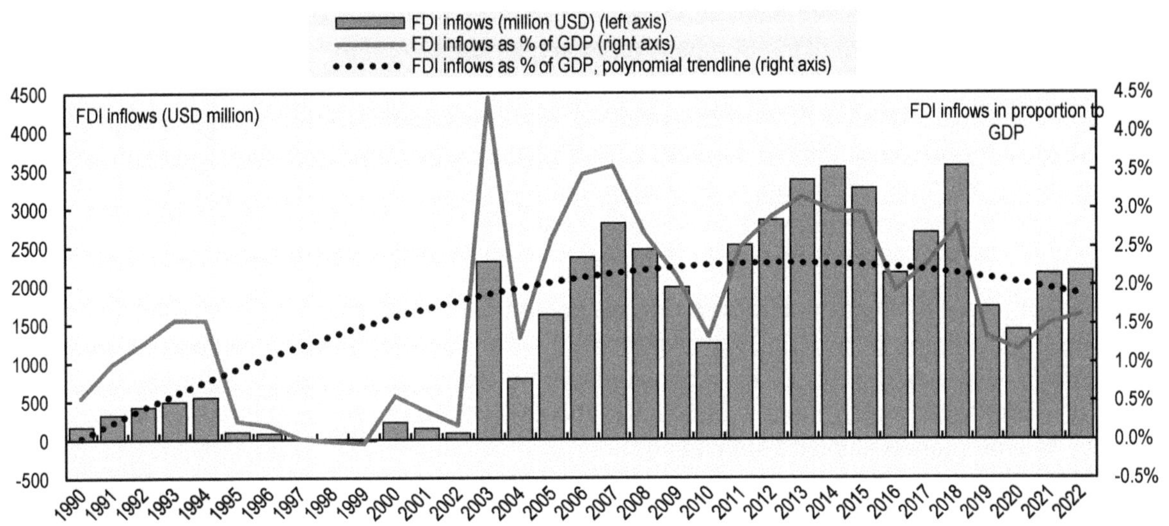

Source: OECD elaboration from IMF (Balance of Payments and International Investment Position Statistics) and World Bank (GDP data).

Morocco has been an important destination for European investors as well as for those stemming from the MENA region. In 2022, investors from the **EU** (49%) and from the **MENA region** (36%) held nearly 85% of the total USD 63 billion inward FDI stock in the country. The share of FDI stock held by European investors grew in the last years, with investors stemming in majority from **France** (27%), and **Spain** (7.8%). Investors from the MENA region are essentially from the **United Arab Emirates**, who held 30% of the inward FDI stock in Morocco in 2022 (Figure A A.2).

Figure A A.2. Origins and total value of inward FDI stock in Morocco (2018-2021)

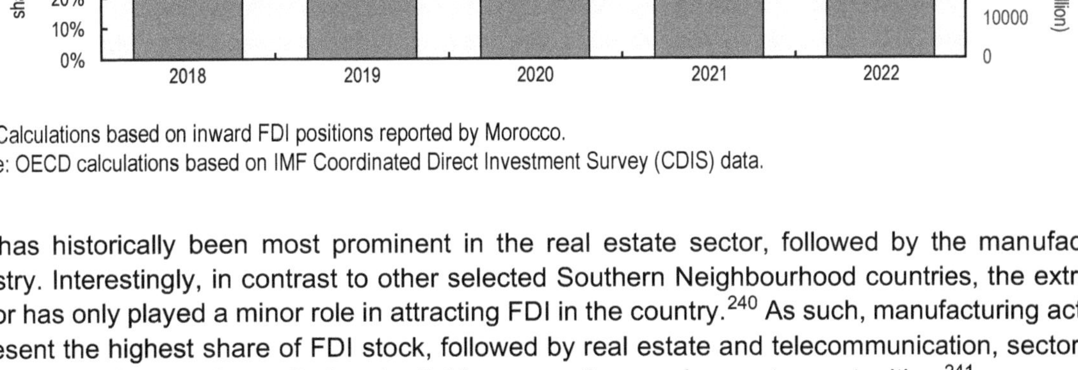

Note: Calculations based on inward FDI positions reported by Morocco.
Source: OECD calculations based on IMF Coordinated Direct Investment Survey (CDIS) data.

FDI has historically been most prominent in the real estate sector, followed by the manufacturing industry. Interestingly, in contrast to other selected Southern Neighbourhood countries, the extractive sector has only played a minor role in attracting FDI in the country.[240] As such, manufacturing activities represent the highest share of FDI stock, followed by real estate and telecommunication, sectors with particular significance due to their potential for generating employment opportunities.[241]

Perceptions of Morocco's business environment by investors appear to be highly favourable and outperforming the other five countries of the Southern Neighbourhood, as indicated by comparative studies.[242] Investors have nevertheless reported facing important bottlenecks in terms of administrative processes in Morocco. A third of the domestic firms and a quarter of foreign-invested firms surveyed by the World Bank in 2020 identified business licensing and permits as a major constraint affecting the investment climate in Morocco.[243] Significant differences in perceptions may be observed following the location of investors in the country, potentially indicating uneven facilitation services across the regions. While practically no firms operating in the regions of Marrakech-Safi, Rabat-Salé-Kénitra or Tanger-Tétouan-Al Hoceïma reported having issues with business licensing, nearly half of firms surveyed in the regions of Fès-Meknès, Souss-Massa or in the Oriental identified it as a major constraint.

In consultation with private and public partners, the government established the Roadmap for Improving the Business Environment 2023-2023 in March 2023. The roadmap is structured around three pillars which aim to improve the structural conditions for investing and entrepreneurship in Morocco, strengthen national competitiveness and optimise the costs of production and develop an environment conducive to entrepreneurship and innovation.

General institutional framework for investment in Morocco

Morocco's approach to investment promotion and facilitation is unique among the Southern Neighbourhood countries considered in this Report. It is characterised by decentralised regional mandates, rather than entrusted to a centralised agency, and a centralised and unified approach to investment-related procedures and decision-making.[244] Investment facilitation in Morocco is primarily undertaken at regional level by Regional Investment Centres (*Centres régionaux d'investissement*, **CRIs**) and Regional Unified Investment Commissions (*Commissions régionales unifiées d'investissement*, **CRUIs**). The facilitation mandate of Morocco's nation-wide IPA – the Moroccan Agency for Investment and Expert Development (*Agence Marocaine de Développement des Investissements*, **AMDIE**) – is more limited although it does work along with CRIs and other regional actors in assisting investors, post-investment monitoring and aftercare services.[245]

Regional investment facilitation agencies and entities: CRIs and CRUIs. CRIs and CRUIs are mandated with wide-ranging powers to effectively support investors in the implementation of their investment projects and facilitate investment-related administrative procedures (these are summarised in Table A A.1). **CRIs** play a pivotal role in Morocco's decentralised approach to investment facilitation across its twelve regions. Their establishment in 2002 was part of the country's broader decentralisation efforts aimed at significantly enhancing the efficiency of investment facilitation and the country's economic and social development.[246] CRIs had performed unevenly and at times inefficiently across the country, impeding the overall effectiveness of the nation-wide investment facilitation strategy.[247] Decree 1-19-18 of 13 February 2019 promulgating La (**Law 47-18**) was adopted among others with a view to harmonise CRI mandates across regions, and thereby enhanced their effectiveness.[248] CRIs operate as OSS to assist and guide investors with investment-related establishment and operation formalities. These procedures are facilitated by the CRIs themselves and via the harmonised CRI-Invest Platform,[249] the exclusive platform shared by CRIs to streamline investment-related formalities and applications through which most of the CRIs' OSS services are provided.[250] CRIs are also required to operate their own websites to publish information relating to the Moroccan regulatory framework for investment and investment procedures and formalities.[251]

Law 47-18 also established a new entity, **CRUIs**, that are mandated with supporting investors in obtaining a number of defined establishment and operation authorisations and formalities required for the implementation of investment projects. These requirements and formalities are explicitly set out in Law 47-18,[252] which nevertheless provides that CRUI powers are broad as the entity may rule on *"all investment-related matters"*. They replace previous regional commissions that processed parallel but uncoordinated investment-related administrative procedures and formalities.[253] Their membership and organisation is designed to centralise and enhance the efficiency of these processes, and their decisions are binding upon CRUI members and the administrations they represent.[254] In contrast to CRIs, whose role is limited to assisting, guiding and supporting investors, CRUIs are entrusted with regulatory powers and either directly decide upon or provide their formal opinion or assent on investment-related administrative acts, in respect of both establishment and operation requirements and formalities.[255] The clearly set out and harmonised mandates of regional CRUIs and the processing and decision-making framework for investment-related established by Law 47-18 contributes to significantly enhancing the predictability of the legal and regulatory framework for investors.

Law 47-18 also established a new entity, **CRUIs**, that are mandated with supporting investors in obtaining a number of defined establishment and operation authorisations and formalities required for the implementation of investment projects. These requirements and formalities are explicitly set out in Law 47-18,[256] which nevertheless provides that CRUI powers are broad as the entity may rule on *"all investment-related matters"*. They replace previous regional commissions that processed parallel but uncoordinated investment-related administrative procedures and formalities.[257] Their membership and organisation is designed to centralise and enhance the efficiency of these processes, and their decisions are binding upon CRUI members and the administrations they represent.[258] In contrast to CRIs, whose role is limited to assisting, guiding and supporting investors, CRUIs are entrusted with regulatory powers and either directly decide upon or provide their formal opinion or assent on investment-related administrative acts, in respect of both establishment and operation requirements and formalities.[259] The clearly set out and harmonised mandates of regional CRUIs and the processing and decision-making framework for investment-related established by Law 47-18 contributes to significantly enhancing the predictability of the legal and regulatory framework for investors.

Commission nationale des investissements. The National Investment Commission (*Commission nationale des investissements,* **CNI**) was established in 2022, and its mandate and structure were reformed further to Decree 2-23-1 of 16 February 2023 (**Decree 2-23-1**). It is chaired by the Head of the Government; its membership comprises principally Ministry and Government branches representatives, and the AMDIE acts as its secretariat.[260] The CNI's mandate under the 2022 Investment Charter relates in great part to the implementation of the incentives regime.[261]

Table A A.1. Summary of investment facilitation missions of CRI OSS and CRUIs

	Missions	
	CRI OSS	**CRUIs**
Establishment	• Assist investors with company establishment procedures • Pre-review investment project files prior to CRUI handover	• Carry out and decide upon preliminary evaluations of investment projects
Operation ***Administrative acts and authorisations***	• Assist investors obtain investment-related administrative acts and authorisations, review their applications with relevant authorities • Prepare administrative acts under the region's authority • Prepare operation authorisations manual (procedures, formalities and documents required)	• Rule on or assent to investment-related authorisations and administrative acts
Operation ***Incentives***	• Monitor execution of Investment Agreements concluded between investors and the Government • Prepare guide outlining eligibility conditions for investment incentives	• Review investment projects' eligibility for investment incentives • Issue opinions on investment projects' access to advantages under investment schemes and on investment agreements related thereto*
Aftercare	• Advise and assist businesses • Monitor investment projects (underway or completed)	/
Resources for investors	• Launch online regional investment platforms (data on the regional investment environment, financing and labour;	/

	Missions	
	CRI OSS	CRUIs
	regulatory framework for investment; regional investment opportunities; investment projects procedures; investor portals for tracking progress of applications) • Digitalise investment applications procedures and formalities	

Note: * Law 47-18, Article 29(c) provides that CRUIs are to examine and give their opinion on investment projects that seek to benefit from investment incentives and on investment agreements related thereto. This aspect of the CRUIs' mandate specifically relates to the investment incentives regime in force under the 1995 Investment Charter. As per Article 35 of the 2022 Investment Charter, this mandate will be complemented – and/or supplanted – by additional measures. Until such measures are adopted, the CNI is responsible for approval all Investment Agreements relating to the Primary Incentives Regime regardless of the total value of the investment project (Decree 2-23-1, Article 29).
Source: OECD compilation on the basis of Law 47-18 and the CRI available websites; non-exhaustive.

Transparency and predictability of the Moroccan legal framework for investment

This section considers Morocco's investment framework and those measures which the country has adopted for facilitating investment, including with respect to accessibility and transparency of the country's legal and regulatory framework for investment, establishment restrictions and conditions, and operation authorisations; and the manner in which investment-related procedures are streamlined.

Legal and regulatory framework for investment. Morocco adopted a new investment law in 2022 (**2022 Investment Charter** or the **Charter**), which replaces and repeals the previous investment legislation in force since 1995, which had been subject to review for a number of years.[262] Law 47-18, the 2022 Investment Charter and its implementing decrees together define the legal regime for domestic and foreign investors across economic sectors,[263] except for agricultural activities which are subject to sector-specific policies.[264] At the time of writing in September 2023, one decree was adopted implementing specific incentives schemes which the Charter introduced, as well as three implementing orders. Two further implementing decrees are scheduled to be adopted by June and December 2023 respectively, in accordance with the calendar set out in the Charter.[265]

The adoption of the 2022 Investment Charter is part of a broader set of structural reforms on administration decentralisations and the streamlining of administrative procedures among others, as set out in detail in the Charter's Preamble.[266] The latter outlines that the Charter rests on three central pillars: the new investment incentives regime and its governance; the harmonisation of decentralised investment facilitation; and foreseen reforms to further enhance the country's business climate.[267] The Charter sets out general principles and rights enjoyed by investors, including freedom of enterprise, free competition, equal treatment irrespective of the nationality of the investor, the right to transfer funds related to investment projects, and legal predictability and good governance.[268]

Transparency and publication. Legislation is published by the Official Printing Directorate (*Direction de l'Imprimerie Officielle*) in the Official Bulletin (*Bulletin Officiel*), which is freely accessible online to the public. Instruments are in theory published in the Arabic official edition and a French translation edition. In practice, legislation is not systematically translated into French (or is translated and published in the French edition of the Official Bulletin but with a significant delay).[269] Further, stakeholders consultations have also highlighted that adopted legislation may at times have a retroactive effect; these considerations may in practice hinder the transparency and predictability of the investment framework. While the country's legal and regulatory framework for investment is not available through a unique, comprehensive portal, a number of CRI portals feature links to the framework's main legal instruments (e.g., the Tanger-Tetouan-Al Hoceima CRI and the Fès-Meknès CRI, by way of example), as required under Law 47-18, thereby contributing to the investment framework's transparency and predictability.

The 2011 Moroccan Constitution requires that public authorities undertake public consultations in their decision-making process and policymaking, and the Moroccan House of Representatives and House of Councillors each publish drafts of laws and regulations. A report examining the draft Charter was prepared and published online on the House of Representatives website in October 2022, alongside the examined draft. The report detailed the Charter's purpose, and how it was debated and amended throughout the elaboration process.[270] It is unclear when these documents, and more particularly, when the draft Investment Charter, was made publicly available, and as such it is difficult to assess whether reasonable time was afforded to investors and interested persons between the Charter's publication and its entry into force. Morocco's legislative frameworks affords an opportunity for the public to comment on drafts laws and bills are available to the public.[271] Based on publicly available information, the Government undertook stakeholder consultations in the development of the Charter starting in February 2022.[272] It is unclear whether these consultations were based on informal exchanges between regulatory authorities and selected stakeholders, or if all potential stakeholders were provided a reasonable opportunity to comment on the draft legislation. Further, no official information sheds light as to whether the outcomes these consultations impacted the adoption of the Charter.

Streamlining of investment-related administrative and other procedures. Morocco has adopted legislation which significantly enhances the transparency and predictability of its investment framework and streamlines authorisation procedures. These measures are summarised in Box A A.1. Unless specified otherwise, they apply to both establishment and operation procedures.

Box A A.1. Streamlining of authorisation procedures, transparency and predictability in Morocco

Morocco adopted Law 55-19 to improve the efficiency of administrative procedures and formalities. It sets out the principles and rules relevant to procedures, timeframes, rights of appeal, and highlights the imperative of digitalisation of administrative procedures. These complement the streamlining requirements set out in Law 47-18 for establishment and operation formalities and procedures undertaken by CRIs and CRUIs. Four decrees implementing Law 55-19 were adopted in May 2023.[273]

Table A A.2. Authorisation procedures in Morocco: streamlining, transparency and predictability

Streamlining of authorisation procedures	Transparency and predictability
CRUIs decide or assent to or give their opinions on all administrative acts depending on the relevant regulatory regime for the realisation of investment projects; decisions adopted by CRUIs bind all those administrations represented therein	Relevant administrations must compile and publish directories listing the administrative acts for which they are competent within 6 months of the publication of Law 55-19 (see, the Idarati national portal, launched in 2021); these must outline the documents required for administrative acts applications
Public administrations may only request from users administrative acts, documents and record required by laws and regulations in force and identified, listed, formalised, transcribed and published on the Idaratildarati national portal	Standardisation of the contents and format of administrative acts
Unless otherwise required by laws and regulations, public administrations shall not ask users for more than one copy of an application for an administrative document (including documents and other items making up the application file)	Standardisation of the general procedure relating to the issuing of administrative acts and document requirements
Unless otherwise required by laws and regulations, public administrations shall not ask users to provide publicly available administrative documents that do not directly concern them	Make available electronic applications for administrative acts on adequate platforms by 2025 (e.g., the CRI-Invest platform)[274]
Public administrations must refrain from requesting from investors documents they may already have in their possession/which can be provided by other public administrations	CRUIs must **reason** their negative decisions, and investors may **appeal negative decisions**. Relevant timeframes and procedures: (i) investors appeal a decision before the *ministerial steering committee* within 10 days of notification of refusal; alternatively, (ii) investors lodge an appeal (*recours gracieux*) with the region's wali for submission to the CRUI; the latter renders the appeal decision within 10 days of receipt. If under (ii) no response is received with these timeframes or a negative decision is rendered further to the *recours gracieux*, then the investor may appeal with the *ministerial steering committee*, which issues a decision within a period of 30 days**
Public administrations may only request additional information relevant to a user's application once; any such request will extend relevant timeframes for the processing of such an application	
CRIs are to submit investment project applications to the CRUIs (in respect of matters which the CRUIs are mandated to issue decisions upon) within **30 days** of receipt of a complete investment project file	
CRUIs are to render their decisions within a maximum of **30 days** from the date of receipt of an investment project file from the region's CRI; this timeframe may only be extended once and only in certain circumstances*	
'Tacit approval' applies if the timeframes envisaged under the relevant legal instruments have expired with respect to certain administrative acts; Decree 2-22-141 provides among others provides a list of nine administrative decisions subject to tacit approval	

Note: *Timeframe for the review and issuance of administrative acts is capped to 60 days; timeframe is capped to 30 days with respect to the review of applications for administrative acts required for the realisation of investment projects (Law 55-19 of 2020, Law 47-18); **Law 47-18 does not outline the implications of an informal appeal as opposed to those of an appeal. Appeal provisions outlined in Law 55-19 concern administrative acts other than those falling within the CRUIs' mandate.

Source: OECD compilation based on Law 47-18 (Articles 15, 29(b), 30, 33, 36, 37), and Law 55-19 (Articles 5-7, 10, 13, 16-19, 24-26, 29); non-exhaustive.

Facilitation of business establishment by foreign investors

Restrictions to foreign investment

Restrictions on foreign investments apply across several sectors, as set out by sector-specific legislation rather than consolidated in a negative list, which negatively impacts the transparency of the investment framework.[275] This significantly hampers the transparency of the investment framework insofar as restrictions to foreign investment are concerned in terms of accessibility to applicable legislation, and the processes by which exemptions – if and when applicable – may be obtained.[276] These restrictions include, among others, foreign equity limits to acquisitions in the air and maritime transport, financial and professional services (including insurance, legal services, audit and accounting, and architectural services), and fishing sectors, among others.

Pre-admission formalities and legal incorporation of companies

Preliminary evaluations of investment projects. CRUIs are tasked with carrying out preliminary economic, social, environmental and urbanistic and employment-creation related evaluations of investment projects submitted by investors. Law 47-18 does not confirm whether this evaluation constitutes an establishment pre-condition for foreign – or all – investments, although information provided by CRI websites (e.g., the Tanger-Tetouan-Al Hoceima CRI) suggests that these might be. Similarly, the Law is not clear as to whether this requirement is relevant to all investment projects, or only those seeking to benefit from investment incentives. The basis upon which these evaluations are carried out is clarified neither by way of regulation nor via the CRI-Invest Platform, which negatively hinders the transparency of the establishment process.[277]

Legal incorporation of companies. CRIs provide information and support to investors to facilitate the legal incorporation of companies. These services are provided by the CRIs themselves, rather than through the CRI-Invest Platform. Many of their websites feature specific company incorporation portals. In their great majority, these outline the pathway for legal incorporation (e.g., the Rabat-Salé-Kénitra CRI, the Guelmim Oued-Noun CRI and the Casablanca-Settat CRI portals). Some also offer company establishment guides (e.g., the Oriental CRI "Setting up a company" guide). When these are featured, they outline in varying degrees the: (i) documents required and formalities relevant for each company incorporation step; (ii) administrations involved at each of these steps; (iii) timeframes and fees associated with these formalities; and the (iv) types of companies and legal forms available under Moroccan law, the procedural requirements and formalities required for their establishment, as well as the factors which investors should consider when deciding upon the most suitable form of incorporation for their business. Different legal entities are available to both Moroccan-owned businesses and foreign-invested enterprises, including partnerships and joint-stock companies, among others.[278]

Some CRIs also facilitate company incorporation services and formalities via their websites, e.g. by providing access to administrative forms relevant to company incorporation procedures (e.g., the Guelmim Oued-Noun CRI, the Marrakech Safi CRI and the Fes Meknes CRI); by featuring online simulation tool designed to assist investors in choosing the company form best suited to their business needs (e.g., the Fes Meknes CRI). Other CRI websites feature company incorporation portals which allow investors to create an account with the CRI for the purposes of setting up their business and/or book a "*business creation*" appointment with a CRI advisor (e.g., the Marrakech Safi CRI, Tanger-Tetouan-Al Hoceima CRI and Casablanca-Settat CRI). It is unclear whether these CRI-specific services and/or portals will in time be merged with the CRI-Invest Platform.

Table A A.3. Facilitating company incorporation in Morocco

Steps	Relevant public administration
Negative certificate* application	CRI or via the official government business creation and support platform ("Direct Entreprise")
Filing of company's incorporation documents and other registration formalities**	Regional tax authorities representation within the relevant regional CRI; alternatively, online
Business tax application	Regional tax authorities representation within the relevant regional CRI
Commercial Registry	Commercial court (appointment online)
National Social Security Fund (CNSS) affiliation	For Moroccan investors: with their affiliated CNSS; unclear for foreign physical or moral persons
***Official Bulletin* publication**	Through the *Official Bulletin*, online

Note: *required for all commercial companies except sole proprietorships; **required for public limited companies, limited liability companies, general partnerships, limited partnerships, and partnerships limited by shares.
Source: OECD compilation based on CRI websites (as and when available); non-exhaustive.

Facilitation of business operation by foreign investors

Regional CRUIs may rule or give their opinion or assent in respect of administrative acts required for the realisation of investment projects, in accordance with requirements and procedures in force.[279] Law 47-18 provides a list of the matters which CRUIs may issue such decisions upon. The operation authorisations which CRUIs are mandated to consider, as listed exhaustively in Law 47-18, fall within three general categories: land-related authorisations, planning permissions, and operating licences and permits.[280] The CRI-Invest Platform outlines these authorisations, as well as the formalities and documents required to successfully complete them, the regulatory frameworks relevant to them, and an estimate timeframe for their successful completion.[281] Law 47-18 also requires that CRIs prepare a manual which outlines the procedures, formalities and documents relevant to investment-related operation authorisations;[282] these were at the time of writing in September 2023 not publicly available. Investors submit their investment file applications directly via the Platform, with the assistance of a CRI advisor, based on the CRI-Invest platform User Guide. These must provide information relating to the investor and the investment (e.g., the industry specific to the projected investment, the description of the investment, the total value of the investment, employment-creation expected as a result of the investment, among others) as well as the authorisations required for the realisation of the investment project.

Separate to those acts and authorisations, activities in a number of sectors are regulated and require a prior authorisation. Two out of the twelve CRIs provide information as to these authorisations (e.g., the Tanger-Tétouan-Al Hoceima CRI). A CRI-affiliated SME support platform also provides a list of regulated activities requiring prior authorisations; it refers to the legal instruments relevant to each of these regulated activities and outlines the pre-conditions and formalities related thereto as well as the competent authorities. Investors may also require licences, permits and other authorisations for the realisation of their investment projects. In that regard, investors may refer to the Rokhas.ma platform for economic authorisations (*autorisations à caractère économique*) and urban planning permits. The platform allows for the submission of applications to the competent authorities and the receipt of authorisations directly via user portals. The Idarati national platform also provides standardised information on all formalities and requirements relevant to administrative acts issues by public bodies and authorities, at national and regional level (procedural steps, relevant authorities, documents required, estimate timeframes, fees).[283] A significant number of these administrative acts have been identified by way of decree, adopted in May 2023.[284] Law 55-19 requires that electronic applications for administrative acts be made available on adequate platforms by 2025. Morocco is currently working on the development of a unified national platform with a view to digitalise procedures and formalities.[285] It is understood that investors are in the meantime required to submit their applications directly to the relevant authorities.[286]

Transparency and predictability of the Moroccan Investment Incentives Regime

The 2022 Investment Charter introduced four new investment incentives schemes (*dispositifs de soutien à l'investissement)* which repeal and replace the previous incentives schemes provided for under the 1995 Investment Charter.[287] These include a Primary Incentives Regime which encompasses Common, Territorial and Sectorial Premiums; and three separate schemes relating to strategic investment projects (*projets d'investissement à caractère stratégique*); medium and small enterprises; and Moroccan businesses expanding into the international market.[288] As per the calendar set out in the 2022 Investment Charter, Decree 2-23-1 and three Orders were adopted to implement the Primary and the Strategic Investment Projects Incentives Scheme in February and March 2023.[289] Two additional decrees are foreseen for the implementation of the two remaining specific incentives schemes.[290] This section sets out the investment incentives available under the Moroccan legal and regulatory framework, their eligibility requirements, and the application requirements and process related thereto.

Types of available incentives and eligibility conditions

Schemes may be cumulated with specific and separate incentives offered at regional level,[291] and additional sectoral incentives may be relevant to specific investment projects, on a case-by-case basis. Incentives under the Strategic Investment Projects Incentives Scheme cannot however be cumulated with Primary Incentives Regime incentives.[292] The three premiums available under the **Primary Incentives Regime** may be cumulated up to a limit of 30% of the total amount of the investment.[293] Investment projects eligible under the Primary Incentives Regime must fulfil either one of the two following conditions: a MAD 50 million investment value and generate 50 to 149 employments; or generate a minimum of 150 employments, independent of investment value.[294] Eligibility criteria and details of how premiums are calculated and applicable rates are set out in Decree 2-23-1.[295] Separately, investment projects may qualify under the **Strategic Investment Projects Incentives Scheme** if their total value equals or exceeds MAD 2 billion and if they fulfil the pre-conditions set out in Decree 2-23-1, e.g., the investment project's foreseen contribution to ensuring water, energy, food and health security, and employment-creation.[296] Investors undertaking investments that fulfil the Scheme's eligibility conditions may negotiate tailored advantages.[297]

CRIs are, under Law 47-18, missioned with preparing and making available to investors guides outlining the Investment Regimes and Schemes and their eligibility conditions. The contents of these guides are to be harmonised across CRIs to ensure that consistent services are provided to investors. These have not seemingly been published yet, but an Investment Charter Guide was published via the AMDIE's website in June 2023. It among others outlines each of the investment incentives schemes, their respective objectives and their eligibility conditions. The CRI-Investment Platform also outlines the available investment incentives schemes, their eligibility conditions and requirements, as well as steps involved in the application process to obtain access to such incentives. However, the websites of some CRIs (e.g., the Tanger-Tetouan-Al Hoceima CRI) have not yet been updated to reflected the reforms brought about the 2022 Investment Charter.

Procedural requirements and processing of applications

CRUIs are specifically mandated with the preliminary evaluation of the eligibility of investment projects under the Investment Incentives Regime and issue opinions as to whether investment projects may benefit from advantages thereunder, regardless of the value of the investment project.[298] This review results with the granting by the CRUI of an administrative act, required before proceeding with their applications for advantages under the Primary Incentives Regime.

Investment Agreements are concluded between the Government and investors and govern the terms and conditions of benefits granted under the investment incentives regime (save for incentives for MSMEs).[299] These are not made publicly available. Their core features and contents are clearly defined by Decree 2-23-1,[300] and they are elaborated, subject to approval and signed either at the regional level or at national level by the CNI, depending on total value of the investment. The conclusion of Investment Agreements also provides access to additional benefits and advantages, including tax- and customs-related, in accordance with the relevant laws and regulations.[301] These are not set out in the 2022 Investment Charter.

Premiums are paid in instalments on the basis of an investment project's progress, the total timeframe of which should not exceed five years, unless stipulated otherwise in a given Investment Agreement.[302] In the event of default under the specific terms and conditions of an Investment Agreement, investors are required to refund the advantages and/or investment premiums granted to the investment project to the Government, within the framework of either the Primary Incentives Regime or the Strategic Investment Projects Incentives Scheme.

Table A A.4. Investment agreements under the Primary Incentives Regime and the Strategic Investment Projects Incentives Scheme: attribution of powers and mandates between competent authorities

Total value of investment	< MAD 250 million	> MAD 250 million	IPSN (i.e., x ≥ MAD 2 billion)
Competent authority	Regional level – CRIs / CRUIs	National level – CNI	
Role of the competent authority	*Carry out a preliminary review of investment projects' eligibility** *Issue opinions on investment projects' access to advantages to incentives regime** Prepare approve and conclude Investment Agreements with investors**	Prepare approve and conclude Investment Agreements under the Primary Incentives Regime and the Strategic Investment Projects Incentives Scheme Determine the strategic nature of investment projects under the Strategic Investment Projects Incentives Scheme	

Source: OECD compilation based on the 2022 Investment Charter and its implementing decrees; non-exhaustive.

Tunisia

Investment climate in Tunisia: a practical overview

Over the years, Tunisia has made considerable efforts to open its economy to foreign investment. The country adopted its first Investment Code in 1969 and created its Agency for the Promotion of Industry and Innovation (APII) the same year. Structural reforms initiated in the late 1980s to enhance Tunisia's attractivity to foreign investors culminated with the adoption of a new Investment Incentives Code in 1993 and the subsequent establishment of the Foreign Investment Promotion Agency (**FIPA**) in 1995.

As a result, FDI inflows in Tunisia gained traction and reached their peak in 2006 at USD 3.2 billion, representing more than 9% of the country's GDP recorded at the time.[303] Economic drawbacks caused by the Global Financial Crisis, and internal political disruptions linked to the Tunisian Revolution considerably impacted FDI inflows into the country, which have been generally decreasing since 2012 despite showing some signs of recovery in 2017 and 2018. External shocks resulting from the COVID-19 pandemic in 2020 brought about additional contraction in terms of FDI inflows (Figure A A.1).

Figure A A.1. FDI inflows in Tunisia (1990-2021)

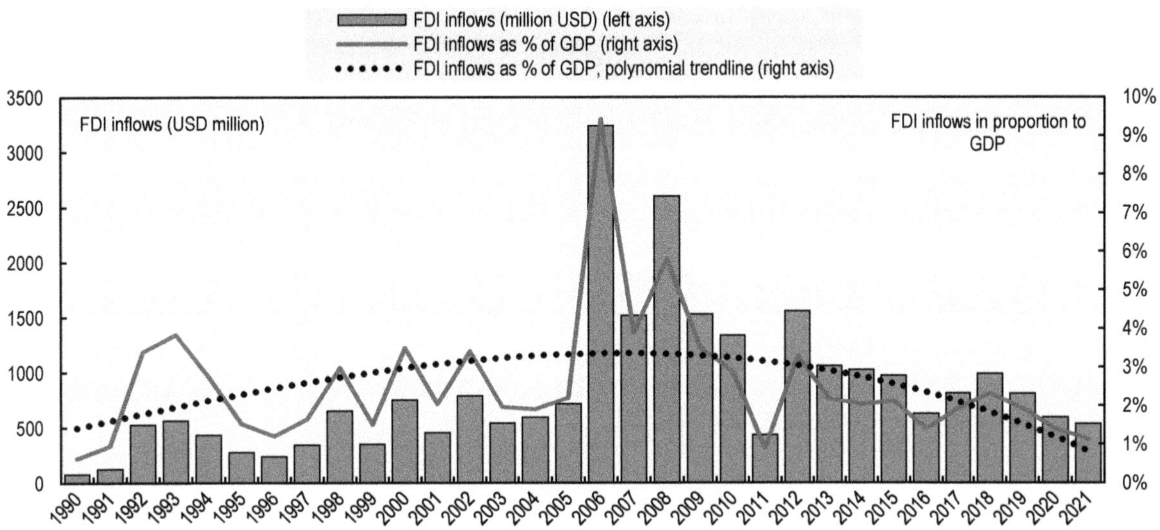

Source: OECD elaboration from IMF (FDI inflows data from the Balance of Payments and International Investment Position Statistics) and World Bank (GDP data).

As for the other five countries of the Southern Neighbourhood, foreign investors in Tunisia appear to stem essentially from the **EU** and from the **MENA region**. In 2021, investors from the EU (48%) – principally from **France**, **Italy**, **Germany** and **Spain,** and from the MENA region (40%, from the **United Arab Emirates** and **Qatar** essentially) held nearly 90% of the total FDI stock in the country in non-energy activities (Figure A A.2).

Figure A A.2. Origins and total value of inward FDI stock in Tunisia (2018-2021)

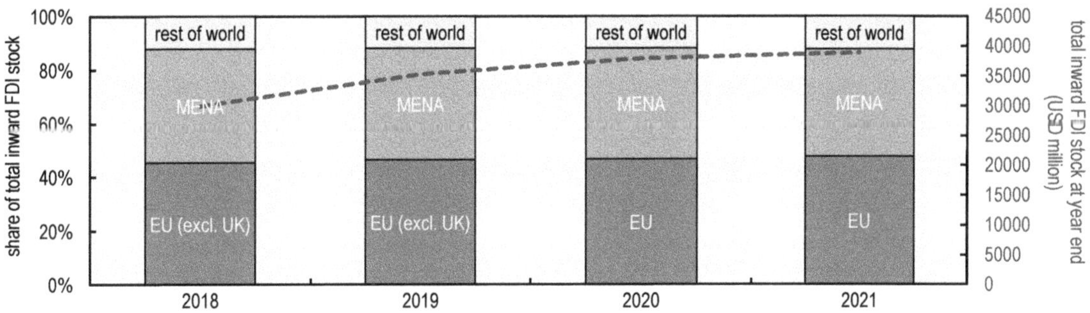

Note: Due to data availability reasons, the FDI stock data by origins excludes the energy sector. Total FDI stock based on reported international investment positions.
Source: OECD elaboration based on FIPA (*Rapports annuels des IDE*) and IMF (International Investment Positions).

FDI were historically geared towards the energy, manufacturing, and services sectors. In 2018, a notable shift occurred, with the manufacturing sector receiving 41% of total flows to Tunisia. The trend has persisted since, with manufacturing activities attracting an increasing amount of share of greenfield investment compared to the years before the financial crisis,[304] creating opportunities for FDI to create better-paid and higher-skilled jobs.[305]

In global indicators developed to assess local business environments, Tunisia fared relatively favourable in comparison to its regional peers, but poorly by international standards.[306] Although a positive consensus appears to exist with respect to the facilitation of pre-establishment matters such as the declaration of investment projects and the setting up of businesses, the main constraint systematically referred to by Tunisian entrepreneurs is access to financing, dealing with tax authorities and administrative burdens.[307] More than a quarter of domestic and foreign-invested firms surveyed by the World Bank in 2020 have also identified business licensing and permits as a major constraint of the country's business and investment climate.[308]

In recent years the Tunisian government has conducted efforts aimed at simplifying business procedures and attracting foreign investment. In that regard the in 2016 established Investment Law provides for a relatively open environment for investments and sets a framework for streamlining the administrative processing of applications through timeframes and online submission portals.[309] In the same light, more recently, Tunisia has made the improvement of its business environment a national priority, as reflected by its Development Plan 2023-2025 and has announced a number of reforms, some of them relating to investment facilitation, in the comprehensive "*National strategy to improve the business climate*", presented in January 2023.[310]

General institutional framework for investment in Tunisia

Tunisia stands out among the other five Southern Neighbourhood countries in that it operates more than one IPA. Tunisia's IPAs carry different, albeit at times overlapping roles. Two principal agencies feature investment facilitation mandates.[311] The Tunisian Investment Authority (*Instance Tunisienne de l'investissement*, **TIA**) was established further to the adoption of the new Tunisian Investment Law in 2016 (**2016 Investment Law** or **Law**).[312] The TIA operates above and together with a number of other agencies, whose respective mandates were not reconsidered further to the adoption of the Law, including the Agency for the Promotion of Industry and Innovation (*Agence de Promotion de l'Industrie et de l'Innovation*, **APII**). The TIA was originally established with the objective of integrating and replacing pre-existing IPAs, the main of which is APII. The TIA's and the APII's mandates are complementary but do not offer the same range of facilitation services for those investment projects that fall within their respective mandates, and investment facilitation for projects which fall under the TND 15 million capital threshold[313] – and outside of the TIA's mandate – is therefore limited. Based on stakeholder consultations, the vision of the TIA's new Director General is that the TIA's digital platform should work as unique front-office for all investors, while back-office functions are still to be carried out by other agencies. The respective mandates and missions are considered in this section. Other sector-specific entities also offer some limited and sector-specific investment facilitation services; these are not considered in this Country Section.[314]

Tunisian Investment Authority (TIA). The TIA was established by the 2016 Investment Law; its governance and mandate were further detailed in the subsequent Government Decree 2017-388 of 9 March 2017 (**Decree 2017-388**).[315] The TIA endorses a number of mandates, including investment policy advocacy among others. It is also features specific investment facilitation missions, namely: reviewing and deciding upon investment incentives applications; and, through a Commission for licences and approvals (*Commission des autorisations et agréments*), deciding upon all applications for chiefly operation approvals and authorisations necessary for the realisation of investments.[316]

Decree 2017-388 provides in that regard that the TIA "may delegate the supervision of investment operations whose value is equal to or inferior to TND 15 million to [the relevant bodies], and that until the time the TIA is established and carries out all of its missions".[317] At the time of writing in September 2023, no decree, order, or other legal instrument has indicated that this transitional period and ensuing delegation of mandate had terminated. Instead, the TIA website confirms capital-based split and complementary mandates between the TIA and other investment promotion agencies, including the APII.[318] Stakeholder consultations, have confirmed that the current working arrangement between the TIA and the APII is that the APII is responsible for all industrial investment project which fall under the

TND 15 million capital threshold, except if they fall within any of the mandates of other sector-specific agencies.

A single interlocutor (*interlocuteur unique de l'investisseur*) operates within the TIA to assist domestic and foreign investment projects and facilitate all stages of establishment and operation phases. The TIA's single interlocutor carries out on behalf of investors the establishment administrative procedures relevant to the incorporation of companies and the mandatory declaration of investments as well as other operation authorisations, and addresses all investor queries and creates a public database of frequent queries and issues raised by investors relevant to the investment process.[319] The TIA showcases its services through its website, which among others outlines the investment process stages from start to finish and provides download links for administrative documents relevant to investment-related formalities (e.g., legal incorporation of companies, investment declarations). The TIA's Investor Guide platform similarly provides practical information on the administrative formalities relevant to establishment and operation phases and requirements and provides the contact details of TIA staff mandated to assist investors at every step of the investment process.

The Agency for the Promotion of Innovation and Industry (APII). The mandate of the APII predates the 2016 Investment Law and is concerned with the implementation of the Tunisian government's policies relative to the promotion of the industrial sector.[320]

The APII's OSS (*guichet unique*) operates both out the APII head office in Tunis and via its regional offices. The agency's website provides contact details to each of the headquarter and regional OSS. The APII OSS's membership includes representatives from a number of investment-related authorities and administrations, including the tax authorities, the Official Printing Office, customs authorities, the Commercial Registry, among others.

The mandate of the APII's OSS is showcased on its OSS online portal, and principally concerns facilitating procedures and providing guidance to investors with respect to investment declarations and company incorporation.[321] Formalities relating to these procedures and requirements can be processed in part via APII dedicated portals (the online investment declaration portal, and separately, the online pre-legal incorporation of companies portal, available only to certain types of companies). Within the APII operates a Single Contact Point, established in collaboration with the Tunisian Ministry of Finance in 2006, which is specifically and exclusively mandated with carrying out on behalf of investors the procedures and formalities relevant to company incorporation within 24 hours of receipt. The APII does not, under the current institutional framework for investment, facilitate any post-establishment authorisations and formalities or access to investment incentives. This suggests that facilitation measures for projects which fall under the TND 15 million capital threshold is limited.

Higher Council for Investment. The Higher Council for Investment (**HCI**) was established by way of the 2016 Investment Law. It is headed by the Prime Minister and its membership includes Ministers whose respective jurisdictions are relevant to investment.[322] The HCI's mandate is closely linked to the investment incentives regime; among others, the HCI is responsible for assessing investor applications for incentives, while decisions for the granting or refusal of investment and incentives and the implementation of investment incentives are dealt with at other levels of the Government and/or administrative entities. Based on stakeholder consultations, it does not convene on a regular basis.

Transparency and predictability of the Tunisian legal framework for investment

This section considers Tunisia's investment framework and those measures which the country has adopted for facilitating investment, including with respect to accessibility to and transparency of the country's legal and regulatory framework for investment, establishment restrictions and conditions, and operation authorisations; and the manner in which investment-related procedures are streamlined.

Legal and regulatory framework for investment. Tunisia overhauled its legal framework for investment with the adoption of the 2016 Investment Law. Save for specific provisions principally concerning incentives schemes, the Law repealed and replaced the Investment Incentives Code of 1993 which previously governed foreign investment activity in the country.[323] The 2016 Investment Law rests on two core pillars: the reform of the investment governance structure and the creation of several investment governance entities among which a new IPA, the TIA; and the introduction of a new investment incentives regime (**Investment Incentives Regime**).

The 2016 Investment Law, its implementing decrees and related instruments[324] together define the legal regime for domestic and foreign investors across economic sectors, and applies to greenfield investments as well as acquisition and ownership operations of enterprises in Tunisia.[325] It establishes the general principle of freedom of investment, and sets out that foreigners enjoy a treatment under the Law no less favourable than that enjoyed by domestic investors in.[326] It guarantees the protection of investor assets against unlawful expropriation and their intellectual property rights and the right to transfer funds related to investment projects.[327]

Transparency and predictability. Tunisia's laws, regulations, decrees, governmental decrees, ministerial orders and notifications, among others, are published in the Official Journal (*Journal Officiel de la République Tunisienne, JORT*) and freely accessible through the website of the Official Printing Office of the Republic of Tunisia, the *Imprimerie Officielle de la République Tunisienne*. The Official Journal's and the Official Printing Office's official language is Arabic, and French translations of the Official Journal are available through the same website portal (also available in French). English translations of the Official Journal are only available for some instruments. Both the TIA and the APII websites outline the principal legal and regulatory instruments of the Tunisian investment framework. The latter also features a number of Fact Sheets, available in Arabic, French and English, which shed light on specific features of the 2016 Investment Law and the newly introduced Investment Incentives Regime.

The Tunisian legislator is required as per its new internal regulations to publish proposed texts and bills on its website.[328] However, the portal is currently not operational, and it remains at the time of writing in September 2023 difficult to assess whether under the Tunisian legislative framework, laws and regulations – or alternatively, documents that provide details about such upcoming instruments – are published in advance, and whether specifically, drafts of the 2016 Investment Law were made publicly available prior to the Law's adoption.[329] It is also unclear whether documents outlining the purpose or rationale of the new investment framework were published prior or after the adoption of the Law. The Tunisian Assembly is required to conduct public consultations over questions deemed *"essential and which determine strategic choices"*.[330] Official government sources do not directly confirm whether such consultations were carried out. However, based on an official presentation prepared in the context of a presentation carried out by Members of Parliament members of the Committee on Finance, Planning, and Development, dated February 2016,[331] over 1500 private sector, public sector, international organisations and non-governmental organisations stakeholders were consulted, as well as regional authorities and committees. The consultations were undertaken between 2012-2013, and subsequently, in 2015. Information as to outcomes of this consultation process, and its impact on the adoption of the final text of the 2016 Investment Law is not publicly available. The legislation was adopted on 30 September 2016, published in the Official Journal on 7 October 2016, and subsequently entered into force on 1 April 2017, thereby allowing a reasonable time between its publication and date of compliance by investors.

Streamlining measures. Tunisia has adopted legislation with a view to enhance the transparency and predictability of its investment framework and streamline authorisation procedures. These are enshrined chiefly in Law 2019-47 and Government Decree 2020-310 of 15 May 2020 (**Decree 2020-310**),[332] and are summarized in Box A A.2. Unless specified otherwise, they apply to both establishment and operation procedures.[333]

Box A A.2. Streamlining of authorisation procedures, transparency, and predictability

Tunisia has adopted a number of overarching measures which bind "Public bodies" and seek to improve the country's business climate by enhancing transparency, reducing procedural timeframes, and streamlining procedures for company incorporation and more generally, all of those procedures relevant to investors and businesses, including by way of Law 2019-47, which among others amended the 2016 Investment Law. Based on stakeholder consultations, implementation of Law 2019-47 remains an issue.

Decree 2020-310 established a Commission for the monitoring and coordination of administrative streamlining mechanisms for investors and businesses and working groups within each Ministry that is concerned with investment, entrusted with monitoring the implementation of the Government Decree.[334]

Table A A.5. Authorisation procedures in Tunisia: streamlining, transparency and predictability

Streamlining of authorisation procedures	Transparency and predictability
Coordinate and share among themselves up-to-date documents which they either hold or are entrusted with issuing, as well as information and data relevant to process investor applications for the realisation of investments, an authorisation to carry out an economic activity, an investment declaration, or company incorporation	Make available and regularly update, through the Ministries' and Public bodies' online portals, all of the information relating to the conditions, timeframes and completion of administrative procedures relevant to investors and businesses
Refrain from requesting from investors any administrative documents not required under the applicable laws and regulations	Make available relevant *cahiers des charges* online for download
Refrain from requesting from investors documents they may already have in their possession/which can be provided by other Public bodies	Investors may correct documents, information, or data in event of error
	Liaise with investors by way of written notice
	Make available online payment options for administrative fees
	Allow investors to follow the review of their applications online
	Paperless administrative forms for investor and businesses applications

Source: OECD compilation based on Law 2019-47 and Government Decree 2020-310; non-exhaustive.

Facilitation of business establishment by foreign investors

- Restrictions to foreign investment

Restrictions on foreign investments apply in several sectors, as set out by sector-specific legislation and commercial legislation, among others, rather than consolidated in a negative list, which negatively impacts the transparency of the investment framework.[335] This significantly hampers the transparency of the investment framework insofar as restrictions to foreign investment are concerned in terms of accessibility to applicable legislation, and the processes by which exemptions – if and when applicable – may be obtained.[336]

These restrictions include foreign equity limits to acquisition and/or greenfield investments in agriculture, transport, fishing and aquaculture, telecommunications and financial services, among others. A number of foreign investment restrictions are also provided under Annex 1 of Decree 2018-417.[337] These appear to partially overlap with restrictions relating to foreign nationals and foreign legal entities carrying out certain commercial activities – including in the sectors of wholesale and retail distribution, media, telecommunications – prior to obtaining "foreign merchant card". Further, a number of commercial activities are also barred to foreigners and foreign investors, and that unless an exemption is granted by the Secretary of State for Planning and Finance.[338]

- Pre-admission formalities and legal incorporation of companies

As outlined above, the TIA's and the APII's respective mandates are complementary on the basis of a capital threshold of TND 15 million, and both entities operate OSS or single interlocutors that facilitate a number of investment procedures, including establishment formalities and requirements.[339] Establishment formalities are broadly split into successive stages: the declaration of an investment project, followed by company legal incorporation. The granting of an "investment declaration certificate" is a necessary pre-condition to the incorporation of a company.

Investment projects declarations. The 2016 Investment Law requires that investment declarations and company legal incorporation of companies be carried out on the basis of a single set of administrative forms (*liasse unique*),[340] and that the TIA's single interlocutor provide investors with their investment declaration certificates and the documents pertaining to the incorporation of their company within one working day of the date of deposit of the complete investment declaration. Specifically with respect to investment declarations, both the TIA single interlocutor and the APII OSS provide investors whose investment's fall within each of IPAs respective mandates information pertaining to the timeline of the process, forms to be considered and filled out and fees to be paid. Both IPAs also provide for the electronic submission of investment declaration applications through the APII's dedicated investment declaration page and through the TIA's dedicated investor portal.

Legal incorporation of companies. Similarly, both the TIA's single interlocutor and the APII's OSS provide investors with information relevant to the legal incorporation of companies. Both IPAs also provide online services for the legal incorporation of companies. The TIA manages this through the same dedicated investor portal. The APII assists investors with the legal incorporation of companies, either through its OSS or via the APII's single intermediary which carries out the relevant legal incorporation formalities on behalf of investors within 24 hours of receipt of a full application. The APII also offers an online pre-legal incorporation of companies portal for certain types of companies only, with a view to expedite the formalities investors are required to complete in person at the APII OSS.

In that regard, foreign-invested enterprises can register under the same commercial forms available to Tunisian-owned businesses. These include partnerships (*societés en nom collectif*, *societés en commandite simple*, joint ventures), limited liability companies (limited liability companies and single-member private limited companies) and joint stock companies (limited companies, joint stock companies and open joint stock companies).[341]

Facilitation of business operations by foreign investors

The 2016 Investment Law has introduced a list of sectors in respect of which both domestic and foreign investors may require licences and authorisations to carry out certain activities. Decree 2018-417 outlines the administrative procedures relevant to obtaining operational licences and other authorisations,[342] with a view to simply and clarify business – and investor – relations with public authorities and administrations. More specifically, it sets out: a comprehensive list of all the economic activities subject to authorisation (a total of 100 activities; Annex 1), a list of administrative authorisations required for the realisation of certain investment projects (143 authorisations; Annex 3), and a list of activities for which pre-authorisations are required (27 activities; Annex 4). Activities within these controlled economic sectors which are not specifically cited in Annex 1 are in principle considered open to private investment activity. Each of these lists is organised on the basis of economic sectors categories, namely: natural resources; land, maritime and air transport activities; financial services (banking, insurance, and securities trading); dangerous or polluting industries; health; education; telecommunications; and certain commercial activities and services.[343]

Stakeholder consultations have clarified that the overall objective of Decree 2018-417 is to gradually review the Annex 1 list to ultimately establish a limited negative list of sectors where prior authorisations are required. Indeed, the enactment of Decree 2019-417 ended another 27 authorisations, and an additional 13 activities were exempt from licensing conditions further to the enactment of Presidential Decree 2022-317.[344] Stakeholder consultations have signalled that additional exemptions are expected to enter into force.

The common procedural framework established further to Decree 2018-417 seeks to streamline the processing of authorisations with a view to enhance the predictability of the framework. The lists set out in each of the Annexes define the pre-conditions and supporting documentation, competent authorities, indicative timeframes and legal frameworks relevant the authorisations. When timeframes for the processing of investor authorisations are not clearly set out, the Decree sets a general timeframe of 60 days for the processing and issuing applications for licences or permits, extendable by 90 additional days in instances where the application requires the assessment of several administrative authorities, or to 180 days if the application requires the approval by the HCI – the conditions or basis upon which the HCI's approval is specifically required are however not clarified.[345] Negative decisions must be motivated and grounds for refusal notified in writing;[346] recourse or appeal mechanisms are however not available to applicants.

Authorisations required for the realisation of investment projects whose capital value exceeds TND 15 million are processed through the TIA Commission for licences and approvals.[347] The Commission, whose membership includes relevant ministries and public bodies, operates within the TIA and is directly responsible for reviewing, deciding upon and ultimately issuing applications for these authorisations, in coordination with the relevant competent authorities, with whom it is required to liaise according to defined procedures and within specified timeframes.[348] The TIA also provides general assistance and guidance to qualifying investors and investments with respect to the entire operation process. In that regard, the TIA Investor Guide provides a general overview of the licensing requirements, the relevant procedures to obtain them and the contact details of dedicated TIA staff and liaison officers. The TIA's dedicated investor portal is also expected to provide online services for investment incentive and authorisation applications. It is not clear whether this feature was at the time of writing in September 2023 operational.

The Law also sets out an overarching 'tacit approval' procedure, whereby a complete authorisation application which has not been explicitly denied by the relevant competent authorities within the pre-defined processing timeframe is deemed approved. In such instances, investors – regardless of the capital value of their investment, i.e., including investments falling under the TND 15 million threshold and that do not fall within the scope of the TIA's facilitation mandate – may apply directly to the TIA to obtain the requested authorisation, following a process and timeframes clearly set out under Decree 2018-417.[349] Aside from this 'tacit approval' mechanism, the procedural and institutional arrangements for operation authorisations for projects whose capital value falls below the TND 15 million threshold and outside of the TIA's mandate is limited, and investors are expected to submit their authorisation applications directly to the relevant competent authorities.

Transparency and predictability of the Tunisian investment incentives regime

Prior to the adoption of the 2016 Investment Law, Tunisia's framework of investment incentives was severely fragmented, featuring over 20 separate mechanisms which had been amended numerous times over the years. The schemes were characterised by their protracted procedures, which hindered the overall effectiveness of the promotion schemes.[350] With a view to facilitate investor access to investment incentives, the 2016 Investment Law reorganised and clarified Tunisia's framework for investment promotion.

The TIA is expected to publish a practical guide on the Investment Incentives Regime in Tunisia, specifically on the process to obtain them and on post-approval stages.[351] No such document appears to have been published as at the time of writing in September 2023, although the TIA's online Investor Guide provides an interactive platform featuring a succinct overview of the different types of incentives available to investors at the regional and national levels. The Investor Guide offers information on the value of incentives, relevant procedures, and contact details of a dedicated TIA liaison officer. It does not however specify in any detail the conditions for obtaining incentives or provide practical information on any post-approval processes, which hinders the transparency of the investment framework insofar as investment incentives are concerned.

Types of available incentives and eligibility conditions. The Tunisian Investment Incentives Regime offers a wide array of financial and fiscal investment incentives to eligible foreign investors, ranging from tax deductions to customs exemptions, loans, grants, or leases of state land. The 2016 Investment Law introduced a new investment incentives regime which consists of four distinct schemes underpinned by well-defined rationales, three of which are available to foreign investors – namely:[352]

- "**Premiums**" for eligible activities, which are in turn divided in four separate categories: (i) premiums for the increase of the value added and competitiveness of the Tunisian economy; (ii) premiums for projects contributing to regional development; (iii) premiums for the projects with high employment capability; and (iv) premiums for projects contributing to sustainable development;[353]
- Loans for the purchase and development of agricultural land;[354] and
- Incentives for qualified "projects of national interest" (**PNI**).[355]

Eligibility to, as well as the procedure and institutional arrangements for requesting and being granted incentives, are principally detailed in Decree 2017-389[356] and its accompanying Joint Ministerial Order of 2017.[357] The Investment Law 2016 sets out practical considerations for the obtention of incentives: they may be individually granted to investors, cumulated – subject to specific conditions and thresholds[358] – or awarded through a bundled package.[359] The Law also explicitly provides for the possibility for investors to change incentives scheme, provided they complete the necessary administrative steps to that effect.[360]

The primary eligibility condition of an investment project to incentives concerns its economic sector or activity:

- Direct investment projects eligible to premiums for the "increase of added value and competitiveness"[361] and to some premiums for the "development of employability capacity"[362] are confined to "priority sectors". Priority sectors, which are considered strategic to the economic development of the country, are set out in a positive list in the Decree 2017-389 (Annex 1, I).[363] They include industry, agriculture, high technology, research and development, and labour-intensive fields, *inter alia*.[364] The second list of economic sectors annexed to the Decree 2017-389 (Annex 1, II) concerns activities that are eligible only to premiums for the improvement of added value and competitiveness, including extractives.[365]
- Activities eligible to premiums for regional development are framed by a negative list annexed to the Decree 2017-389 (Annex 1, III) which sets out sectors barred from obtaining these premiums. They include extractive industries, financial and insurance activities, telecommunication services, wholesale and retail trade, non-renewable electricity generation and distribution, and transport services, among others.[366]
- Premiums for sustainable development are specifically geared towards water and air pollution control projects; projects applying green technologies to prevent pollution at its source or to control the exploitation of resources; and projects involving the installation of collective depollution equipment.[367]

Additional eligibility conditions for incentives may include the geographic location of the investment project, especially for incentives geared towards regional development, or even professional qualifications.

The eligibility of a project to qualify as a PNI is not assessed by reference to a positive – or negative – list of sectors or activities. Rather, PNI scheme eligibility is conditioned upon a minimum investment capital requirement, performance requirements in terms of employment of local workers, and their contribution to national economic priorities, subject to the discretionary appreciation of the relevant authorities.[368]

Further, the 2016 Investment Law provides information with regards to the capital amount of incentives available to investment projects and their practical implementation (duration and disbursement of funds especially).[369] The total amount of promotion incentives a project may receive is often subject to a maximum capital ceiling,[370] and the amount each incentive depends on the general project or the implementation costs for which it is specifically granted.[371]

Procedural requirements and processing of applications. The 2016 Investment Law provides, as a preliminary condition, that requests for incentives may be submitted only one year from the date of the declaration of an investment project. Two distinct procedures exist for the granting of incentives: one for PNI, and a separate procedure for all other incentives available under the Investment Incentives Regime (premiums, equity participations and agricultural land loans, respectively):

- For *projects of national interest*: incentives are effectively granted further to the adoption of a governmental decree, following the recommendations formulated by the HCI and the TIA on the applications for such incentives.[372]
- For *other incentives*: premiums, equity participations and agricultural land loans are granted further to a "decision of the Minister in charge of the sector or their delegate". Decisions to grant these incentives are based on a preliminary assessment of applications by the commissions established within the relevant authorities.[373]

The Law and its implementing instruments frame the administrative processing of applications as well as the competent authorities' discretion in their assessment thereof with a view to reduce the potential for arbitrary or discriminatory outcomes. This is done by:

- Setting a detailed list of documents required for the applications for incentives under Decree 2017-389, thereby limiting the possibility for authorities to request additional supporting documentation or to impose additional conditions upon investors to obtain incentives.
- Defining clear timeframes for the processing of applications by the relevant authorities. Granting or refusing applications for incentives must be decided within one month of the filing of a complete application,[374] and investors must be notified of the results of the committee's deliberations within seven days as of signing the decision by the competent minister.[375]
- Requiring that decisions which reject a request for incentives be clearly motivated and grounds for the refusal of an investor's application be explicitly mentioned.[376]
- Allowing investors to request the review of decisions refusing to grant incentives within 30 days from their issuance. In case of review, the application for incentives is referred to the same commission that carried out its first assessment and may be supplemented by additional documentation.[377]

The HCI is responsible for the assessment of applications for the *project of national interest* incentives scheme.[378] The assessment of investor applications with respect to the remainder of the schemes falls within the mandate of special commissions at national and regional levels, which were established within relevant authorities (the TIA, and more specifically, its *pôle des primes et des incitations* and *pôle de l'évaluation et du contrôle des primes et des incitations*; APII, APIA, ONTT).[379] The allocation of tasks between these authorities is contingent upon the economic sector relevant to a given investment, as well as the investment capital.[380]

These commissions are also responsible for re-examining applications for incentives when decisions refusing to grant incentives are challenged by investors. Final decisions to grant or refuse incentives to an investment project are taken, further to recommendations formulated by the competent assessing authorities, either at government level with respect to *projects of national interest* incentives,[381] or ministerial level with respect to all other incentives.[382]

The release of approved premiums is subject to detailed rules and procedures under Articles 12 to 14 of the Decree 2017-389. Their disbursement is separated in two separate stages, subject to an assessment by the relevant authorities of the implementation of the project based on supporting documentation and on-site visits by representatives of relevant sectoral agencies.

Promoted investments are subject to the scrutiny of relevant administrative authorities following Article 21 of the 2016 Investment Law. Investors are required to report annually to the relevant authority on the effective implementation of the investment project.[383] Incentives may be withdrawn by the TIA[384] in defined situations as set out under Article 20, especially if the investment project is not carried out within four years of the investment declaration,[385] or in case of illegal misappropriation of the initial object of the investment. The withdrawal of incentives may be accompanied by sanctions, especially in case of delays in their reimbursement by the investor.[386]

Notes

[1] Ministerial order dated 28 September 2022 portant nomination des membres du conseil d'administration de l'agence algérienne de promotion de l'investissement.

[2] Interministerial order dated 24 November 2022 fixant l'organisation interne de l'agence algérienne de promotion de l'investissement.

[3] AAPI's role and mandate are outlined on its website. The website contains information on Algeria and its investment opportunities, a presentation of AAPI, and information essential for investors such as the various incentive schemes, OSS services, forms to fill out and a complaints register. The website also provides an online version of the 2022 Investment Law.

[4] In order to assist investors, guidelines are available online (in French and Arabic) outlining the different steps required to register an investment through the portal. Investors are required to create an account in order to access the guidelines.

[5] Decree 22-299 of 8 September 2022, Article 4.

[6] Article 37 of the AAPI Decree provides that "*En attendant la mise en place des guichets uniques prévus par l'article 18 ci-dessus, les dispositions du présent décret ainsi que les effets induits par la période de transition sont pris en charge par le guichet unique décentralisé créé par l'article 22 de l'ordonnance n° 01-03 du Aouel Joumada Ethania 1422 correspondant au 20 août 2001*".

[7] 2022 Investment Law, Articles 19-21 and AAPI Decree, Articles 18-26.

[8] 2022 Investment Law, Articles 25. Registration consists of the issuing of a certificate, accompanied by a list of goods and services eligible for incentives.

[9] AAPI Decree, Article 19 and 2022 Investment Law, Articles 19-20.

[10] AAPI Decree, Article 20.

[11] AAPI Decree, Article 20.

[12] AAPI Decree, Article 26 para. 10. The designation of these additional administrative authorities requires a joint order issued by the Prime Minister, the Finance Minister, and the Authority in charge of civil servants (AAPI Decree, Article 6).

[13] 2022 Investment Law, Article 16.

[14] Decree 22-297 of 8 September 2022 on the composition and functioning of the National Investment Council (in French), JORF, issue No. 60.

[15] 2022 Investment Law, Article 17.

[16] Presidential Decree 22-296 of 4 September 2022 on the composition and functioning of the Higher National Commission of Appeals related to Investment (in French), JORF, issue 60.

[17] HCNRLI Decree, Article 6.

[18] Previously, the investment regime was governed by Investment Law 16-09 of 3 August 2016. However, the new 2022 Investment Law provides that the provisions of Law 16-09 are repealed (except for its Article 37). The executive regulations of Law 16-09 remain in force until the adoption of the executive regulations of the 2022 Investment Law (Article 40).

[19] 2022 Investment Law, Article 2.

[20] 2022 Investment Law, Articles 4-5.

[21] 2022 Investment Law, Article 3.

[22] Decree 22-296 of 8 September 2022 on the HCNRLI (**Decree 22-296**); Decree 22-297 of 8 September 2022 on the CNI (**Decree 22-297**); and Decree 22-298 of 8 September 2022 on the AAPI (**Decree 22-298**).

[23] Decree 22-300 of 8 September 2022 on activities, goods and services ineligible to certain advantages and the minimum funding thresholds for remittance guarantee (**Decree 22-300**); Decree 22-302 of 8 September 2022 on incentives for high stakes "*structuring investments*" (**Decree 22-302**); and Decree 22-301 of 8 September 2022 on incentives for "*zones of particular interest*" (**Decree 22-301**).

[24] Decree 22-299 of 8 September 2022 setting out the procedures for investment registration, disposal or transfer of investments, as well as the procedures for the payment of investment applications (**Decree 22-299**); and Decree 22-303 of 8 September 2022 on the monitoring of investments and the measures to be taken in case of breaches of duties and commitments (**Decree 22-303**).

[25] See e.g., Algérie Eco, "*Abdelouahab Ziani : « Le nouveau code de l'investissement va libérer et booster les investisseurs »*", 8 May 2022.

[26] See, OECD (2021), Middle East and North Africa Investment Policy Perspectives, OECD Publishing, Paris.

[27] See, OECD (2015), Policy Framework for Investment, 2015 Edition, OECD Publishing, Paris.

[28] 2020 Complementary Finance Law, Article 49.

[29] Law 04-08, Article 25 and Decree 15-234, Article 4.

[30] Law 04-08, Article 4(2).

[31] Law 04-08, Article 24.

[32] Article 544 of the Algerian Commercial Code, amended by Law 22-09.

[33] Law 04-08 dated 14 August 2004 concerning the conditions of operation of commercial activities; Law 13-06 dated 23 July 2013 modifying and completing Law 04-08 dated 14 August 2004 concerning the conditions of operation of commercial activities; Law 18-08 dated 10 June 2018 modifying and completing Law 04-08 dated 14 August 2004 concerning the conditions of operation of commercial activities.

[34] Law 04-08, Article 4.

[35] Law 04-08, Article 5bis 1.

[36] Law 04-08, Article 5bis 2.

[37] Decree 15-57 on the storage and/or distribution of oil and gas products.

[38] Decree 14-165 on the wholesale trade of fishing and aquaculture products; Decree 13-176 on the manufacture, storage and distribution of lubricants and regeneration of waste oils; Decree 22-383 on the dealing of new cars; Decree 09-181 on the importation of raw materials destined for resale in its same state.

[39] Decree 22-384 on the construction of vehicles.

[40] Decree 14-153 on the opening and operation of laboratories.

[41] Decree 09-19 on the collection of special waste.

[42] AAPI Decree, Article 26.

[43] 2022 Investment Law, Article 22.

[44] 2022 Investment Law, Article 2.

[45] 2022 Investment Law, Article 24.

[46] 2022 Investment Law, Article 24.

[47] 2022 Investment Law, *op. cit.*, Articles 27, 29 and 31.

[48] 2022 Investment Law, *op. cit.*, Article 35.

[49] 2022 Investment Law, *op. cit.*, Articles 27, 29 and 31.

[50] Decree 22-300, Article 26; separately, Article 3.b, Decree 22-300 of 8 September 2022, setting the lists of activities, goods and services non-eligible to advantages, and fixing the minimum thresholds of financing to benefit of the transfer guarantee, published in issue No. 60 of the Official Gazette (available in Arabic and French), on 18 September 2022.

[51] Decree 22-301 of 8 September 2022, on the list of areas that are among the zones to which the State accords a particular interest in terms of investment, published in in issue No. 60 of the Official Gazette (available in Arabic and French), on 18 September 2022 (p. 38-41), as amended in issues No. 64 and 65 of the Official Gazette, for the Arabic text, and issue No. 65 of the Official Gazette, for the French text.

[52] Decree 22-300, Article 3.a.

[53] Decree 22-300, Articles 3-6.

[54] Among the goals enumerated by the first Article of the Investment Law, the following goals are considered the essential ones to be fulfilled by structuring investments: (i) import substitution, (ii) export diversification , (iii) integration in global and regional value chains, and (iv) the acquisition of technology and know-how, as per Article 15, Decree 22-302, Article 15.

[55] Article 16, Decree 22-302 of 8 September 2022, setting the criteria to qualify as structuring investments, the conditions of benefiting of incentives during the operational phase, and the evaluation schemes, published in in issue 60 of the Official Gazette (available in Arabic and French), on 18 September 2022.

[56] 2022 Investment Law, Article 18 and Decree 22-298, Article 4.5.

[57] 2022 Investment Law, Article 25.

[58] 2022 Investment Law, Article 25, para. 1.

[59] Decree 22-299.

[60] Decree 22-299, Articles 6-8.

[61] Decree 22-298, Article 4.5 and Article 26.1.

[62] 2022 Investment Law, Article 25, para. 2.

[63] 2022 Investment Law, Article 25 and Decree 22-299, Article 5, para. 2.

[64] 2022 Investment Law, Articles 32-33. See also, para. 0.

[65] Decree 22-302, Article 22.

[66] Decree 22-299, Article 9.

[67] Presidential Decree 22-296 of 8 September 2022, Articles 6-7, on the composition and functioning of the High National Appeals Commission related to Investment, published in issue No. 60 of the Official Gazette (available in Arabic and French), on 18 September 2022.

[68] Decree 22-302, Article 18.

[69] 2022 Investment Law, Article 31, para. 2 and Decree 22-302, Article 19.

[70] 2022 Investment Law, Article 32, para. 1.

[71] 2022 Investment Law, Article 32, para. 3.

[72] Decree 22-299, Articles 15-17.

[73] 2022 Investment Law, Article 36.

[74] Decree 22-303, Articles 7-10.

[75] Decree 22-303, Article 11.

[76] As at September 2019, 10 ISCs were established and operational across the country, and an additional 27 were at the time in the process of being set up across all 27 governorates (OECD, 2020[4]). See also, ISC Investor Guide, "*Investor Service Centres in Governorates*".

[77] 2017 Investment Law, Article 22; 2017 Executive Regulations, Articles 17 *et seq*. Among these conditions is that the application must be a joint-stock company exclusively dedicated to accreditation activity, to have technical personnel with 10 years of experience, and to purchase an insurance policy for the benefit of GAFI with a minimum amount of EGP one million. Furthermore, the operational licence of the accreditation activity is valid for one year and must be renewed (2017 Executive Regulations, Article 17). Similar structures exist in other sector-based legislations (e.g., industry, tourism, medium and small enterprises (see e.g., Law 15 of 2017 on the facilitation of the licensing procedures of industrial establishments, published in the Official Gazette, Law 8 of 2022 on hotels and touristic establishments, and Law 152 of 2020 on the development of medium, small and micro projects).

[78] 2017 Executive Regulations, Article 28. GAFI has not published any list of such licensed Offices. According to information provided by the Egyptian authorities to the OECD Secretariat, GAFI announced establishing only one Approval Office in March 2020.

[79] 2017 Investment Law, Articles II and VIII, repealing Law 8 of 1997 on Investment Guarantees and Incentives (as amended) and every provision that contradicts the Investment Law.

[80] Investment Law 72 of 31 May 2017, which has entered into force on 1 June 2017, as amended by Law 141 of 2019 (**2017 Investment Law**); Prime Minister Decree 2310 of 2017 adopting Executive Regulations to the Investment Law promulgated by Law 72 of 2017, as amended, namely by: Prime Minister Decrees 2731 of 2019, 1199 of 2020, 2467 of 2020, 910 of 2021, 2300 of 2022, and 4426 of 2022 (**2017 Executive Regulations**). Cabinet Decree 2140 of 2023 was adopted in June 2023, amending the 2017 Executive Regulations; it principally eases the conditions for operation in a private free zone. When relevant, the 2017 Investment Law and its related instruments are also hereafter referred to as the "*2017 Investment Law*".

[81] Cabinet Decree 57 of 2022 on the conditions of qualifying an investment project as strategic or national in implementation of the provisions of Article 20 of the 2017 Investment Law (**Cabinet Decree 57 of 2022**); and Prime Minister Decree 104 of 2022; Prime Minister Decree 981 of 2022; Prime Minister Decree 1775 of 2022; President Decree 141 of 2023.

[82] 2017 Investment Law, Definitions, namely, investment activities in a defined set of sectors; see also, 2017 Executive Regulations, Part I, Chapter I, which lists those "*investment activities*" governed by the Law, sector-by-sector (investment activities carried out in those sectors are referred to as "*Investment Projects*" throughout the law and in this country sections).

[83] 2017 Investment Law, Articles 2-8.

[84] See also, OECD (2020), *OECD Investment Policy Reviews: Egypt 2020*, OECD Investment Policy Reviews, OECD Publishing, Paris.

[85] 2017 Investment Law, Articles, 68 and 71; 2017 Executive Regulations, Articles 44-59.

[86] Egypt has in that regard been working on a regulatory reform program for a number of years, including in respect of the development of an Egyptian Legislation Register. It remained unclear at the time of writing in September 2023 whether this platform is operational.

[87] These are namely, Prime Minister Decrees 2731 of 2019 and 1199 of 2020. English translations prepared by GAFI feature disclaimers that provide that translations of the official Arabic texts are provided for "*convenience and information purposes only*" and that in the event of discrepancies, inconsistencies, conflict or other between the original Arabic instrument and its translation, the former will prevail. Separately, another version for the Law and the 2017 Executive Regulations is available on the Invest in Egypt promotion website, but only in Arabic (both the 2017 Investment Law and the 2017 Executive Regulations without incorporating any subsequent amendments).

[88] The law was however published the website of Youm7, a local privately owned daily newspaper on 29 December 2016; *Full text of the new investment law after its approval by the Council of Ministers*, Youm7, 29 December 2016.

[89] 2017 Investment Law, Article II.

[90] No governmental and/or official sources provide insight as to the 2017 Investment Law consultation process. It was at the time however reported in the local press, see e.g., *Sisi chairs second meeting of Supreme Council for Investment* (unofficial translation from Arabic), Al Masry Al Youm, 4 December 2016; *Dalia Khorshid: Preparation of the final draft of the investment law December 14* (unofficial translation from Arabic), Shorouk News, 5 December 2016; *The Minister of Investment announces the development of alternatives to special free zones and maintaining the current one* (unofficial translation from Arabic), Al Masry Al Youm, 8 January 2017; *Dalia Khorshid: New Investment Law Issued After Community Dialogue* (unofficial translation from Arabic), El Balad, 19 November 2016.

[91] See, OECD (2021), *Middle East and North Africa Investment Policy Perspectives*, OECD Publishing, Paris.

[92] See, OECD (2020), *OECD Investment Policy Reviews: Egypt 2020*, OECD Investment Policy Reviews, OECD Publishing, Paris.

[93] See, the ISC Investor Guide.

[94] 2017 Investment Law, Article 70; 2017 Executive Regulations, Article 30.

[95] See e.g., a Central Bank of Egypt preapproval is required for the establishment of a bank (Law 194 of 2020 on the promulgation of the Central Bank and Banking Sector Law, Articles 63-65).

[96] Companies Law 159 of 1981, as amended. The English translation of the Companies Law provided via the GAFI website does not reflect the latest amendments to the law.

[97] The 2017 Investment Law (Article 48) distinguishes between the incorporation of companies under the Law and under the Companies Law 159 of 1981. See also, the ISC Investor Guide and GAFI's e-services guide.

[98] 2017 Investment Law, Definitions, "*Investment Project*"; 2017 Executive Regulations, Part I, Chapter I.

[99] 2017 Executive Regulations, Article 1.

[100] 2017 Investment Law, Article 21, which outlines among other that outlines that the entity "*shall provide*" a wide range of incorporation and corporate-related services.

[101] The ISC Investor Guide lists those Competent Authorities represented at the ISC Cairo headquarters, and their physical offices therein. No indication is provided as to whether these Competent Authorities are represented at other branches and/or whether these formalities can equally be carried out at other branches.

[102] 2017 Investment Law, Article 54; 2017 Executive Regulations, Articles 127-128. The Law requires that both GAFI and the ISC automate and integrate via a unique platform all of those services which fall within their mandates, and more specifically pertaining to the legal incorporation of companies, the standardisation of fees and a certain number of corporate forms and documents, with a view to replace existing – presumably paper-based – formalities falling within the GAFI and ISC's mandates. GAFI's e-services portal is available both in Arabic and partly in English.

[103] 2017 Investment Law, Article 51; see also, ISC Investor Guide.

[104] The 2017 Investment Law prescribes the completion of these formalities within 15 days of receipt of an investor request (Article 51); the 2017 Executive Regulations do not impose any time limit or cap, and simply require that streamlining provisions be set up in that regard.

[105] 2017 Investment Law, Article 54; 2017 Executive Regulations, Articles 127-128.

[106] 2017 Investment Law, Article 21.

[107] See, footnote 76.

[108] 2017 Investment Law, Article 19; 2017 Executive Regulations, Article 16. The Law provides that this Guide should be prepared and published within 90 days of the Law's entry into force, while the 2017 Executive Regulations requires that it be made available within 60 days of its entry into force.

[109] At the time of writing in September 2023, only one guide (the Gas Market Regulatory Authority Guide) was available in English as well as French. Additional translations are planned to be made available via the GAFI website (information provided further to consultations with GAFI, August 2023).

[110] Information provided further to consultations with GAFI, August 2023.

[111] 2017 Investment Law, Articles 48 and 50; 2017 Executive Regulations, Articles 32, 37, 38 and 127.

[112] Information provided further to consultations with GAFI, August 2023.

[113] Supplemental streamlining measures have been introduced via sectoral instruments, see e.g., Law 15 of 2017 on the Simplification of Industrial Licences, which seeks to reduce the timeframes relevant to obtaining licenses required to establish new factories.

[114] 2017 Investment Law, Article 27.

[115] 2017 Investment Law, Article 18; Cabinet Decree 982 of 2022, Article I.

[116] 2017 Investment Law, Article 18; Cabinet Decree 982 of 2022, Article I.

[117] 2017 Investment Law, Article 18; Cabinet Decree 982 of 2022, Article II.

[118] 2017 Investment Law, Article 21.

[119] 2017 Executive Regulations, Article 7.

[120] 2017 Investment Law, Articles 5, 83-84; 2017 Executive Regulations, Articles 129-133. The timeframes and procedures are defined as follows: (i) complaints must be submitted within 15 days from of notification of decision making the object of complaint; (ii) the Grievance Committee must settle the matter with a reasoned decision within 30 days from the date of closing of hearings and submissions. The decision rendered is final and binding on all competent authorities but does not prejudice the investor from resorting to legal action.

[121] 2017 Investment Law, Article 5; 2017 Executive Regulations, Articles 7, 8, 58, 59 and 124. See also, 2017 Investment Law, Article 81, whereby GAFI is also mandated with monitoring compliance with the provisions of the 2017 Investment Law and may in that regard request that investors comply with their rights and obligations thereunder and if applicable, impose a certain number of determined sanctions, including the suspension of benefits under the incentives schemes, the revocation of licences, among others. In this context, investors must also be provided with a similar "*grace period*".

[122] 2017 Investment Law, Articles 24-25.

[123] 2017 Investment Law, Article 22; 2017 Executive Regulations, Article 24.

[124] 2017 Investment Law, Article 22; 2017 Executive Regulations, Articles 25 and 29.

[125] 2017 Investment Law, Articles 55 *et seq*.

[126] 2017 Investment Law, Section III, Chapter 6; 2017 Executive Regulations, Articles 44-59.

[127] 2017 Investment Law, Article 26; 2017 Executive Regulations, Articles 44-59.

[128] 2017 Investment Law, Article VIII.

[129] These are not considered within the scope of this country section.

[130] 2017 Investment Law, Article 9.

[131] 2017 Investment Law, Article 12, as amended by Law 141 of 2019, Article I; Cabinet Decree 22 of 2020, Article I; 2017 Executive Regulations, Articles 10-13.

[132] 2017 Investment Law, Article 12; Law 141 of 2019 (amending the 2017 Investment Law), Article I, complementing 2017 Investment Law, Article 12, which introduces projects for the expansion of existing investments that aim to increase the production capacity of the investment project as eligible to the Scheme, subject to certain rules and conditions; Cabinet Decree 6 of 16 February 2020, which was adopted to clarify the conditions for the implementation of the above-cited amendment, and provided that further criteria and technical pre-conditions would be issued via GAFI Board of Directors resolutions (Article I). These were not at the time of writing publicly available. See also, Memoranda of 15 July 2020 and GAFI Board of Directors Technical Secretariat Letter No. 2809/M5, which all pertain to criteria, rules and conditions pertaining to eligibility to the Special Incentives Scheme. Whether these are publicly and readily available remains unclear.

[133] "*Investment costs*" is defined in the 2017 Investment Law, Article 11; 2017 Executive Regulations, Article 11.

[134] 2017 Investment Law, Article 11; 2017 Executive Regulations, Article 11, as amended by subsequent implementing decrees amending the definitions of the sectors.

[135] 2017 Investment Law, Article 11.

[136] 2017 Executive Regulations, Article 13.

[137] 2017 Investment Law, Article 12(3).

[138] 2017 Investment Law, Article 13.

[139] 2017 Executive Regulations, Articles 12-13.

[140] 2017 Executive Regulations, Article 42.

[141] 2017 Investment Law, Article 20.

[142] 2017 Investment Law, Article 20.

[143] Cabinet Decree 56 of 2022.

[144] In that regard, the Egyptian Cabinet recently approved an amendment to the 2017 Investment Law, extending the eligibility conditions under the Mechanism to cover those companies established prior to the entry into force of the 2017 Investment Law. The adopted text of the amendment was available for consideration at the time of writing in September 2023. See, Cabinet Meeting No. (244), Press Release, 21 June 2023 (last accessed on 12 September 2023).

[145] Cabinet Decree 56 of 2022, Article II.

[146] Cabinet Decree 56 of 2022, Article I.

[147] 2017 Executive Regulations, Article 42, as amended by Prime Minister Decree 2300 of 2022, Article I; and Prime Minister Decree 4426 of 2022, Article I.

[148] 2017 Investment Law, Article 13.

[149] 2017 Investment Law, Article 9. In that regard, the Egyptian Cabinet recently approved an amendment to the 2017 Investment Law, whereby all businesses – those established before and after the entry into force of the 2017 Investment Law – benefit from incentives under the General Scheme. The adopted text of the amendment was available for consideration at the time of writing in September 2023. See, Cabinet Meeting No. (244), Press Release, 21 June 2023 (last accessed on 12 September 2023).

[150] 2017 Executive Regulations, Articles 42-43. The existence of this unit is confirmed by the Golden Licence Guidebook; however, its establishing instrument (Prime Minister Decree 1156 of 2020) is not publicly available.

[151] 2017 Executive Regulations, Article 43; as amended by Prime Minister Decree 2300 of 2022, Article I.

[152] 2017 Investment Law, Articles 14, 71(4).

[153] See e.g., 2017 Executive Regulations, Article 13.

[154] In that regard, the ISC Investor Guide provides background as to the formalities for requirements relevant to the Special and Additional Schemes, namely the determination of the start date of the investor's activity.

[155] 2017 Investment Law, Article 79.

[156] 2017 Executive Regulations, Article 126.

[157] 2017 Investment Law, Article 81; 2017 Executive Regulations, Article 124.

[158] 2017 Investment Law, Article 83.

[159] See the government portal's webpage on the JIB.

[160] OECD (2022), *FDI Qualities Review of Jordan*, OECD Publishing, Paris, p. 11.

[161] World Bank, *Doing Business – Economy Profile: Jordan (2020).*

[162] *U.S. Department of State (2021), Investment Climate Statement: Jordan.*

[163] OECD (2022), *FDI Qualities Review of Jordan*, OECD Publishing, Paris, p. 11.

[164] World Bank (2019), *Enterprise Surveys: Jordan*.

[165] OECD (2022), *FDI Qualities Review of Jordan,* OECD Publishing, Paris, p. 12.

[166] Jordan MoI, Jordan's Investment Ministry Streamlines Processes, Paving the Way for Modern Economic Vision.

[167] See for instance the MoI's press release on the establishment of the MoI.

[168] The Jordan Investment Commission (JIC) was established in 2014, against the backdrop of stagnating FDI inflows following the global financial crisis of 2008/2009 as well as the protests of 2011/2012 which diminished investors' confidence in the stability of the Jordanian business environment. The establishment of the JIC aimed explicitly at streamlining the institutional framework for investment promotion and facilitation. It was entrusted with a broader mandate than its predecessor – the Jordan Investment Board (JIB) – which it absorbed, alongside two other agencies operating in the country: (1) the Export Promotion Department of the Jordan Enterprise and Development Corporation; and (2) the Development and Free Zones Commission. See, OECD (2019), *Mapping Investment Promotion Agencies: Middle East and North Africa*, OECD Publishing, Paris, p. 22.

[169] The 2022 Investment Environment Law does not apply to all investments in Jordan across all economic sectors. The Law's Article 2 confines the legislation's material scope to "*any industrial, commercial, agricultural, service, tourism, information technology or creative industry activity*", and excludes specifically "banking, money exchange or regulated professional activities as per special legislations" from the scope of the Law's provisions. In turn, the facilitation mandate of the MoI, as defined by the Law, is limited to investments in certain sectors.

[170] Decree 7 of 2023 on the Regulation of the Investment Climate, pursuant to Article 51, para. (a) of the Investment Environment Law (Law 21 of 2022), Official Gazette, Issue No. 5842, 12 February 2023, Article 181.C.

[171] 2022 Investment Environment Law, Article 8. The MoI published a draft Investment Promotion Strategy developed with the support of the World Bank Group in mid-March 2022.

[172] 2022 Investment Environment Law, Article 8(C)(6) and 11(D), Instructions No. 5 of 2023.

[173] The regulations, instructions and decisions issued under the Investment Law (2014) shall continue to be in effect until they are cancelled, amended, or replaced by others in accordance with the provisions of this Law or its implementing instruments. According to the Regulation, Article 194, 13 regulations have been repealed; these regulations concern (1) the issuance of construction permits in development and free zones, (2) investors' grievances, (3) the establishment of free and development zones, (4) regulating foreign investments, (5) land recovery in development and free zones, (6) customs' clearance in development zones, (7) the income tax decrease in the less developed regions, (8) the investment window, (9) the investment incentives, (10) the general sales' tax in development and free zones, (11) the regulation of the investment environment and registration of establishments in development and free zones, (12) regulation on the employment and employees of development and free zones, and (13) the customs duties procedures in free zones.

[174] 2022 Investment Environment Law, Article 2.

[175] 2022 Investment Environment Law, Article 3.

[176] The Council of Ministers adopted in 2018 a new code of practices for the governance of governmental policies and legislative instruments to enhance regulatory transparency and predictability. The

guidebook accompanying the policy (June 2022), accentuates the role of public consultations for good regulatory practices. See also, the Jordanian Policy on Electronic Participation of 2021.

[177] 2022 Investment Environment Law, Article 5(A).

[178] Decree 7 of 2023 on the Regulation of the Investment Climate, pursuant to Article 51, para. (a) of the Investment Environment Law (Law 21 of 2022), Official Gazette, Issue No. 5842, 12 February 2023.

[179] See, OECD (2021), *Middle East and North Africa Investment Policy Perspectives*, OECD Publishing, Paris.

[180] 2022 Investment Environment Law, Article 3(C).

[181] 2022 Investment Environment Law, Article 35(B).

[182] See, para. 0 on the material scope of the Law.

[183] USAID LENS was a five-year project (2014-2019) aimed at supporting small business growth and better economic planning to strengthen Jordanian communities against economic adversity. One of the core objectives of the project was to enhance the business environment in Jordan by improving the business registration process for medium and small enterprises (MSEs). This included upgrading the CCD's server storage capacity to handle more data for registered businesses and developing a business registration manual. Background information on USAID LENS can be found on the project's website at: https://jordanlens.org/.

[184] 2022 Investment Environment Law, Article 37. For a description of these sectors, see, para. 0.

[185] 2022 Investment Environment Law, Article 37(C).

[186] 2022 Investment Environment Law, Article 37(B).

[187] 2022 Investment Environment Law, Article 37(D) and (E).

[188] 2022 Investment Environment Law, Article 40(A) and (B).

[189] Investment Environment Law, Article 40(E).

[190] 2022 Investment Environment Law, Article 40. Among the prohibited grounds of refusals are the protection of a monopoly or dominant position, or the restriction of an investment.

[191] 2022 Investment Environment Law, Article 42(C).

[192] 2022 Investment Environment Law, Article 3.A.

[193] 2022 Investment Environment Law, Articles 9.B and 51.

[194] Regulation 7 of 2023, Article 27.E.

[195] Regulation 7 of 2023, Article 32.B.

[196] Regulation 7 of 2023, Article 37.E.

[197] This inventory was developed by Jordan with the support of the World Bank in 2016. It was available on the Jordan Investment Commission's (JIC) website and was regularly updated by a dedicated JIC team. Due to recent institutional reshufflings and the JIC's absorption into the newly created MoI in 2021, the inventory is no longer available and a new inventory reflecting incentives offered under the recent 2022 Investment Environment Law has not yet been developed.

[198] The Investment Promotion Strategy (2023-2026), published in June 2023, provides that the MoI *"will completely revamp its website drawing from multiple examples of good practice IPA websites around the world"* and is expected to launch an electronic platform entitled 'Invest in Jordan' (*Invest.Jo*) which, among others, will highlight the advantages and incentives granted according to the Investment Environment Law, alongside other relevant information on the country's investment framework (p. 21).

[199] The Aqaba SEZ is explicitly excluded from the scope of the Investment Environment Law (see, Article 50) and is governed by the Aqaba Special Economic Zone Law (Law 32 of 2000), as amended, published in issue No. 4453 of the Official Gazette, on 31 August 2000 (p. 3423-3441). See, the Aqaba SEZ official website for more details.

[200] It should be noted that even if an economic activity qualifies for the additional advantages, it may not benefit of the subsidisation of energy in case that its operational cost invoice exceeded 20% of the total operational cost, as per Article 29.B, Regulation 7 of the year 2023, *op. cit.*

[201] Investment Environment Law, Article 13.A.

[202] Investment Environment Law, Article 14.B.

[203] See, para. 0 on the material scope of the Law.

[204] Regulation 7 of 2023, Article 2.A.

[205] Council of Ministers' approval on issuing the schedule of fixed assets, production requirements and inputs, and spare parts necessary to exercise the economic activity subject to a zero-rate general sales' tax, published issue No. 5848 of the Official Gazette, on 16 March 2023 (pp. 1336-1420).

[206] Regulation 7 of 2023, *op. cit.*, Articles 23.C and 23.D.

[207] Regulation 7 of 2023, Article 18.

[208] Regulation 7 of 2023, Article 19.

[209] Regulation 7 of 2023, Article 22.

[210] Regulation 7 of 2023, Article 20.

[211] Regulation 7 of 2023, Article 21.

[212] Regulation 7 of 2023, Article 28.A. "Strategic economic activities" eligible for additional incentives are defined by reference to two cumulative conditions: (i) they fulfil at least two of the criteria to qualify for the additional incentives, and (ii) they meet minimum capital thresholds that are listed in reference to their economic sector (e.g., agriculture, information technology, renewables, tourism, and education), or set at JOD 100 million in non-listed sectors. The Regulation states two additional conditions specific to the single approval: (i) taking one of the corporate forms available under the Jordanian Companies

Law (excluding limited liability companies), and (ii) that the investor has not been convicted of an economic crime (Regulation 7 of 2023, Article 36.A).

[212] Investment Environment Law, Article 13.B.

[213] Investment Environment Law, Article 13.B.

[214] Regulation 7 of 2023, Article 29.A.

[215] Regulation 7 of 2023, Article 26.

[216] 2022 Investment Environment Law, Article 14.A.

[217] Regulation 7 of 2023, Articles 27.E, 32.B, 37.E.

[218] Regulation 7 of 2023, Article 15.

[219] Regulation 7 of 2023, Article 24.A.

[220] Regulation 7 of 2023, Article 23.

[221] Regulation 7 of 2023, Article 32.B.

[222] Regulation 7 of 2023, Article 26.

[223] 2022 Investment Environment Law, Article 13.E.

[224] Regulation 7 of 2023, Article 36.B.

[225] It is unclear if this committee is (or is expected to be) a permanent body under the authority of the MoI or would function on an *ad hoc* basis. Article 3 of the draft instructions on the revocation of the single approval (published on the official website of the MoI, in Arabic), seems to point towards a permanent committee in charge of assessing single approval applications.

[226] 2022 Investment Environment Law, Article 13.E and Regulation 7 of 2023, Article 37.

[227] Regulation 7 of 2023, Article 37.

[228] Regulation 7 of 2023, Article 37.E.

[229] In accordance with Schedule No. 2 on the services rendered by the OSS, row 94, in implementation of Regulation 7 of 2023, Article 3.B,

[230] Regulation 7 of 2023, Articles 15.B, 15.D, 16 and 17.

[231] Regulation 7 of 2023, Article 15.D.

[232] Regulation 7 of 2023, Articles 15.D, 16 and 17, in implementation of 2022 Investment Environment Law, Article 11.

[233] 2022 Investment Environment Law, Article 11.

[234] Regulation 7 of 2023, Article 27.E.

[235] Regulation 7 of 2023, Article 37.E.

[236] Regulation 7 of 202, Article 27.C.

[237] 2022 Investment Environment Law, Article 11 and Regulation 7 of 2023, Article 17.A.

[238] Regulation 7 of 2023, Article 37.D. The draft instructions regarding the revocation of the single approval are available for public consultations on the official website of the MoI, in Arabic.

[239] OECD (2021), *Middle East and North Africa Investment Policy Perspectives*, OECD Publishing, Paris, p. 19.

[240] OECD (2018), *Examen des statistiques d'investissements directs internationaux au Maroc, OECD Publishing, Paris, p. 13.*

[241] U.S. Department of State (2023), *Investment Climate Statement: Morocco.* Compare OECD (2021), *Middle East and North Africa Investment Policy Perspectives*, OECD Publishing, Paris, p. 22.

[242] World Bank, *Doing Business – Economy Profile: Morocco (2020).*

[243] World Bank, *Doing Business – Economy Profile: Morocco (2020).*

[244] In that regard, the Investment Charter clarifies that public policies for investment promotion are defined by the State, which are then subsequently implemented at regional level, both by the competent regional government authorities (including among others the CNI), and the CRIs and CRUIs (Article 3). Law 47-18 in that regard provides that the CRIs contribute, within the limits of their territorial jurisdiction, to the implementation of the State's policy on the development, promotion and attraction of investment at regional level, and for providing regional level and overall support for businesses, in particular small and medium-sized SME's and very small enterprises (Article 4). It also specifies in that regard that CRIs, together with the relevant regions and administration, draw up and implement regional development, promotion strategies *in accordance with government guidelines and directives* among others (Article 4(3)). Law 47-18 also provides that, as part of implementing investment policies, governmental authorities keep CRIs informed of any national, sectoral or cross-sectoral strategies, general guidelines, programmes and development projects decided by the government with a view to promote investment; CRIs are also kept informed of decisions taken by the deliberative bodies of the local authorities relating to investment promotion and the economic development of the said communities (Article 5; see also, Articles 6-7).

[245] The AMDIE is Morocco's nation-wide IPA. It was established in 2017 with the adoption of Decree 1-17-49 of 30 August 2017 promulgating Law 60-16 on the establishment of the AMDIE (**Law 60-16**) and replaces and merges the mandates of the previous *Agence marocaine de development des investissements* and the *Centre marocain de promotion des exportations and the Office des foires et expositions de Casablanca*. Investments in the agriculture, fishing, crafts and tourism sectors fall outside of its mandate. Its mandate does not specifically concern investment facilitation, but rather the implementation of the Government strategy for the development, encouragement, and promotion of national and foreign investments and of exports.

[246] Lettre royale relative à la gestion déconcentrée de l'investissement, 9 January 2002 (**Royal Letter of 2002**).

[247] See, the Moroccan Court of Auditors' Annual Report (2015), specifically the "*Evaluation de l'expérience des Centres régionaux d'investissement*", which identified several shortcomings hindering the overall effectiveness of CRIs in facilitating investment in the country since their establishment in 2002. See also, Royaume du Maroc, Le Chef du Gouvernement, Les cahiers des reformes, *Réformes des centres régionaux d'investissement – une réforme au service de la promotion de l'investissement dans les régions du Maroc*, Edition 2019 (2019).

[248] In that regard, a government ministry responsible for investment was established and the supervision of the CRIs was transferred to the Head of Government in order to strengthen synergies and public action between various stakeholders involved in investment at both central and regional levels – see, Decrees 2-23-310 and 2-23-414 of 18 May 2023. The role of CRIs and CRUIs may further evolve as Law 47-18 appears to be currently under review (information corroborated by stakeholder consultations, August 2023).

[249] Law 47-18, Articles 4(a)(1), (2), (5) and (6).

[250] Among others, Investors may through the CRI-Invest Platform directly (i) submit investment project files to the CRIs (ii) find information relating to relevant administrative establishment and operation formalities and (iii) complete these (save for incentives-related formalities), with the assistance and guidance of a CRI advisor allocated to their project. Investors may follow the CRUI's review of their investment project file and the issuance of establishment and operation administrative acts and authorisations in real time. Investors may also lodge appeals further to any negative decisions rendered by the relevant CRUI through the platform. See, the CRI-Invest platform User Guide, prepared and published by the Moroccan Government in October 2020.

[251] Law 47-18, Articles 4(a)7, 4(a)9. The CRIs' websites are listed on the Government's website through its National Portal for Regional Authorities. To date, all of the 12 CRIs' websites are up-and-running, namely: the Marrakech – Safi CRI, the Rabat-Salé-Kénitra CRI, the Oriental CRI, the Guelmim Oued-Noun CRI, the Casablanca-Settat CRI, the Beni Mellal-Khenifra CRI, the Fes-Meknes CRI, the Tanger – Tétouan – Al Hoceima CRI, the Souss Massa CRI, the Dakhla Oued Eddahab CRI, the Drâa-Tafilalet CRI, and the Laâyoune – Sakia Al Hamra CRI.

[252] Law 47-18, Article 29.

[253] Royal Letter of 2002, para. 3.

[254] Among others, CRUIs hold meetings on a need-basis, and their membership varies depending on the items which they are expected to discuss at any given meeting and may include any of the representatives envisaged under Law 47-18, including the governor of the relevant prefecture and representatives from regional authorities and administrations. While investors cannot themselves attend CRUI deliberations, they may be invited by the CRUI's chair to provide information relevant to the CRUI's review of their investment project file (Law 47-18, Articles 31-39). In that regard, law 47-18 provides that the relevant government authorities shall take the necessary steps to provide heads of decentralised departments under their authority with the prerogatives required to take decisions falling within the remit of their respective administrations in connection with the examination of files relating to investment projects.

[255] Law 47-18, Article 33.

[256] Law 47-18, Article 29.

[257] Royal Letter of 2002, para. 3.

[258] Among others, CRUIs hold meetings on a need-basis, and their membership varies depending on the items which they are expected to discuss at any given meeting and may include any of the representatives envisaged under Law 47-18, including the governor of the relevant prefecture and representatives from regional authorities and administrations. While investors cannot themselves attend CRUI deliberations, they may be invited by the CRUI's chair to provide information relevant to the CRUI's review of their investment project file (Law 47-18, Articles 31-39). In that regard, law 47-18 provides that the relevant government authorities shall take the necessary steps to provide heads of decentralised departments under their authority with the prerogatives required to take decisions falling within the remit of their respective administrations in connection with the examination of files relating to investment projects.

[259] Law 47-18, Article 33.

[260] Decree 2-23-1, Articles 18-27. A previous *Commission des Investissements* had been established under the former investment regime (*Loi cadre 18*-95).

[261] Law 47-18, Articles 40-41. 2022 Investment Charter, Articles 34-36 set out further aspects of the CNI's mandate, including: carrying out periodic assessments of the effectiveness of the Charter's new Investment Incentives Regime and, if and when appropriate, put forward possible amendments; and monitoring the implementation of the 2022 Investment Charter and any subsequent decrees adopted for its implementation.

[262] The 2022 Investment Charter entered into force on 15 December 2022, as a *loi cadre* (defined under Moroccan law as legislation that outlines the fundamental objectives of the economic, social, environmental and cultural activity of the State). Instruments adopted to implement the Investment Charter of 1995 remain in force until they are repealed or replaced in accordance with the provisions of the 2022 Investment Charter (2022 Investment Charter, Article 39).

[263] The current Moroccan legal and regulatory framework for investment, as considered in this Report, rests on the following instruments: Decree 1-17-49 of 30 August 2017 promulgating Law 60-16, pertaining to the establishment of the AMDIE (**Law 60-16**); Decree 1-19-18 of 13 February 2019 promulgating Law 47-18, reforming CRIs and establishing CRUIs (**Law 47-18**) and accompanying Decree 2-19-67 of 17 April 2019 enacting Law 41-18; Decree 1-22-76 of 9 December 2022 promulgating Framework Law 03-22, pertaining to the new investment charter (**2022 Investment Charter**); Decree 2-23-1 of 16 February 2023, pertaining to the implementing of certain incentive schemes (**Decree 2-23-1**). See also, Decree 1-20-06 promulgating Law 55-19 of 6 March 2020, pertaining to the streamlining of administrative procedures and formalities (**Law 55-19**). When relevant, the 2022 Investment Charter and its related instruments and amendments are also hereafter referred to as the "2022 Investment Charter". As per applicable Moroccan legislation, entry into force of legislation takes place on the date of their publication in the Official Bulletin.

[264] 2022 Investment Charter, Article 7.

[265] 2022 Investment Charter, Preamble, Article 39.

[266] See, Decree 2-17-618 of 26 December 2017, pertaining to administration decentralisation; Decree 1-20-06 of 6 March 2020 promulgating Law 55-19 and its implementing regulations, pertaining to the streamlining of administrative procedures and formalities. See also, Decree 1-20-103 of 31 December 2020 promulgating Law 76-20, pertaining to the establishment of the Mohammed VI Fund for Investment.

[267] 2022 Investment Charter, Preamble, Articles 3-5 and 22-30. These include: facilitating access to property for investment projects and the development of special economic zones; improving and facilitating access to finance; and advancing ongoing reforms for the streamlining of investment-related administrative procedures and formalities at the regional level.

[268] 2022 Investment Charter, Article 2. No implementing decree is adopted – or is foreseen to be adopted – in that regard.

[269] See e.g., Law 55-19, which was published in the Arabic version of the Official Bulletin on 19 March 2020, and subsequently published in its French edition on 20 May 2021.

[270] Similar explanatory notes were published with respect to the adoption of Law 47-18. Further, the Minister of Investment presented the draft Decree 2-23-1 before the CGEM in February 2023, after its approval by the Cabinet in January of this year – see e.g., *Jazouli presents basic investment support system to CGEM members* (unofficial translation from Arabic), Bayane Al Youme, 9 February 2023.

[271] House of Representatives Internal Regulations, Article 137; 2011 Moroccan Constitution, Article 33. See also, the website of the Secretary General of the Government, which features a dedicated portal for draft laws and regulations accessible to the public, and which also provides for opportunities for comment.

[272] See e.g., *A new investment charter and many questions* (unofficial translation from French), Tel Quel, 28 February 2022; *Interview with Ali Seddiki: "The Investment Charter will reverse the distribution between public and private"* (unofficial translation from French), L'Opinion, 30 October 2022.

[273] These pertain to the 'tacit approval' mechanism (Decrees 2-22-141 and 2-22-387 of 11 May 2023); investment-related administrative acts and decisions which competent authorities (in most instances, Ministries) should issue within the prescribed 30-day timeframe (Decree 2-22-385 of 11 May 2023); and administrative decisions which require technical expertise and/or public inspection and in relation to which the 30-day timeframe may be extended (Decree 2-22-386 of 11 May 2023).

[274] See, Open Government Partnership, Morocco Action Plan Review 2021-2023, *Digitalization of administrative acts and procedures* (last accessed on 11 September 2023). The development of a unified national platform is currently being carried out in collaboration with the Open Government Partnership, with a view to digitalise *"a first batch of the most used procedures and formalities, with the aim of completing the digitalisation process of all administrative procedures and formalities by 2025"*.

[275] See, OECD (2021), *Middle East and North Africa Investment Policy Perspectives*, OECD Publishing, Paris.

[276] See, OECD (2015), *Policy Framework for Investment, 2015 Edition*, OECD Publishing, Paris.

[277] The CRI-Invest Platform provides information on the environmental assessment forming this preliminary evaluation only. Stakeholder consultations with the AMDIE have indicated that, in the

context of this preliminary evaluation process, assist and advise investors in the preparation of their investment project applications with a view to ensure that all required pre-conditions are met and approvals are granted by the relevant CRUI.

[278] Several legal instruments govern these commercial forms and companies, including but not limited to Law 5-96 pertaining to general partnerships, limited partnerships, partnerships limited by shares, limited liability companies and joint ventures; and Law 17-95 pertaining to public limited companies.

[279] Law 47-18, Articles 29(b) and 30.

[280] Law 47-18, Article 29(b).

[281] See Box A A.1 for the rules pertaining to the CRUI decision-making, relevant timeframes, and appeals procedures.

[282] Law 47-18, Article 4(a)(9).

[283] Launched further to Law 55-19 to streamline administrative procedures and formalities; see Box A A.1. See also, Guide prepared relative to the streamlining of administrative procedures and formalities (*Simplification des procedures et des formalités administratives*) prepared by *Secretariat de la Commission de la simplification des procedures et des formalités administratives*).

[284] Decree 2-22-385 of 11 May 2023 sets out an exhaustive list of 281 administrative acts and decisions, along with the relevant competent authorities to which applications must be submitted and estimate timeframes for the processing and delivery of authorisations. This timeframe is subject to the submission of a complete application file and may run longer in instances where the application file is incomplete and/or where the relevant competent authority makes a request for additional information. It is also subject to further extension under specific and limited circumstances. See Law 55-19, Articles 6, 10 and 16-17, Decree 2-22-386 of 11 May 2023.

[285] See, Open Government Partnership, Morocco Action Plan Review 2021-2023, *Digitalization of administrative acts and procedures* (last accessed on 11 September 2023). The development of a unified national platform is currently being carried out in collaboration with the Open Government Partnership, with a view to digitalise *"a first batch of the most used procedures and formalities, with the aim of completing the digitalisation process of all administrative procedures and formalities by 2025"*.

[286] The Idarati platform nevertheless carries a binding effect on public administrations as they cannot request documents from applicants other than those which they list on the platform (Law 55-19, Article 3).

[287] 2022 Investment Charter, Article 39; Decree 2-23-1, Article 28.

[288] 2022 Investment Charter, Articles 8, 19-21. The 2022 Investment Charter does not apply to investment projects carried out in the agricultural sector, which are governed by a separate investment and incentives regime. Real estate and trade investment projects are not eligible to the Primary Incentives Schemes (Article 7).

[289] Order 3-12-23, 3-13-23 and 3-14-23 of 1 March 2023.

[290] 2022 Investment Charter, Article 40. These implementing decrees are not considered in this Country Section.

[291] 2022 Investment Charter, Article 6.

[292] 2022 Investment Charter, Article 18.

[293] 2022 Investment Charter, Article 16; Decree 2-23-1, Articles 10-11. Investment projects undertaken with respect to wind, hydraulic or solar power are capped at MAD 30 million of cumulated incentives benefits.

[294] The term "*steady employment*" is defined under Decree 2-23-1 and Prime Minister Order 3-13-23, Article 1.

[295] Decree 2-23-1, Article 1, 7-8; 2022 Investment Charter, Article 12-15. These are also further defined in the Decree's implementing Orders adopted in March 2023.

[296] Decree 2-23-1, Article 15.

[297] 2022 Investment Charter, Article 17.

[298] 2022 Investment Charter, Article 29.

[299] 2022 Investment Charter, Article 9.

[300] Decree 2-23-1, Articles 23 and 26.

[301] 2022 Investment Charter, Article 10.

[302] Decree 2-23-1, Articles 3-4.

[303] According to the Foreign Investment Promotion Agency (FIPA), the privatisation of *Tunisie Telecom* accounted for 67.5% of total FDI inflow in 2006.

[304] OECD (2020), *OECD Review of Foreign Direct Investment Statistics: Tunisia*, OECD Publishing, Paris, p. 10 and 22.

[305] OECD (2021), *Middle East and North Africa Investment Policy Perspectives*, OECD Publishing, Paris, p. 22.

[306] World Bank, *Doing Business – Economy Profile: Tunisia (2020)*.

[307] U.S. Department of State (2023), *Investment Climate Statement: Tunisia.*

[308] World Bank (2020), *Enterprise Surveys: Tunisia*.

[309] OECD (2021), *Middle East and North Africa Investment Policy Perspectives*, OECD Publishing, Paris, p. 65.

[310] http://www.mdici.gov.tn/wp-content/uploads/2023/01/Strategie_nationale_pour_l_amelioration_du_climat_des_affaires-1.pdf, p. 36-37.

[311] The Foreign Investment Promotion Agency (FIPA) is one of Tunisia's investment promotion agencies. It was established in 1995, as a publish institution, under the Ministry of Development, Investment and International Cooperation. Its mandate is narrow, and it focuses on investment promotion activities. It does not carry any investment facilitation mandate, nor does it perform any such functions. More specifically, it promotes inward foreign investment, as well as innovation and regional development, and acts primarily as an "*image builder*". For more information, see OECD (2019), *Mapping of Investment Promotion Agencies: Middle East and North Africa*, OECD Publishing, Paris.

[312] Law 2016-71 of 30 September 2017 promulgating the investment law.

[313] Equivalent at the time of writing in September to +/- EUR 4.5 million.

[314] These include among others the Agency for the Promotion of Agricultural Investment (whose main mission is to promote private investment in the fields of agriculture, fishing and associated services, as well as in primary processing activities integrated into agricultural and fishing projects); the Tunisian National Tourist Office, the Tunisian National Office for Handicrafts (ONAT implements the State's strategy for safeguarding and developing the Tunisian craft sector, notably by promoting investment and supporting job creation, innovation and creativity, as well as developing policies for preserving the country's craft heritage; the body provides limited facilitation services, including business registration, access to finance, and specific sectoral incentives); and the Tunisian Export Promotion Centre. These agencies fall under the remit of different Ministries and have a different sector-based mandates.

[315] Government Decree 2017-388 of 9 March 2017, establishing the structure and organisation of the High Council for Investment, the administrative and financial organisation of the TIA and the Tunisian Fund for Investment. The TIA's governance structure is set out in Decree 2017-388 of 9 March 2017, Articles 8-22. Among others, its *Executive Body* encompasses several units mandated with investment policy advocacy (*pôle des politiques d'investissement et des réformes*), assessing investment incentives applications and post-execution monitoring, (*pôle des primes et des incitations*, *pôle de l'évaluation et du contrôle des primes et des incitations*), and providing investor support (*pôle d'encadrement de l'investisseur*) in respect of the services provided by the TIA's *Interlocuteur unique de l'investisseur*, or OSS. See also, the TIA's organisation chart.

[316] 2016 Investment Law, Article 14; Decree 2017-388 of 9 March 2017, Article 7; Law 2019-47 of 3 June 2019, Article 11.

[317] Decree 2017-388 of 9 March 2017, Article 40.

[318] The TIA specifies that facilitation for projects whose capital falls under the TND 15 million threshold is carried out by the APII (see, here with respect to investment declarations; although the French and Arabic versions of the website do not provide the same; and here with respect to the mandate of the Commission for licences and approvals). The APII does not define the scope of its mandate by reference to capital threshold however. Further, the FIPA exclusively refers to the APII's OSS with respect to legal incorporation in Tunisia, irrespective of the value of the investment project. See also, the TIA's institutional brochure, which provides that the TIA delivers different services *"depending on the capital value of the investment"*, and that it provides assistance, guidance and advice only to projects under a TND 15 million threshold; whereas investment projects whose value exceeds this threshold enjoy a streamlining of administrative and other procedures, the direct processing (on behalf of investors) of applications, operation and aftercare, among others.

[319] 2016 Investment Law, Article 15; 2019-47 of 3 June 2019, Article 11.

[320] Law 91-38 of 8 June 1981 establishing the APII, as amended including by Decree 2003-178 of 21 January 2003 and Decree 2001-1567 of 2 July 2001. See also, *OECD (2019), Mapping of Investment Promotion Agencies: Middle East and North Africa*, OECD Publishing, Paris.

[321] The APII also provides *"other types of services"* through three of its branches (Tunis, Sousse and Sfax), including customs-related formalities, issuance of residence permits, and employment-related formalities.

[322] Decree 2017-389 of 9 March 2019.

[323] 2016 Investment Law, Articles 27 *et seq.*

[324] The current Tunisian legal and regulatory framework for investment, as considered in this Report, rests on the following instruments: Law 2016-71 of 30 September 2016 promulgating the investment law (**2016 Investment Law**), which entered into force on 1 April 2017; Government Decree 2017-388 of 9 March 2017, establishing the structure and organisation of the High Council for Investment, the administrative and financial organisation of the TIA and the Tunisian Fund for Investment (**Decree 2017-388**); Government Decree 2017-389 of 9 March 2017, relating to financial incentives for investments established within the framework of the 2016 Investment Law, complemented by the Joint Ministerial Order of the Minister of Development, Investment, and International Cooperation, the Minister of Finance, the Minister of Industry and Commerce, the Minister of Agriculture, and the Minister of Tourism, Arts and Crafts of 28 April 2017 (**Decree 2017-389**, **Joint Ministerial Order of 2017**); Government Decree 2017-390 of 9 March 2017, establishing and setting out the organisation of a management unit for the review of authorisation required to carry out certain economic activities (**Decree 2017-390**); Government Decree 2018-47 of 11 May 2018, publishing the exclusive list of economic activities subject to authorisation and the list of administrative authorisations for the implementation of projects and their streamlining (**Decree 2018-47**), as amended by Presidential Decree 2022-317 of 8 April 2022 (**Decree 2022-317**); Order of the Minister of Development, Investment and International Cooperation of 8 November 2019, setting out the composition and organisation of the Commission for licences and approvals (including the relevant timeframes for the granting of authorisations) (**Order of 2019**); and Law 2019-47 of 29 May 2019, relating to the improvement of the business climate (**Law 2019-47**). When relevant, the 2016 Investment Law and its related instruments and amendments are also hereafter referred to as the *"2016 Investment Law"*.

[325] 2016 Investment Law, Article 3.

[326] 2016 Investment Law, Articles 4 and 7.

[327] 2016 Investment Law, Articles 8 *et seq.* In some instances, the transfer of foreign currency abroad may require the prior authorisation of the Central Bank of Tunisia. Decree 2018-417 provides in that regard that the Central Bank should address requests for the authorisation of transfer of capital in foreign currency abroad within 90 days of the submission of the request. If this time period lapses without the Central Bank issuing a decision as to the authorisation request, then the 'tacit approval' provided for under Decree 2018-417 will apply.

[328] See, *Règlement intérieur de l'Assemblée des représentants du peuple du 2 mai 2023*, Articles 66-67 (last accessed on 18 September 2023).

[329] See, Tunisia Country Section, para. 0 et *seq*. It is worth noting that Tunisia has in recent years undertaken a number of commitments in collaboration with the Open Government Partnership. These include a right to information commitment in 2018, which sought to strengthen the right of access to information, which yielded overall moderate results. Tunisia has also committed, between 2016 and 2018, to reform its open data legal and regulatory framework at national level with the establishment of an online open data portal, as well as modernise its regulatory framework to enforce the right to access to information. The objectives underlying these two commitments were not fully met by Tunisia.

[330] Assembly of the Representatives of the People, Internal Regulations, Article 143 ("*questions essentielles qui déterminent les choix stratégiques*").

[331] The document was located on the website of Tustex, a Tunisian media platform dedicated to financial and economic reporting. The veracity and accuracy of this document was not confirmed.

[332] Government Decree 2020-310 of 15 May 2020, relating to the streamlining of administrative procedures, the shortening of timeframes, the use of modern means of communication and the adoption of transparency in respect of public bodies-investor relations.

[333] Tunisia has launched a nation-wide public e-consultation process and a wider public-private dialogue with the aim of addressing perceived obstacles to an improved business climate and to identify relevant structural reforms, ultimately with a view to stimulate investment. These discussions are *inter alia* articulated around the 13 policy areas identified in the World Bank's B-Ready Project (formerly Doing Business) While this has not been explicitly highlighted, this process may ultimately result in reforming Law 2019-47. See, E-Consultation - Portail de la participation publique (e-participation.tn) for more information (last accessed on 28 July 2023).

[334] Decree 2020-310, Commission de suivi et de coordination des mécanismes de simplification des procédures administratives au profit des investisseurs et des entreprises économiques.

[335] See, OECD (2021), Middle East and North Africa Investment Policy Perspectives, OECD Publishing, Paris.

[336] See, OECD (2015), Policy Framework for Investment, 2015 Edition, OECD Publishing, Paris.

[337] Decree 2018-417, Annex 1. These restrictions concern notably activities pertaining to the natural resources, land, sea and air transport, banking and finance, insurance and financial markets, health, education, telecommunications sectors, and other economic activities related to certain services and commercial activities.

[338] The conditions relating to the application for and issuance of a "*foreign merchant card*" are set out in Decree-Law 61-14 of 30 August 1961, as amended, and related Order of 14 September 1961. The relevant authority mandated to consider applications for foreign merchant cards and their issuance enjoy a degree of discretionary power in its decision-making process.

[339] Additional entities may also provide facilitation services relating to some aspects of establishment requirements, namely APIA, ONTT, ONA and CEPEX, yet their roles are more limited and they do not operate specific OSS.

[340] 2016 Investment Law, Article 15; Decree 2017-388, Chapter I.

[341] The characteristics, requirements and other matters relating to the constitution of companies are governed by the *Code des sociétés commerciales* of 2000, as amended. Law 2019-47 has introduced new provisions amending and repealing provisions of the *Code* with a view to streamline procedures and requirements for the legal incorporation of companies.

[342] 2016 Investment Law, Article 4; Decree 2018-417, Annex 1. The 2016 Investment Law has alleviated several licensing requirements for a number of activities in controlled economic sectors. These liberalised activities, as listed in Annex 2 of Decree 2018-417, have been open to private investment at least since 1 January 2019 (Decree 2018-417, Article 4).

[343] Decree 2018-417 of 2017, Article 3. Decree 2018-417 also sets out some establishment conditions and requirements relating to the exercise of a number of economic activities.

[344] Presidential Decree 2022-317, Annexes 1 and 2. In 2017, it set up a *special management unit* tasked with identifying and phasing out additional licensing requirements, in coordination with relevant Ministries and government agencies (Decree 2017-390).

[345] Decree 2018-417, Article 6.

[346] 2016 Investment Law, Article 4.

[347] 2016 Investment Law, Article 14; Decree 2017-388 of 9 March 2017, Article 7; Law 2019-47 of 3 June 2019, Article 11. Initially, the TIA's OSS was mandated with liaising with the relevant authorities and agencies on behalf of the investor to obtain relevant licences and permits for the implementation of projects (2016 Investment Law, Article 15). Are excluded from the Commission's mandate those activities or investment projects pertaining to the hydrocarbons, energy and air transport sectors, or those requiring licences or authorisations granted by regulatory authorities (e.g., the Bank of Tunisia, the Financial Market Council, or the General Insurance Committee) – see, Order of 2019.

[348] 2016 Investment Law, Article 15bis; Law 2019-47, Article 11.

[349] Decree 2018-417, Article 9; Law 2019-47, Article 15. See also, the TIA Investor Guide portal. The 'tacit approval' principle does not apply with respect to two categories of activities, namely: activities which require licensing by sectoral regulatory authorities ("*competent authorities*" as defined under the Decree 2018-417), such as the Central Bank of Tunisia, the Financial Market Council, or the General Insurance Committee (Decree 2018-417, Article 2); and licences for activities specified under Annex 4 of Decree 2018-417, which include the production and distribution of defence and military equipment, oil exploration, telecommunications, the production and distribution of medicine and pharmaceutical products, and transport activities, *inter alia*.

[350] See, WTO, Trade Policy Review: Tunisia (2016), Report by the Secretariat, 10 October 2016, WT/TPR/S/341/Rev.1, p.36. The Review accounts for 30 amendments to the Investment Incentives Code since its adoption in 1993, and 150 amendments to the Code's 33 implementing Decrees.

[351] Decree 2017-389, Article 15.

[352] Decree 2017-389, Article 21(4). Foreign natural persons are not eligible to obtain incentives for equity participation by the Tunisian Investment Fund (TIF).

[353] 2016 Investment Law, Article 19.

[354] 2016 Investment Law, Article 27.

[355] 2016 Investment Law, Article 20.

[356] Decree 317-389. It should be noted that an English translation of the Decree is available in the *JORT*, but does not include its Annexes.

[357] Joint Ministerial Order of 2017.

[358] See e.g., the 2016 Investment Law, Article 19, allows for cumulation of premiums provided the combined value of granted premiums does not exceed one third of the investment costs. This calculation does not take into account the State's spending on infrastructure, or other premiums granted under some specific schemes.

[359] The qualification of an investment as a "*project of national interest*" allows the investment to benefit from a bundle of incentives ranging from tax deductions to grants for infrastructure development (2016 Investment Law, Article 20).

[360] 2016 Investment Law, Article 22.

[361] 2016 Investment Law, Article 19(1).

[362] Decree 2017-389, Article 3(3).

[363] Decree 2017-389, Annex 1, I.

[364] Decree 2017-389, Annex 1, I ("*Liste des secteurs prioritaires*").

[365] Decree 2017-389, Annex 1, II ("*Liste des filières économiques*").

[366] Decree 2017-389, Annex 1, III ("*Liste des activités exceptées du bénéfice des incitations du développement régional*").

[367] Decree 2017-389, Article 3(4).

[368] Decree 2017-389, Article 16. These national economic priorities are vaguely described in Article 1 of the 2016 Investment Law as including the increase of the added value and competitiveness of the Tunisian economy at the regional and global scales, especially by developing identified priority sectors (as listed in Annex 1 of the Decree 2017-389); creating employment; promoting an equal regional development; and contributing to the country's SDG's.

[369] Decree 2017-389, Article 24: The repayment term agricultural land loans is fixed at 25 years, including a 7-year grace period, and the interest rate is fixed at 3%. The interest amounts for the 7-year grace period shall be distributed over the 18 annuities of repayment.

[370] Decree 2017-389, Article 17: Incentives for PNIs may not exceed one third of the investment costs or TND 30 million (equivalent at the time of writing in September 2023 to EUR 9 million). This calculation considers the State's funding granted for infrastructure work.

[371] Decree 2017-389, Article 2, 18. See also, 2016 Investment Law, Article 12.

[372] 2016 Investment Law, Article 20; Decree 2017-388, Article 7(4).

[373] Decree 2017-389, Articles 9-10.

[374] Decree 2017-389, Article 11.

[375] Joint Ministerial Order of 2017, Article 12. The decision to postpone the examination of the application could be signed by the president of the committee in case of an existing delegation.

[376] Decree 2017-389, Article 11.

[377] Decree 2017-389, Article 11.

[378] 2016 Investment Law, Article 12.

[379] Decree 2017-389, Article 9. The composition, powers, and functioning of these committees are set out in Joint Ministerial Order of 2017.

[380] Decree 2017-389, Article 9; Joint Ministerial Order of 2017, Article 2.

[381] 2016 Investment Law, Article 20.

[382] Decree 2017-389, Article 10.

[383] Decree 2017-389, Article 14.

[384] 2016 Investment Law, Article 22.

[385] This delay can be exceptionally extended once, for two additional years after an administrative decision is adopted to that effect.

[386] 2016 Investment Law, Article 22.

Annex B. Investment and policy frameworks for renewable energy and green hydrogen production in the Southern Neighbourhood

The growing concerns over climate change, the need to improve trade balances as well as to find new and more sustainable sources of economic growth and job creation all call for an acceleration in the regional efforts to transition towards cleaner and more sustainable energy sources. The Southern Mediterranean region has long been recognised as a global powerhouse in the field of energy production, primarily due to rich reserves of fossil fuels in some countries, and more recently, due to the local abundance of renewable energy resources (Hawila, 2014[1]) and the potential of green hydrogen, produced from renewable power via the electrolysis process, as a versatile low-carbon energy vector.

Renewable energy investments already provide many benefits for economic development in the Southern Neighbourhood including enhanced energy security, reduced fuel import dependency, improved energy access, low-carbon industrial development and job creation (IRENA, 2013[2]). Renewable energy capacity has grown substantially in some of the countries in the region, in particular Jordan and Egypt (Figure A A.1). The total investment in clean energy in the five countries has been estimated at USD 3 billion in the last year where data is available (2021 for Jordan and Morocco, 2022 for Egypt, Tunisia and Algeria) (Climatescope, 2023[3]). As deployment grows, so does the impetus to develop domestic manufacturing capacity as well as research and development capacities. The importance of renewable energy and hydrogen in the region further increased since the full-scale invasion of Ukraine by Russia, which sent shockwaves through the global energy market. It comes as no surprise, therefore, that boosting renewable energy and green hydrogen capacity development features prominently in today's trade relations between the European Union and the countries in the Southern Mediterranean.

The region has emerged as a promising place for green hydrogen production. The use of hydrogen is expected to grow significantly around the globe, playing a significant role in broader industrial decarbonisation, provision of flexible power generation and potentially nationwide transportation such as Heavy Goods Vehicles (HGVs). There is also significant interest in the role of liquid hydrogen and hydrogen carriers (ammonia or synthetic fuel) to decarbonise shipping and aviation, which could see large scale deployment post 2030 (OECD, 2022[4]).

Figure A B.1. Installed renewable energy capacity in selected countries of the Southern Mediterranean

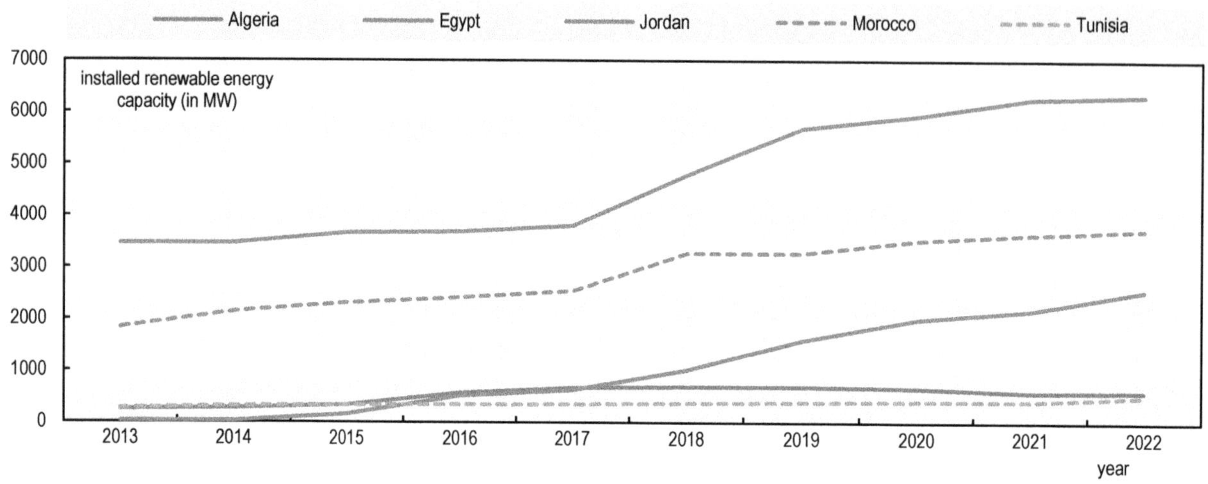

Source: OECD elaboration from IRENA Renewable Energy Capacity Statistics 2023.

Scope, objectives and report structure

The aim of this Annex is to inform the potential for future Sustainable Investment Facilitation Agreements (SIFAs) negotiations with five selected Southern Neighbourhood partners – Morocco, Egypt, Algeria, Tunisia and Jordan, specifically with respect to possible investments in renewable energy and green hydrogen.

The EU Angola SIFA contains a series of provisions which encourage Parties to implement reforms to maximise the positive benefits of inward FDI to their sustainable development, and at the same time using FDI itself as a lever to advance their SDGs. With respect to investments specifically to achieve environmental goals, the agreement stresses commitments to internationally recognised standards and agreements, such as, for instance, the Paris Agreement. While the interpretation of the SIFA principles for investment at large is already addressed in the main Report (OECD, 2023[5]), we translate these high-level principles into detailed investment readiness factors specifically relevant to renewable energy and green hydrogen development in section 2 of this chapter ((i) market potential and state of development, ii) strength and predictability of regulatory framework and non-regulatory policies, iii) strength and predictability of financial support, iv) infrastructure readiness and other complementary resources). We subsequently analyse these readiness factors for each of the five countries using available information, outlined in the methodology section below. The information is summarised in country factsheets to provide a convenient overview.

The research on this Annex was conducted through desk research. Information was compiled directly from legal texts as well as from academic and grey literature, including reports from governmental agencies and their websites, industry organisations, as well as reports and datasets from key international organisations in the energy space such as the Organisation for Economic Cooperation and Development (OECD), the International Energy Agency (IEA) and the International Renewable Energy Agency (IRENA), the World Bank (WB) and others. The growing work of the OECD on green hydrogen under the Clean Energy Finance and Investment Mobilisation (CEFIM) programme has been instrumental in gathering information on this emerging industry. Given the need for information to be recent, press releases and specialised press articles were likewise an essential source of information. Not all information is available in the public domain so targeted consultations with government experts might be needed to comprehensively cover all the criteria.

This chapter excludes assessment of the countries' general financial stability and ability to attract domestic and foreign investment and we therefore leave out factors which play a role in shaping the general investment environment in the surveyed countries, such as political stability or the rule of law. It also excludes addressing any of the general regulatory aspects explicitly mentioned in the EU Angola SIFA, such as restrictions and conditions applying to investment, business registration, acquisition and registering of property, construction permits, resolving insolvency and others or any general-purpose infrastructure that facilitates investment at large such as roads or railways.

Methodology for assessing the state of readiness for investment in renewable energy and green hydrogen in the Southern Mediterranean

Further development of renewable energy and green hydrogen capacity in the Southern Mediterranean is intertwined, since green hydrogen production relies on low-cost supply of renewable power. In order to accelerate the deployment of both, a supportive regulatory environment, strong and predictable financial incentives and strategic investments into relevant infrastructure will be essential. The development of green hydrogen capacity in particular remains a risky undertaking so creating an enabling environment is a specific challenge. New OECD analysis suggests that achieving the economic viability of green hydrogen requires, *inter alia*, new financing instruments (OECD, 2022[4]).

In this section, we identify the key factors that contribute to a country's reading readiness for renewable energy and green hydrogen investments. We describe each factor and which elements it includes below. The approach to the assessment is distinct from IRENA Renewables Readiness Assessment (RRA) (IRENA, 2013[2]), which mostly focuses on ratcheting up policy support renewable energy at a high level, the World Bank Regulatory Indicators for Sustainable Energy (RISE) (World Bank, 2015[6]), which focus mainly on renewable energy, energy efficiency and specifically the 7th Sustainable Development Goal as well as the UNFCCC Climate Investment Readiness Index (CIRI) (UNFCCC, n.d.[7]), which has a broader thematic and geographical scope. We nevertheless adapt relevant elements from these frameworks where appropriate.

Market potential and state of development

The availability of domestic natural resources typically galvanises political interests in their development. Likewise, awareness among investors is largely driven by the available domestic resources. We therefore examine the countries' solar and wind energy potential and where appropriate, also other renewables. The current state of development of renewable energy (in terms of installed capacity) and green hydrogen deployment (in terms of the number of projects in the pipeline) is key as an indicator of political will, capacity to implement relevant projects and as an indicator of accumulated know-how.

Given the fact that hydrogen is an energy vector, rather than a resource in its own right and the term 'green hydrogen' refers to hydrogen sourced from renewable energy sources, domestic renewable energy resources are also a relevant market potential determinant for green hydrogen development. The existing installed renewable energy capacity is additionally relevant as higher penetration rates are also generally associated with a stronger imperative to manage the variable electricity output and reduce eventual curtailment, which creates further incentives for green hydrogen capacity development as a means of mitigating these issues. We highlight the pipeline of green hydrogen projects, especially where these are in advanced stages of preparation and have achieved a financial close.

We also analyse the country's dependence on fossil fuel imports it typically provides a strong additional incentive for pursuing investments in renewable energy and green hydrogen and additionally provide a brief overview of the state of the domestic renewable energy manufacturing sector, with a particular focus on the production assets.

Strength and predictability of regulatory framework and non-regulatory policies

We provide a comprehensive overview countries' policy environment related to renewable energy and green hydrogen. We consider both regulatory and non-regulatory polices such as renewable energy and green hydrogen plans, strategies, targets and any other legislation directly relevant to renewable energy and green hydrogen development as well as the broader institutional framework. The ambition of the regulation, as well as clarity and predictability are taken into account. Since predictability is something that is difficult to assess ex-ante, we proxy this indirectly by considering commitments to international climate negotiations, consideration of whether targets are binding or not and sufficiently long-term. Any past retro-active revisions of legislation detrimental to renewable energy and green hydrogen development would also be captured in this section. In the case of green hydrogen, national strategies and roadmaps are mostly, but not always, a key source of information. Wherever the intention to export green hydrogen or its derivatives are mentioned, this is stated.

Strength and predictability of financial support

We evaluate common types of financial incentives and support mechanisms available to investors pursuing renewable energy and green hydrogen projects. projects. We consider both technology push and market pull instruments that directly and indirectly alter or de-risk the payoff associated with renewable energy and green hydrogen projects during their life cycle. This means that we consider financial incentives and instruments such as research and innovation incentives, targeted tax incentives, subsidies, feed-in tariffs, availability of power purchase agreements (PPA), grants, access to project financing, the degree of involvement of foreign investors and availability of public-private partnerships as well as access to e.g. green bonds (OECD, forthcoming[8]; OECD, forthcoming[9]). We consider also financial incentives in downstream sectors, that are intended to increase the demand for renewable energy or green hydrogen respectively. Direct engagement with companies involved in green hydrogen project development emphasised the key role of Development Finance Institutions (DFIs), Multilateral developments banks (MDBs) (OECD, 2022[4]), so this is another element that is assessed.

Infrastructure readiness and availability of complementary resources

A country's general infrastructure affects its ability to implement large scale projects, including those in renewable energy and green hydrogen. In this section, we however, only address the availability and quality of infrastructure specifically necessary for renewable energy and green hydrogen projects. For a country to be able to add additional renewable energy capacity, it is vital to have a transmission grid that is capable of supporting the intermittent nature of renewable energy and transport renewable power from where it is produced to where it is needed. We pay specific attention to cross-border grid interconnection capacity as these enable trade, helping to bring the aggregate costs down and to facilitate grid balancing. With respect to infrastructure needed for green hydrogen development, it is essential that renewable energy and hydrogen production capacity and transport infrastructure are co-located to minimise costs (OECD, 2022[4]). We therefore focus on plans for such co-location as well as port infrastructure (IEA, 2019[10]). The availability of complementary resources, mainly water, is also included.

Summary Factsheet: Algeria

Table A B.1. Market potential and state of development in Algeria

Renewables		
	Availability of renewable energy resources	Abundant solar and wind resources (IRENA, 2022[11])
	Contribution of renewables incl. hydro to total primary energy supply	0.12% (2021 or latest) (OECD, 2023[12])
	Current renewable energy capacity installed (wind and solar)	599 MW total; solar 460 MW (out of which CSP 25 MW); wind 10 MW (2022) (IRENA, 2023[13])
	Domestic renewable energy industry	The Algerian solar power supply chain grew significantly in last decade. Algerian telecoms and renewables company Milltech, for instance, built a 100 MW annual capacity solar module factory in the industrial zone of Boukerana in Chelghoum El Aid, in the Mila province in the north east of the country. There is no known manufacturing capacity in wind power (PV Magazine International, 2020[14]).
Green hydrogen		
	Existing green hydrogen capacity/project pipeline (including derivatives)	2 in planning (ESMAP, 2023[15])
	Existing blue hydrogen capacity/project pipeline (including derivatives)	None
Cross-cutting		
	Fossil fuel import dependency	Major hydrocarbon producer and exporter. According to latest World Bank figures net energy exports are at 177.1% of energy use (World Bank, 2023[16]).

Table A B.2. Strength and predictability of regulatory framework and non-regulatory policies in Algeria

Renewables		
	Renewable energy strategies and targets	Increase share of renewables in electricity generation to 27% by 2030 and install 15 GW of renewable power generation capacity by 2035 (International Trade Administration, 2023[17])
	Establishment of dedicated agency/body to support development	Yes, the National Observatory for the Promotion of Renewable Energies
	Other relevant regulation (e.g. local content rules, investment at large)	Algeria's Law on Renewable Energy Promotion establishes a general structure for the deployment of a renewable energy policy and sets production targets. There is no legal framework for local content specifically for renewables (IEA, 2023[18]).
Green hydrogen		
	Green hydrogen strategies/roadmaps	Hydrogen strategy exists, however, lacks the commitment to produce hydrogen using renewable energy only (Hydrogen Insight, 2023[19]).
	Green hydrogen cost target, if any	No explicit cost reduction target.
	Green hydrogen capacity target, if any	The strategy specifically targets the production and export of 30 to 40 TWh of (gaseous and liquid) hydrogen and derivatives by 2040.
	Establishment of dedicated agency/body to support development	Yes
	Any other relevant regulation (e.g. certification/standards)	The removal of the 51/49% rule, which required majority shareholding by Algerian national residents, by the Supplemental Finance Law for 2020, as amended ("LFC 2020"), brought new opportunities for foreign investors. While certain activities in strategic sectors continue to be subject to the rule, renewable energy is not listed (IEA, 2023[18]).
	Green hydrogen export provisions	Algeria aims to supply Europe with 10% of its renewable hydrogen needs by 2040 (Enerdata, 2023[20]).
Cross-cutting		
	UNFCCC participation and greenhouse gas reduction/renewable energy/green hydrogen commitments in Nationally Determined Contribution (NDC)	NDC includes a target to reduce greenhouse gases emissions by 7%-22% to 2030; 27% of electricity generated from renewable sources of energy by 2030.

Table A B.3. Strength and predictability of financial support in Algeria

Renewables		
	Feed-in tariffs	Yes, for solar PV and wind, not for CSP currently (IEA, 2023[18])
	Other operational support (e.g. contract for difference/feed-in-premium policies/long-term power purchase agreements)	Renewable power projects subject to a specific regime based on a 20-year power purchase agreement.
	Competitive auctions	Yes, in a recent (July 2023) round A total of 90 bids were submitted by Algerian and foreign companies. Among the successful proposals, 50 came from foreign developers, 18 were filed by local companies and nine were made by consortiums of both local and international companies (RenewablesNow, 2023[21]).
	Tax incentives and other financial support	None
Green hydrogen		
	Financial support (including co-investment commitments) available or planned specifically for green hydrogen installation/production	None
Cross-cutting		
	Financial investment support for clean investments in general (e.g. green bonds etc.)	No specific support
	Carbon markets	No domestic carbon pricing mechanisms or participation in international carbon markets.
	History/robust pipeline of international co-investment in renewable energy or green hydrogen projects	Yes (International Trade Administration, 2023[17])

Table A B.4. Infrastructure readiness and availability of complementary resources in Algeria

Renewables		
	Grid sufficiency for additional renewable energy capacity	Algeria's transmission and distribution grid is well developed in the north of the country, with interconnections to Morocco and Tunisia. In the South, however, the grid is isolated and susceptible to technical challenges (IRENA, 2020[22]).
	Grid access and transmission rules for renewable energy projects	Law 02-01 grants independent power producers the right to access the grid. According to the Executive Decree 06-429 the TSO is responsible for building the connection infrastructure up to 50 km. For the domestic market, transmission fees are paid by consumers and are determined by the CREG (IEA, 2023[18]).
	History of curtailing renewable energy production due to insufficient grid capacity	No evidence found.
Green hydrogen		
	Grid planning reflecting possible hydrogen production sites	No evidence found.
	Port/other maritime infrastructure	There are two existing Algerian LNG export terminals - Arzew/Bethouia (20.8 mln tonne per year) and Skikda (7.7mln tonnes per year).
	Availability of water	Water stress levels are high to extremely high in coastal areas in the North of the country.
	Any other relevant infrastructure	Algeria's existing hydrocarbons infrastructure offers an interesting basis to build up its hydrogen potential (PtX hub, 2023[23]). Infrastructure plans include an expansion of an existing gas pipeline corridor that will go through Tunisia and Italy (Pipeline journal, 2023[24]). The energy ministries of Italy, Germany, and Austria signed a letter of support for the development of a hydrogen-ready pipeline between North Africa and Europe involving Italy's gas grid operator (IMF, 2023[25]; IRENA, 2022[26])

Summary Factsheet: Egypt

Table A B.5. Market potential and state of development in Egypt

Renewables		
	Availability of renewable energy resources	Abundant solar and wind energy resources (IRENA, 2022[27]).
	Contribution of renewables incl. hydro to total primary energy supply	6.2% (2021 or latest) (OECD, 2023[12])
	Current renewable energy capacity installed (wind and solar)	6322 MW total; solar 1724 MW; wind 1643 MW (2022) (IRENA, 2023[13])
	Domestic renewable energy industry	Egypt has a comparative advantage in different segments of the renewables value chain, particularly in the downstream segments of project development, operation and maintenance. Several local players, including cable manufacturers and EPC contractors, have been active within the renewable energy market and hold a considerable market share for all renewable energy technologies (solar PV, CSP and wind). (Renewable Energy Agency, n.d.[28])Electrical components (cables, transformers) and turbine towers for the wind energy industry have been mostly produced by local companies. Egypt has little local capacity in the solar sector. It has a number of small companies that are involved in supplying solar water heaters. Aside from this small sector, Egypt does not have much capacity to locally produce the components of solar power plants (African Development Bank, 2012[29]).
Green hydrogen		
	Existing green hydrogen capacity/project pipeline (including derivatives)	24 projects (ESMAP, 2023[15])
	Existing blue hydrogen capacity/project pipeline (including derivatives)	At least 1 project
Cross-cutting		
	Fossil fuel import dependency	Substantial fossil fuel imports but also planning expansion of domestic production. (net energy exports are at 7.4% of energy use) (World Bank, 2023[16]).

Table A B.6. Strength and predictability of regulatory framework and non-regulatory policies in Egypt

Renewables		
	Renewable energy strategies and targets	The 2035 Integrated Sustainable Energy Strategy is currently being revised and waiting the approval of the supreme council for energy to reflect 33% of energy generated from renewable energy by 2025, 48% by 2030, 55% by 2035, and 61% by 2040 (IEA, 2023[18]).
	Establishment of dedicated agency/body to support development	Yes, New and Renewable Energy Authority (NREA).
	Other relevant regulation (e.g. local content rules, investment at large)	30% local content for wind farms in 2018 and was expected to increase the share to 70% by the end of 2020 (IRENA, 2018[66]). No known localisation provisions with respect to workforce in particular.
Green hydrogen		
	Green hydrogen strategies/roadmaps	Yes (being developed with the help of EBRD) (International Renewable Energy Agency, 2023[30])
	Green hydrogen cost target, if any	Yes, the country is aiming to produce green hydrogen at the lowest cost worldwide by 2050 at $1.7 per kg (ESI Africa, 2023[31]).
	Green hydrogen capacity target, if any	Aiming to produce up to 8% of world hydrogen supply.
	Establishment of dedicated agency/body to support development	Yes, National Council for Green Hydrogen and its Derivatives is established.
	Any other relevant regulation (e.g. certification/standards)	No evidence found of a certification scheme being implemented or planned. Package of tax and non-tax incentives approved by Cabinet and currently before the Parliament (December 2023); 20% local content to qualify for incentives.
	Green hydrogen export provisions	Egypt aims to be one of the largest exporters of clean hydrogen in the region (Green Hydrogen Organisation, n.d.[32]).

Cross-cutting		
	UNFCCC participation and greenhouse gas reduction/renewable energy/green hydrogen commitments in Nationally Determined Contribution (NDC)	In a recent update to this first NDC, Egypt brought forward its renewable energy target by five years. The country will now target 42% of energy demand from renewables by 2030, rather than 2035. It also committed to reduce emissions by 33% in the electricity sector, 65% in the oil and gas sector and 7% in the transportation sector by 2030 compared to business-as-usual, conditional on external support (UNFCCC, 2023[33]).

Table A B.7. Strength and predictability of financial support in Egypt

Renewables		
	Feed-in tariffs	Yes, in the past feed-in tariff support system for solar PV and wind projects with capacity less than 50 MW (IEA, 2023[18]) was established. No new projects will be implemented based on FIT.
	Other operational support (e.g. contract for difference/feed-in-premium policies/long-term power purchase agreements)	The power purchase agreements for feed-in tariffs for solar installations will last 20 years, for wind projects 25 years. The system is open only for solar PV and wind technologies (IEA, 2023[18]).
	Competitive auctions	Yes (International Renewable Energy Agency, 2023[30])
	Tax incentives and other financial support	A reduction of 2% in customs on new and renewable energy equipment. Recipients of the feed-in tariff support are also eligible to profit from the renewable tax incentive provided by the government of Egypt (IEA, 2023[18]).
Green hydrogen		
	Financial support (including co-investment commitments) available or planned specifically for green hydrogen installation/production	Extensive package of dedicated incentives recently approved. A new incentive package of pending parliament approval, which includes a wheeling charge methodology modification with potential room for giving discount to green hydrogen developers (IEA, 2023[18]).
Cross-cutting		
	Financial investment support for clean investments in general (e.g. green bonds etc.)	In 2020, Egypt became the first country in the Middle East and North Africa to issue a sovereign green bond (World Bank, 2022[34]).
	Carbon markets	A recent decree provides for the establishment of a voluntary carbon market platform within the Egyptian Stock Exchange (EGX) for the trading of carbon emissions reduction certificates (CERs). The CERs are tradeable financial instruments for greenhouse gases and are to be issued in favour of entities establishing projects reducing GHG emissions after obtaining the approval of the relevant authorities which are not currently specified (Baker Mackenzie, 2023[35]).
	History/robust pipeline of international co-investment in renewable energy or green hydrogen projects	Yes

Table A B.8. Infrastructure readiness and availability of complementary resources in Egypt

Renewables		
	Grid sufficiency for additional renewable energy capacity	A substantial grid expansion and reinforcement is underway to accommodate the rapidly growing renewable capacity, including cross-border interconnectors.
	Grid access and transmission rules for renewable energy projects	Independent power producers can enter bilateral electricity purchase contracts with eligible consumers and sell them produced electricity directly. The Egyptian Electricity Transmission Company (EETC) must allow for conclusion of such contract and make grid network available. In this case, EETC is allowed to charge and collect greed access fee for grid usage (IEA, 2023[18]).
	History of curtailing renewable energy production due to insufficient grid capacity	No evidence found.
Green hydrogen		
	Grid planning reflecting possible hydrogen production sites	Yes, at the end of 2022, the government granted so-called "golden licences", a combination of land leasing, construction permitting and operating rights to two green hydrogen projects in the industrial zone of Ain Sokhna, a port town on the Red Sea, 55km south of the Suez Canal (Hydrogen Insight, 2022[36]).

Port/other maritime infrastructure	The importance of sea ports is recognised in the green hydrogen strategy. . Private companies (SCATEC, Maersk) are investing in the Suez Canal Zone ports to produce green fuel from green hydrogen.
Availability of water	The hydrogen strategy noted that barriers to developing a hydrogen economy included freshwater scarcity. The government plans to build 47 seawater desalination plants over 30 years. The first 21 plants are expected to produce around 3.3 mn cbm/d of water.
Any other relevant infrastructure	The Suez Canal is a transit route for oil and liquefied natural gas (LNG) shipments traveling northbound from the Persian Gulf to Europe and to North America.

Summary Factsheet: Jordan

Table A B.9. Market potential and state of development in Jordan

Renewables	
Availability of renewable energy resources	Abundant wind and solar resources (IRENA, 2022[37])
Contribution of renewables incl. hydro to total primary energy supply	8% (2021 or latest) (OECD, 2023[12])
Current renewable energy capacity installed (wind and solar)	2,555 MW total; solar 1,914 MW; wind 614 MW (2022) (IRENA, 2023[13])
Domestic renewable energy industry	Jordan has been actively pursuing domestic solar industry development. Numerous domestic businesses specialise in solar panels, inverters, and other renewable energy technologies. Firms like Philadelphia Solar have established substantial operations. Petra Solar Jordan, another key player, specialises in the design and manufacture of innovative solar panels. There is a plan to invest JOD 100 mn (c. USD 140.9 mn) to build a solar cell production plant in Amman (Enterprise Climate, 2023[38]).
Green hydrogen	
Existing green hydrogen capacity/project pipeline (including derivatives)	Four MoUs signed in 2023 between the Ministry of Energy and private developers and at least 10 more in the pipeline (Jordan Times, 2023[39])
Existing blue hydrogen capacity/project pipeline (including derivatives)	0 projects
Cross-cutting	
Fossil fuel import dependency	High dependency on imported hydrocarbons putting a strain on national budget. According to latest World Bank figures net energy imports are at 96.8% of energy use (World Bank, 2023).

Table A B.10. Strength and predictability of regulatory framework and non-regulatory policies in Jordan

Renewables	
Renewable energy strategies and targets	Jordan plans to generate 50% of electricity from renewables by 2030 (Reuters, 2021[40]).
Establishment of dedicated agency/body to support development	There is no dedicated renewable energy agency that oversees the development of the renewable energy sector, this competency falls under the Energy and Minerals Regulatory Commission (EMRC) and the Ministry of Energy and Mineral Resources (MEMR).
Other relevant regulation (e.g. local content rules, investment at large)	A 35% requirement local content requirement was proposed in Jordan's last renewable energy tender, with tariff prices reflecting the degree of localisation. All equipment used in renewable energy projects is exempt from import and sales tax (Climatescope, 2021[41]).
Green hydrogen	
Green hydrogen strategies/roadmaps	Green Hydrogen roadmap has been devised, to be followed by a more comprehensive strategy (RenwablesNow, 2023[42])
Green hydrogen cost target, if any	NA
Green hydrogen capacity target, if any	NA
Establishment of dedicated agency/body to support development	National Green Hydrogen Committee was established in 2023
Any other relevant regulation (e.g. certification/standards)	The Jordanian Energy Ministry is currently working on a strategy to set technical and legal standards to produce green hydrogen from solar and wind (PtX Hub, 2023[43]).

	Green hydrogen export provisions	The intention to produce green hydrogen for export has been stated by public officials (The Jordan Times, 2023[44]).
Cross-cutting		
	UNFCCC participation and greenhouse gas reduction/renewable energy/green hydrogen commitments in Nationally Determined Contribution (NDC)	Updated NDC goal increased greenhouse gas reduction commitment 14% to 31% by 2030 compared to BAU. The NDC emphasizes the use of renewable energy and energy efficiency measures to support GHG mitigation efforts, with a target of increasing the share of renewable energy in electricity generation by 35% in 2030 compared to Business As Usual (BAU) scenario (UNFCCC, 2021[45])

Table A B.11. Strength and predictability of financial support in Jordan

Renewables		
	Feed-in tariffs	Yes, for solar energy. The prices are described as a "ceiling tariff", with PV set at USD 0.163/kWh and CSP at USD 0.183/kWh. The tariffs do not include different tranches for size (IEA, 2023[18]).
	Other operational support (e.g. contract for difference/feed-in-premium policies/long-term power purchase agreements)	Yes, long-term power purchase agreements are available to private power producers.
	Competitive auctions	Yes
	Tax incentives and other financial support	Customs duties, sales tax exemption for systems, equipment and devices related to renewable energy (Ministry of Energy and Mineral Resources, 2023[46]).
Green hydrogen		
	Financial support (including co-investment commitments) available or planned specifically for green hydrogen installation/production	None
Cross-cutting		
	Financial investment support for clean investments in general (e.g. green bonds etc.)	The Jordan Renewable Energy & Energy Efficiency Fund (JREEEF) provides renewable energy subsidies to privately owned and operated facilities, interest rate subsidies on commercial loans, a Public Equity Fund to support the deployment of private investment in the sector, a renewable energy guarantee facility to ease credit access for energy efficiency and renewable energy project developers and research and technical cooperation grants for targeted programmes and feasibility studies (IEA, 2023[18]).
	Carbon markets	Jordan was the first developing country to build Monitoring, Reporting and Verification (MRV) and GHG Registry systems to international standards that are the key building blocks for future emissions trading. To prepare for its MRV system, Jordan enacted a climate change bylaw in 2019 setting the institutional and regulatory framework on climate change across the government (World Bank, 2023[47]).
	History/robust pipeline of international co-investment in renewable energy or green hydrogen projects	Yes

Table A B.12. Infrastructure readiness and availability of complementary resources in Jordan

Renewables		
	Grid sufficiency for additional renewable energy capacity	The lack of capacity to handle higher shares of renewables in the transmission and distribution infrastructure is a key hurdle for further growth, however, Jordan is already starting to address the technical challenges by pushing ahead with upgrades to the grid and creation of a new grid installation called Green Corridor (IRENA, 2021[48]).
	Grid access and transmission rules for renewable energy projects	NEPCO (National Electricity Power Company) is expected to purchase the entire amount of electricity produced by private producers and will provide grid access to each individual renewable energy project (IEA, 2023[18]).
	History of curtailing renewable energy production due to insufficient grid capacity	Yes, the country introduced an indefinite suspension of new projects over 1 megawatt (MW) since January 2019, which has introduced uncertainty to the sector. This suspension only ended in 2022.
Green hydrogen		
	Grid planning reflecting possible hydrogen production sites	No evidence of such planning found.

Port/other maritime infrastructure	Aqaba port's readiness and needed infrastructure for the export of hydrogen is currently being studied.
Availability of water	Severe water scarcity, could be potentially partly mitigated through desalination (UNICEF, 2022[49]).
Any other relevant infrastructure	The possibility of adapting current gas network is being studied.

Summary Factsheet: Morocco

Table A B.13. Market potential and state of development in Morocco

Renewables	
Availability of renewable energy resources	Abundant solar and wind energy resources (IRENA, 2022[26])
Contribution of renewables incl. hydro to total primary energy supply	9.4% (2021 or latest) (OECD, 2023[12])
Current renewable energy capacity installed (wind and solar)	3,727 MW total; solar 858 MW (out of which CSP 540 MW); wind 1,556 MW (2022) (IRENA, 2023[13])
Domestic renewable energy industry	Morocco has witnessed a considerable growth of its solar energy industry in particular and there are a number of domestic players. Almaden, a photovoltaic module factory covering an area of 7,000 m², is the first of its kind in Morocco and Africa. The site is dedicated to the production of monocrystalline, polycrystalline and dual-glass panels and has an annual production capacity of 250 MW (Dome Solar, n.d.[50]). Gamesa Siemens built a wind turbine blade factory in Tangier, northern Morocco, however production there closed down in early 2023 due to supply chain issues (Reuters, n.d.[51])
Green hydrogen	
Existing green hydrogen capacity/project pipeline (including derivatives)	9 projects (ESMAP, 2023[15])
Existing blue hydrogen capacity/project pipeline (including derivatives)	None
Cross-cutting	
Fossil fuel import dependency	High dependency on imported hydrocarbons. According to latest World Bank figures net energy imports are at 90.7% of energy use (World Bank, 2023[16]).

Table A B.14. Strength and predictability of regulatory framework and non-regulatory policies in Morocco

Renewables	
Renewable energy strategies and targets	Target of 42% of total generation capacity by 2020, and 52% by 2030. Target to rely 100% on renewables by 2050 (IEA, 2023[18]).
Establishment of dedicated agency/body to support development	Yes, the Moroccan Agency for Sustainable Energy (MASEN)
Other relevant regulation (e.g. local content rules, investment at large)	Yes, MASEN set a 30% local content targetthat gave preferences to local labour, materials and service used for the solar power industry, with the aim of contributing to regional economic development and building local buy-in (World Resources Institute, n.d.[52]). This target is voluntary and therefore not a pre-condition for a license or support (World Bank, 2018[53]).
Green hydrogen	
Green hydrogen strategies/roadmaps	Yes
Green hydrogen cost target, if any	Cost reduction as a priority but no concrete target
Green hydrogen capacity target, if any	Roadmap includes reference and optimistic scenarios for demand exports but does not mention capacity targets
Establishment of dedicated agency/body to support development	Yes, the Hydrogen National Commission
Any other relevant regulation (e.g. certification/standards)	Mentioned in strategy but no concrete proposal.

	Green hydrogen export provisions	In the short term (2020-2030) the focus is on both exports, mainly to Europe, and the use of green hydrogen as an industry feedstock. In the medium term (2030-2040), Morocco will focus on using green hydrogen as an energy storage vector to ensure grid stability, but also in public and heavy trucks transports. In the long term (2040-2050), the strategy foresees higher levels of exports and use in industrial heat, railway, maritime, and aviation transport, as well as passenger vehicles (International Trade Administration, 2024[54]).
Cross-cutting		
	UNFCCC participation and greenhouse gas reduction/renewable energy/green hydrogen commitments in Nationally Determined Contribution (NDC)	Updated NDC commits the country to reducing its greenhouse gas emissions by 18.3% by 2030 compared with the business-as-usual (BAU) scenario. With international support this could reach 45.5% by 2030 compared with the BAU scenario (UNFCCC, 2023[33])

Table A B.15. Strength and predictability of financial support in Morocco

Renewables		
	Feed-in tariffs	No feed-in tariffs (IEA, 2023[18])
	Other operational support (e.g. contract for difference/feed-in-premium policies/long-term power purchase agreements)	Private power purchase agreements (PPAs) are available for a period of up to 25 years (IEA, 2023[18]).
	Competitive auctions	Yes, since 2010, the Moroccan government is tendering new solar and wind capacity through auctions in order to meet country's renewable energy targets (International Renewable Energy Agency, 2023[30]).
	Tax incentives and other financial support	Incentives include tax exemptions, reduced customs duties on renewable energy equipment.
Green hydrogen		
	Financial support (including co-investment commitments) available or planned specifically for green hydrogen installation/production	None, except a targeted international investment commitment. Norad, the Norwegian Agency for Development Cooperation to co-invest in green hydrogen projects in Morocco.
Cross-cutting		
	Financial investment support for clean investments in general (e.g. green bonds etc.)	Moroccan Agency for Solar Energy issued the country's first ever Green Bond. These bonds with total value were issued through private placement following the authorization of the Moroccan Authority of Capital Market (AMMC).
	Carbon markets	No, but a carbon tax is under consideration (World Bank, 2023[55]).
	History/robust pipeline of international co-investment in renewable energy or green hydrogen projects	Yes

Table A B.16. Infrastructure readiness and availability of complementary resources in Morocco

Renewables		
	Grid sufficiency for additional renewable energy capacity	Morocco prioritises improving its infrastructure to accommodate renewable energy projects, including through interconnections with neighbouring countries.
	Grid access and transmission rules for renewable energy projects	Law 13-09 provides for a right of access to the national low-voltage, medium-voltage, high-voltage and extra-high-voltage electricity grid for electricity produced by independent operators from renewable energy sources, within the limits of available technical capacity (IEA, 2023[18]).
	History of curtailing renewable energy production due to insufficient grid capacity	The issue was addressed through Law No. 40-19, which stipulates the maximum amount of installed capacity from renewable energy sources that the national electricity grid can accommodate without facing management constraints.
Green hydrogen		
	Grid planning reflecting possible hydrogen production sites	No evidence found of such planning.
	Port/other maritime infrastructure	The Port of Tangier has joined forces with the German port of Hamburg through a letter of intent signed in 2020 covering, among other things, the export of green hydrogen.
	Availability of water	High water stress coincides with good solar and wind resources, which may be a barrier to green hydrogen development unless there is sufficient desalination capacity.
	Any other relevant infrastructure	NA

Summary Factsheet: Tunisia

Table A B.17. Market potential and state of development in Tunisia

Renewables	
Availability of renewable energy resources	Abundant solar, wind and biomass resources (IRENA, 2022[56])
Contribution of renewables incl. hydro to total primary energy supply	11.5% (2021 or latest) (OECD, 2023[12])
Current renewable energy capacity installed (wind and solar)	508 MW total; solar 197 MW, wind 245 MW (2022) (IRENA, 2023[13])
Domestic renewable energy industry	There are a substantial number of solar equipment suppliers operating within Tunisia's solar market. Most of these entities can only manufacture and distribute equipment for small and medium solar projects and for large-scale solar projects, equipment tends to be imported. One domestic producer, Ifri-Sol has of module production capacity of 750MW and plans to increase it to 1 GW by the end of this year. Its panel factory is located in Enfidha, in north-eastern Tunisia (Solarfeeds.com, n.d.[57]).
Green hydrogen	
Existing green hydrogen capacity/project pipeline (including derivatives)	2 projects in planning (ESMAP, 2023[15])
Existing blue hydrogen capacity/project pipeline (including derivatives)	None
Cross-cutting	
Fossil fuel import dependency	Decline in domestic hydrocarbon production. According to latest World Bank figures net energy imports are at 36.2% of energy use (World Bank, 2023[16]).

Table A B.18. Strength and predictability of regulatory framework and non-regulatory policies in Tunisia

Renewables	
Renewable energy strategies and targets	Tunisia raised its renewable energy target from 30% to 35% by 2030 compared to the trend scenario in 2022. Specific targets of installing 1,000 MW of wind power capacity and 3.8 GW of solar by 2030 are also in place.
Establishment of dedicated agency/body to support development	Yes, National Agency for Energy Management
Other relevant regulation (e.g. local content rules, investment at large)	In May 2019, Parliament passed a bill to improve the business climate, permitting businesses to create separate special-purpose vehicles entirely dedicated to power generation. This policy change allows companies to produce power for their own consumption at more competitive prices.
Green hydrogen	
Green hydrogen strategies/roadmaps	No hydrogen strategy yet but government working on establishing a new legal framework to promote the production and use of green hydrogen and its derivatives in the local market.
Green hydrogen cost target, if any	NA
Green hydrogen capacity target, if any	NA
Establishment of dedicated agency/body to support development	NA
Any other relevant regulation (e.g. certification/standards)	NA
Green hydrogen export provisions	Tunisia envisions exporting between 5.5 and 6 million tonnes of green hydrogen annually to Europe by 2050 (Hydrogen Europe, 2023[58]).
Cross-cutting	
UNFCCC participation and greenhouse gas reduction/renewable energy/green hydrogen commitments in Nationally Determined Contribution (NDC)	In 2021, Tunisia pledged in its updated NDC to reduce its carbon intensity (emissions relative to gross domestic product) by 45% by 2030 compared to its 2010 level.

Table A B.19. Strength and predictability of financial support in Tunisia

Renewables	
Feed-in tariffs	The value of the feed-in tariff is decided by the Ministry of Energy (IEA, 2023[18]).
Other operational support (e.g. contract for difference/feed-in-premium policies/long-term power purchase agreements)	Selected developers sign power purchase agreements with state energy company Societe Tunisienne de l'Electricite et du Gaz (STEG) for a concession period of 20 years under a build-own-operate (BOO) model (IEA, 2023[18])
Competitive auctions	Yes (International Renewable Energy Agency, 2023[30])
Tax incentives and other financial support	Reduced VAT on renewable energy components and customs tariffs if there is no local equivalent available. There is also a reduced corporate income tax, depending on the firm's income and location of the project (IEA, 2023[18]).
Green hydrogen	
Financial support (including co-investment commitments) available or planned specifically for green hydrogen installation/production	In December 2020, the Tunisian Ministry for Energy Mines and Renewable Energy signed a EUR 31 million Memorandum of Understanding with the German Federal Minister for Economic Cooperation and Development (BMZ) for developing its green hydrogen market (Energycentral, 2023[59]).
Cross-cutting	
Financial investment support for clean investments in general (e.g. green bonds etc.)	Fonds de Transition Energétique offers grants, equity financing and improved loan terms to firms willing to invest in renewable energy (mostly for own consumption projects)
Carbon markets	Tunisia plans to establish conditions that will allow it to initiate a carbon pricing programme to support its energy transition policy and the mitigation of greenhouse gas emissions (ANME, 2023[60]).
History/robust pipeline of international co-investment in renewable energy or green hydrogen projects	Yes

Table A B.20. Infrastructure readiness and availability of complementary resources in Tunisia

Renewables	
Grid sufficiency for additional renewable energy capacity	Tunisia's national grid is connected to those of Algeria and Libya, but various other projects to expand electricity transmission and distribution networks across North Africa are in the planning stage.
Grid access and transmission rules for renewable energy projects	Before connecting its power station to the Tunisian national grid, a producer must first obtain approval from STEG (IEA, 2023[18]).
History of curtailing renewable energy production due to insufficient grid capacity	No evidence found.
Green hydrogen	
Grid planning reflecting possible hydrogen production sites	No evidence found.
Port/other maritime infrastructure	Plans to upgrade port/maritime infrastructure to facilitate green hydrogen trade are so far undefined.
Availability of water	Water, a main source for the production of green hydrogen, is in short supply in Tunisia, however, the State intends to set up desalination plants in the south and the midland.
Any other relevant infrastructure	The already-available Transmed gas pipeline that connects Algeria to Italy through Tunisia is an important asset for investors considering exports to Europe. Tunisia is planning to set up a pipeline network to transport green hydrogen from Gabès and Tataouine to the Cap-Bon region.

References

African Development Bank (2012), *Clean Energy Development in Egypt*. [29]

ANME (2023), , https://www.anme.tn/?q=en/content/carbon-pricing (accessed on August 2023). [60]

Baker Mackenzie (2023), , https://insightplus.bakermckenzie.com/bm/capital-markets/egypt-a-voluntary-carbon-market (accessed on August 2023). [35]

Climatescope (2023), *https://www.global-climatescope.org/markets/*. [3]

Climatescope (2021), *Global Climatescope - Jordan*, https://2021.global-climatescope.org/markets/jo/ (accessed on August 2023). [41]

Dome Solar (n.d.), *Photovoltaic roof of a solar panel factory in Morocco - Dome Solar*, https://dome-solar.com/en/photovoltaic-installations/photovoltaic-roof-of-a-solar-panel-factory-in-morocco/ (accessed on 1 March 2024). [50]

Enerdata (2023), *Algeria considers exporting renewable hydrogen to Germany | Enerdata*, https://www.enerdata.net/publications/daily-energy-news/algeria-considers-exporting-renewable-hydrogen-germany.html (accessed on 1 March 2024). [20]

Energycentral (2023), , https://energycentral.com/news/germany-grants-tunisia-%E2%82%AC30-million-develop-green-hydrogen-market (accessed on September 2023). [59]

Enterprise Climate (2023), *Jordan increases investment in its local solar industry supply chain + Iran is nearing completion on the largest lead and zinc processing factory in the region | Enterprise*, https://climate.enterprise.press/stories/2023/08/27/today-jordan-increases-investment-in-its-local-solar-industry-supply-chain-iran-is-nearing-completion-on-the-largest-lead-and-zinc-processing-factory-in-the-region-102318/ (accessed on 1 March 2024). [38]

ESI Africa (2023), , https://www.esi-africa.com/news/egypt-council-set-up-to-target-green-hydrogen-investment/ (accessed on December 2023). [31]

ESMAP (2023), *Scaling Hydrogen Financing for Development*. [15]

Green Hydrogen Organisation (n.d.), *Egypt Profile*, https://gh2.org/countries/egypt (accessed on 1 March 2024). [32]

Hawila, D. (2014), "Renewable energy readiness assessment for North African countries", *Renewable and Sustainable Energy Reviews*. [1]

Hydrogen Europe (2023), *Tunisia Hydrogen Export*, https://hydrogeneurope.eu/tunisia-can-export-over-5-5mt-of-green-h2-to-europe-by-2050/ (accessed on 1 March 2024). [58]

Hydrogen Insight (2023), , https://www.hydrogeninsight.com/policy/algeria-aims-to-supply-europe-with-10-of-its-clean-hydrogen-needs-by-2040-in-new-national-h2-roadmap/2-1-1426265 (accessed on December 2023). [19]

Hydrogen Insight (2022), , https://www.hydrogeninsight.com/production/egypt-grants-final-approval-to-5-5bn-green-hydrogen-and-ammonia-project-near-suez-canal/2-1-1374608 (accessed on August 2023). [36]

IEA (2023), , https://www.iea.org/policies/ (accessed on August 2023). [18]

IEA (2019), *The Future of Hydrogen*. [10]

IMF (2023), *North Africa Hydrogen Mirage*, https://www.imf.org/en/Publications/fandd/issues/2023/09/north-africa-hydrogen-mirage-rabah-arezki (accessed on August 2023). [25]

International Renewable Energy Agency (2023), *North Africa: Policies and Finance for Renewable Energy Deployment*. [30]

International Trade Administration (2024), *Morocco - Energy Profile*, https://www.trade.gov/country-commercial-guides/morocco-energy (accessed on 1 March 2024). [54]

International Trade Administration (2023), , https://www.trade.gov/country-commercial-guides/algeria-renewable-energy (accessed on December 2023). [17]

IRENA (2023), *Renewable Capacity Statistics 2022*. [13]

IRENA (2022), , https://www.irena.org/-/media/Files/IRENA/Agency/Statistics/Statistical_Profiles/Africa/Algeria_Africa_RE_SP.pdf (accessed on September 2023). [11]

IRENA (2022), , https://www.irena.org/-/media/Files/IRENA/Agency/Statistics/Statistical_Profiles/Africa/Egypt_Africa_RE_SP.pdf (accessed on September 2023). [27]

IRENA (2022), , https://www.irena.org/-/media/Files/IRENA/Agency/Statistics/Statistical_Profiles/Africa/Tunisia_Africa_RE_SP.pdf (accessed on September 2023). [56]

IRENA (2022), *Energy profile: Jordan*, https://www.irena.org/-/media/Files/IRENA/Agency/Statistics/Statistical_Profiles/Middle%20East/Jordan_Middle%20East_RE_SP.pdf (accessed on September 2023). [37]

IRENA (2022), *Energy profile: Morocco*, https://www.irena.org/-/media/Files/IRENA/Agency/Statistics/Statistical_Profiles/Africa/Morocco_Africa_RE_SP.pdf (accessed on September 2023). [26]

IRENA (2021), , https://www.irena.org/-/media/Files/IRENA/Agency/Publication/2021/Feb/IRENA_RRA_Jordan_2021.pdf (accessed on September 2023). [48]

IRENA (2020), , https://coalition.irena.org/-/media/Files/IRENA/Coalition-for-Action/Publication/Scaling-up-Renewable-Energy-Investment-in-Emerging-Markets/IRENA-Coalition-for-Action_Algeria_2020.pdf?la=en&hash=B8B4328E567A8633CB3846D7843502E3C5491437. [22]

IRENA (2013), *Renewables Readiness Assessment: Design to Action*. [2]

Jordan Times (2023), *Jordan takes strides towards green ammonia production with four key MoUs Jordan takes strides towards green ammonia production with four key MoUs*, https://jordantimes.com/news/local/jordan-takes-strides-towards-green-ammonia-production-four-key-mous (accessed on December 2023). [39]

Ministry of Energy and Mineral Resources (2023), , https://www.memr.gov.jo/ebv4.0/root_storage/en/eb_list_page/renewable_energy__energy_efficiency_law_-_english.pdf (accessed on July 2023). [46]

OECD (2023), , https://data.oecd.org/energy/renewable-energy.htm#indicator-chart. [12]

OECD (2023), *Main SIFA study*, OECD publishing. [5]

OECD (2022), *Green hydrogen opportunities for emerging and developing economies*, OECD Working Paper Series. [4]

OECD (forthcoming), *Financing cost impacts on cost competitiveness of green hydrogen in emerging and developing economies.* [9]

OECD (forthcoming), *Financing solutions to foster industry decarbonisation in emerging and developing economies.* [8]

Pipeline journal (2023), , https://www.pipeline-journal.net/news/algerias-ambitious-subsea-green-hydrogen-pipeline-meet-10-europes-h2-demand (accessed on December 2023). [24]

PtX Hub (2023), , https://ptx-hub.org/jordan/ (accessed on December 2023). [43]

PtX hub (2023), , https://ptx-hub.org/algeria/ (accessed on August 2023). [23]

PV Magazine International (2020), *Another solar module factory in Algeria – pv magazine International*, https://www.pv-magazine.com/2020/03/09/another-solar-module-factory-in-algeria/ (accessed on 1 March 2024). [14]

Renewable Energy Agency, I. (n.d.), “Renewable energy outlook: Egypt (executive summary)”. [28]

RenewablesNow (2023), , https://renewablesnow.com/news/algeria-accepts-77-bids-in-2-gw-solar-auction-829339/ (accessed on September 2023). [21]

RenwablesNow (2023), , https://renewablesnow.com/news/jordan-devises-green-hydrogen-roadmap-841064/ (accessed on December 2023). [42]

Reuters (2021), , https://www.reuters.com/world/middle-east/jordan-plans-generate-50-electricity-renewables-by-2030-state-tv-2021-11-16/ (accessed on December 2023). [40]

Reuters (n.d.), *Siemens Gamesa plans to sell its Morocco turbine blade factory | Reuters*, https://www.reuters.com/markets/deals/siemens-gamesa-plans-sell-its-morocco-turbine-blade-factory-2022-11-17/ (accessed on 1 March 2024). [51]

Solarfeeds.com (n.d.), *Top Solar Panel OEM Suppliers in Tunisia*, https://www.solarfeeds.com/solar-panel/oem/c/tunisia/ (accessed on 1 March 2024). [57]

The Jordan Times (2023), *Jordan aims to lead region in green hydrogen exports — Gov’t | Jordan Times*, https://jordantimes.com/news/local/jordan-aims-lead-region-green-hydrogen-exports-%E2%80%94-govt (accessed on 1 March 2024). [44]

UNFCCC (2023), , https://unfccc.int/NDCREG (accessed on July 2023). [33]

UNFCCC (2021), , https://unfccc.int/sites/default/files/NDC/2022-06/UPDATED%20SUBMISSION%20OF%20JORDANS.pdf (accessed on August 2023). [45]

UNFCCC (n.d.), *Climate Investment Readiness Index.* [7]

UNICEF (2022), *Tapped out: The costs of water stress in Jordan.* [49]

World Bank (2023), , https://www.worldbank.org/en/news/feature/2022/05/24/countries-on-the-cusp-of-carbon-markets (accessed on July 2023). [47]

World Bank (2023), *Carbon pricing dashboard*, https://carbonpricingdashboard.worldbank.org/ (accessed on July 2023). [55]

World Bank (2023), *World Development Indicators*, https://databank.worldbank.org/source/world-development-indicators/Series/EG.IMP.CONS.ZS#. [16]

World Bank (2022), , https://www.worldbank.org/en/news/feature/2022/03/02/supporting-egypt-s-inaugural-green-bond-issuance (accessed on July 2023). [34]

World Bank (2018), *Climate Investment Fund Fiche*. [53]

World Bank (2015), *Readiness for Investment in Sustainable Energy (RISE) methodology*. [6]

World Resources Institute (n.d.), *Morocco: Ensuring A Large-scale Renewable Installation Benefits Local Communities | World Resources Institute*, https://www.wri.org/update/morocco-ensuring-large-scale-renewable-installation-benefits-local-communities (accessed on 1 March 2024). [52]

www.ingramcontent.com/pod-product-compliance
Ingram Content Group UK Ltd.
Pitfield, Milton Keynes, MK11 3LW, UK
UKHW051502290926
15471UKWH00008B/1375

9 789264 942165